WHONIVERSE

THE UNOFFICIAL PLANET-BY-PLANET GUIDE TO THE UNIVERSE OF THE DOCTOR, FROM GALLIFREY TO SKARO

LANCE PARKIN

BARRON'S

First edition published in 2016 by
Barron's Educational Series, Inc.

Copyright 2015 © RotoVision
Level 4 Sheridan House, 114 Western Road,
Hove BN3 1DD, England

Every effort has been made to trace the copyright
holders of material quoted in this book. If application is
made in writing to the publisher, any omissions will be
included in future editions.

All inquiries should be addressed to:
Barron's Educational Series, Inc.
250 Wireless Blvd
Hauppauge, New York 11788
www.barronseduc.com

Publisher: Mark Searle
Editorial Director: Isheeta Mustafi
Commissioning Editor: Alison Morris
Editor: Angela Koo
Design: JC Lanaway

Text and sourcing of images by Lance Parkin

Metro Books
122 Fifth Avenue
New York, NY 10011

Library of Congress Control Number: 2014956090

ISBN: 978-0-7641-6798-0

Printed and bound in China
9 8 7 6 5 4 3 2 1

DEDICATION

For Brie

CONTENTS

INTRODUCTION

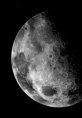

This book is not a list of every planet that has been seen or mentioned in the television series *Doctor Who*. Nor is it a place where dry facts about the diameter of those worlds and the distance from their sun or suns are reeled off. *Doctor Who*, the series and the character, has always had a much more haphazard, cobbled-together approach to traveling the universe. While the Doctor has occasionally claimed to be on a scientific expedition, and to be a legitimate explorer, it's clear he just enjoys popping in on spectacular and peculiar places and meeting the people who live there. This book is therefore a celebration of some of the more interesting, significant, or bizarre places in the *Doctor Who* universe. It hopefully serves as a good overview of the weird terrain the TARDIS travels through, and it should contain at least a few obscure references that will surprise and delight even the most seasoned *Doctor Who* fan.

There are around 1,000 television episodes of *Doctor Who*, but the TV series is the tip of the iceberg. There are countless comic strips, novels and novellas, short stories, audio adventures, video games, and even a handful of stage plays. The notion of a "*Doctor Who* purist" is almost a contradiction in terms because, as soon as they could, *Doctor Who* stories were borrowing liberally from sources other series would dismiss as "non-canonical." This book draws material from all sorts of sources, from the current TV show to candy cigarette cards kids collected in the 1960s.

Doctor Who fans have been hard at work for decades cataloging the series, interviewing the people behind the scenes, and scouring the picture archives. This may be the legacy of *Doctor Who*: hundreds of years from now, if anyone is interested in how television was made, no show's production has been as meticulously documented. This is a roundabout way of apologizing that no book about *Doctor Who* could possibly contain pictures that are all entirely unseen. This book has an eclectic mix of illustrations from all sorts of places. Where the TV series was occasionally held back by budgetary or other practical considerations, artists have been able to let rip with epic landscapes and creature designs. The books and comic strips have shown us things the TV series has only hinted at.

Each planet in this book is represented by a double-page spread—several in the cases of Earth, Gallifrey, and Skaro. Some are arranged as Timelines, where the important stories set on those planets are laid out in the order they were broadcast or published. Other are Fact Files, with a slightly more eclectic approach to the information.

The book is arranged so that it starts with an overview of the universe as a whole and then looks at Earth's Solar System, before moving on to other human colony planets. The second half of the book looks at the planets where the aliens come from: the Time Lords, Daleks, and Cybermen get their own sections, and then we see the home planets of the most notable monsters and other creatures the Doctor and his friends have encountered.

Finally, everything is rounded up with a look at how the universe ends and (because this is *Doctor Who*, and the Doctor wouldn't let something like the final end of the universe put a stop to things) what happens after that.

THE UNIVERSE

THE BIG BANG

Over 13 billion years ago, our universe began with what the human race calls the "Big Bang" and the Time Lords know as "Event One."[1] This was the biggest explosion in history. It released a vast blast of energy, some of which coalesced into matter. At the beginning of all beginnings, there was a force of Good (order) and Evil (chaos), and both shattered in the explosion.[2] There were beings before our universe, and others sprang into existence at the dawn of time. Those who survived are immensely powerful—the inspirations for legends of gods and demons.

HISTORY

Because of the exotic conditions, and the possibility of exploiting them, the Big Bang has been the target of a number of time travelers—the Doctor himself has hinted that he was there.[3] The Urbankan Monarch believed he was God and plotted to travel to the start of the universe to meet himself.[4] The Council of Eight seeded crystals into the fabric of the early universe, allowing them to map the whole of history.[5]

The Master once sent the fifth Doctor's TARDIS crashing toward the Big Bang, where it would be obliterated,[6] while another renegade Time Lord, the Rani, wanted to recreate the conditions of the early universe to increase her scientific knowledge.[7] The universe was destroyed in 2010 when the TARDIS exploded ... but the eleventh Doctor was able to trigger a second Big Bang to recreate it almost exactly.[8]

ABOVE: Moments after the Big Bang, as seen in *Castrovalva*.

OPPOSITE: The Black Guardian has existed since the dawn of time.

BEHIND THE SCENES

A diverse set of stories have established that those few beings able to master the forces at the beginning of the universe have the ability to shape reality. We've only seen the Big Bang once, in *Castrovalva* (Christopher H. Bidmead), although the eleventh Doctor set a second one off in "The Big Bang" (Steven Moffat, 2010).

FIRST APPEARANCE

Castrovalva *(1982)*

INHABITANTS

Fenric, the Guardians, the Council of Eight, the Weeping Angels, the Beast

FACT FILE

THE MASQUE OF MANDRAGORA, SPEARHEAD FROM SPACE

The first native intelligent beings of our universe were creatures of energy, like the Mandragora Helix and the Nestene Consciousness.

THE RIBOS OPERATION

Near-omnipotent beings, the Guardians, created the Key to Time, an object capable of rebalancing the forces of order and chaos in the universe. Its six segments were hidden across time and space.

"THE IMPOSSIBLE PLANET" / "THE SATAN PIT"

Before the universe began, the Disciples of Light chained the Beast in a pit on the planet Krop Tor, an impossible planet orbiting a black hole.

"BLINK"

The Weeping Angels are very nearly as old as the universe. They are hunters, quantum locked so you can never see them move.

THE COMING OF THE TERRAPHILES

Early on the universe sees "the Dark Time, the Time of Chaos." The Battle for the Balance was fought between the archangels of Law and those of Chaos, and it was won by the ruthless Miggea, Queen of Seirot, representing Law.

FOOTNOTES
[1] *Castrovalva* • [2] *The Curse of Fenric* • [3] *Destiny of the Daleks, The Curse of Fenric* • [4] *Four to Doomsday* • [5] *Timeless* • [6] *Castrovalva* • [7] *Time and the Rani* • [8] *"The Big Bang"*

TERMINUS

While the events of the dawn of time were observed and recorded by the Time Lords, the reason the Big Bang occurred was a mystery until the fifth Doctor arrived on Terminus in the 35th century. At that time, the vast space structure was being used as a colony for sufferers of Lazar's disease, where the organization Terminus Incorporated experimented with crude radiation treatments by exposing victims to radiation leaking from the spaceship's engines. What intrigued the Doctor was that Terminus was at the dead center of the universe.

HISTORY

Terminus wasn't built by the corporation controlling it; they had simply occupied a vast, derelict structure. The treatment of the diseased was overseen by the mysterious Garm, a doglike being who was extremely strong and who Terminus Inc. was enslaving using a sonic device. The Doctor discovered that one of the engines was seriously damaged and threatening to overload. This had happened before—the pilot had been able to eject fuel into a void, then attempted to time-jump into the future to escape the blast. The pilot had died, but Terminus had been saved. What the Doctor realized was that the explosion of the ejected fuel was actually the Big Bang. If a second fuel dump took place now, it would detonate with enough force to destroy the universe. With the help of the Garm, the Doctor was able to prevent the ship's computer from automatically dumping more fuel.

ABOVE: A rare view of the whole of Terminus.

LEFT: The Garm, a mysterious denizen of Terminus.

FIRST APPEARANCE
Terminus (1983)

LOCATION
Exact center of the universe

INHABITANTS
The pilot, the Garm

BEHIND THE SCENES

The TV story Terminus (Stephen Gallagher) established Terminus and saw Nyssa leaving the show. The Doctor met up with an older Nyssa in the book Asylum (Peter Darvill-Evans, 2001), and the audio stories Circular Time (Paul Cornell, Mike Maddox, 2007) and Cobwebs (Jonathan Morris, 2010), in which she rejoined the TARDIS crew for a time.

TIMELINE

2010

🎧 **COBWEBS**

Nyssa dedicates her time to curing
another plague, Richter's Syndrome.

1986

🎧 **SLIPBACK**

👤 **SIXTH DOCTOR**

✎ **ERIC SAWARD**

The Doctor lands on the large
spacecraft *Vipod Mor*, which
has a mad computer. The
Doctor escapes as the ship
begins plummeting back in
time, set to blow up—the
explosion will be the cause of
the Big Bang. It's possible that
the *Vipod Mor* ignites the fuel
Terminus has dumped.

2010

🎧 **COBWEBS**

👤 **FIFTH DOCTOR**

✎ **JONATHAN MORRIS**

Nyssa marries a dream specialist
named Lasarti, and they have two
children: a girl, Neeka, and a son
named after Adric.

2001

📖 **ASYLUM**

👤 **FOURTH DOCTOR**

✎ **PETER DARVILL-EVANS**

The Doctor's companion, Nyssa, remains
on Terminus to help find a better cure
for Lazar's Disease. She succeeds in
eradicating it within five years.

THE STRUCTURE OF THE UNIVERSE

Our universe has a discrete shape and size, with Earth's galaxy in the middle, Frontios (in the Veruna system) very far out,[1] and Terminus at the exact center.[2] The Minyans, Morestrans, and a Daemon have all traveled to its very edge. Time Lords mastered transmat technology when the universe was less than half its present size.[3] The Doctor has mentioned "corners of the universe" several times and didn't correct a member of the Sisterhood of Karn who referred to "the nine corners of the universe."[4] The universe had a distinct start (the Big Bang, p. 10), and it will have a distinct end.

HISTORY

The universe as we experience it normally has five dimensions: the three we are familiar with, plus the fourth dimension ("time") and the fifth ("space").[5] There are beings who exist in only two dimensions, such as the Boneless,[6] and those who exist in seven, like the Legion.[7] The Doctor once encountered Fenric in the Shadow Dimensions.[8] The universe is held together by physical laws, chiefly the laws of cause and effect. It is subject to the laws of entropy, which state that any closed system will become less ordered over time—the people of Logopolis (p. 196) have kept the universe alive by creating holes called CVEs that open it up. Logopolis is a "cold, high place overlooking the universe," according to the Master. From there, the Watcher was able to take the TARDIS "beyond space and time" to observe the whole universe.[9]

ABOVE: The fourth Doctor's last adventure saw a threat to the entire universe.

BELOW LEFT: The entire universe, as seen in the classic TV story, *Logopolis*.

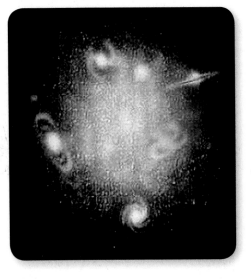

BEHIND THE SCENES

The Doctor has seen the extremities of the universe in the TV stories *Planet of Evil* (Louis Marks, 1975) and *Underworld* (Bob Baker & David Martin, 1978), and the comic *Voyage to the Edge of the Universe* (Paul Neary / David Lloyd, 1981). Thanks to the Master, the universe faced collapse in *Logopolis* (Christopher H. Bidmead).

FIRST APPEARANCE
📺 Logopolis *(1981)*

INHABITANTS
Minyans, Morestrans, Sisterhood of Karn, Boneless, Legion, Logopolitans

FOOTNOTES
[1] *Frontios* • [2] *Terminus* • [3] *Genesis of the Daleks* • [4] *The Brain of Morbius* • [5] *An Unearthly Child* • [6] *"Flatline"* • [7] *Lucifer Rising* • [8] *The Curse of Fenric* • [9] *Logopolis*

FACT FILE

▢ PYRAMIDS OF MARS

Every point in space and time can be expressed as a set of space-time coordinates. Space-time coordinates are based on the "galactic center"—for example, Gallifrey is 10-0-11-0-0 by 0-2 from galactic center zero.

▢ THE MIND ROBBER, WARRIORS' GATE

The TARDIS has twice landed and shown a row of zeroes as coordinates; on both times it has entered a white void. On the first occasion this led to the Land of Fiction; on the second it led to the Gateway, a structure used by the Tharils that linked N-Space with the pocket universe E-Space (p. 18).

▢ THE TIME MONSTER

The Chronovores, beings that feed on time itself, exist outside the universe.

▢ THE INVISIBLE ENEMY

Most of the intelligent life encountered by the Doctor exists in the "macro world," but there is also a "microcosm," a universe of viruses and other microscopic organisms. The Nucleus of the Swarm, an intelligent virus, used the dimensional stabilizers of the TARDIS to grow to macro size and sought to spread throughout both worlds.

▢ PLANET OF EVIL, UNDERWORLD
◯ VOYAGE TO THE EDGE OF THE UNIVERSE

The edge of the universe is, variously, close to the antimatter universe; a churning mass of creation where planets form; a white void where you can walk to the boundary of a mirror-image universe and gain immense powers by merging with your counterpart. Reports agree that traveling there is a lengthy, dangerous process.

▢ THE SUN MAKERS

The TARDIS has "boundary parameters" that prevent—or should prevent—it from traveling too far into the future. If unattended, it risks going "right through the time spiral."

▢ ENLIGHTENMENT

Beyond the universe is nothingness. The Eternals existed in the endless wastes and echoing void of Eternity. Ageless and utterly bored, they would come to prey on mortals, toying with them for their amusement.

▢ THE BLUE ANGEL

Underneath the universe is the Obverse, which the Time Lords know very little about. It is a mysterious realm where time and space are "barely on speaking terms," and so none of the laws of physics apply.

POCKET UNIVERSES

Alongside the universe are many pocket universes—relatively small realms where the laws of physics are not always the same as they are in ours. Because of this, and because they can be difficult to reach, pocket universes have often come to be occupied (accidentally or by design) by powerful entities who would rather avoid detection by authorities like the Time Lords.

HISTORY

Most pocket universes are created accidentally and are unstable, but the most powerful beings are capable of controlling the very nature of reality within them, or even building their own. Such beings are the gods of their domain. Because the laws of physics are different, time can flow at a different rate from the outside universe. It seems that willpower can exert an influence on some pocket universes. When Brimo the Time Witch fell into a blank dimension, she learned she could create solid objects just by thinking about them. She drew the energy she needed from our universe, creating a dangerous time rift.[1]

ABOVE: A chamber in the Celestial Toyroom, the realm of the Celestial Toymaker.

RIGHT: One of the Gods of Ragnarok, masters of the Dark Circus.

FIRST APPEARANCE
📺 The Celestial Toymaker *(1966)*

INHABITANTS
The Celestial Toymaker, the Master of the Land of Fiction, Brimo, the Gods of Ragnarok, the Celestis, Faction Paradox

FOOTNOTE
1 🔍 *The Time Witch*

TIMELINE

📺 THE CELESTIAL TOYMAKER
👤 FIRST DOCTOR
✏️ BRIAN HAYLES

The Doctor already knows about the Toymaker before being drawn to his pocket dimension, the Toyroom. The Toymaker is as old as the universe and plays games to stave off eternal boredom, enslaving those who lose. The Doctor masters his Trilogic Game, while his companions Steven and Dodo evade more physical traps.

1966

1968

📺 THE MIND ROBBER
👤 SECOND DOCTOR
✏️ PETER LING

The Land of Fiction is a realm controlled by a computer where characters from stories are brought to life and where the Doctor has to be careful not to become fictional and thereby trapped in its story.

1988–89

📺 THE GREATEST SHOW IN THE GALAXY
👤 SEVENTH DOCTOR
✏️ STEPHEN WYATT

The Gods of Ragnarok operate from a pocket universe called the Dark Circus.

1997

📖 ALIEN BODIES
👤 EIGHTH DOCTOR
✏️ LAWRENCE MILES

During one of the Time Wars, a faction of Time Lords converts themselves to beings of pure intelligence—the Celestis—and flee the war by hiding in a pocket dimension called Mictlan.

📺 "THE DAY OF THE DOCTOR"
👤 ALL 13!
✏️ STEVEN MOFFAT

2013

The combined efforts of 13 incarnations of the Doctor manage to save Gallifrey (pp. 116–21) from destruction at the end of the Last Great Time War by moving Gallifrey into a pocket dimension.

📺 "HIDE"
👤 ELEVENTH DOCTOR
✏️ NEIL CROSS

When the Doctor and Clara investigate legends of a ghost at Caliburn House, they discover the "Witch" is a time traveler, Hila Tacorien, struggling to get out of a collapsing pocket universe called the Hex.

2012

📺 "THE DOCTOR'S WIFE"
👤 ELEVENTH DOCTOR
✏️ NEIL GAIMAN

A malevolent entity named House lives in a pocket universe and feeds on the artron energy of Time Lords it lures to its domain with fake distress signals.

1999

📖 INTERFERENCE
👤 EIGHTH DOCTOR
✏️ LAWRENCE MILES

When Britain switches to the Gregorian calendar in September 1752, eleven days are "lost." Faction Paradox purchases them from the British government and uses them to create a pocket universe base of operations, the Eleven-Day Empire.

E-SPACE

One of the most notable pocket universes is Exo-Space, also known as E-Space. (Our universe is known as Normal-Space, or N-Space). E-Space was formed when matter was drained from our universe through a Charged Vacuum Emboitment (CVE) to prevent our universe from becoming a closed system, and thus subject to entropy.

HISTORY

Time-space coordinates in E-Space are negative numbers, and one indication that it is smaller than our universe is that space has a slight greenish tinge. Other than that, the conditions seem similar to our universe, and while it is far smaller, it is large enough to contain many stars and a number of Earthlike planets. The fourth Doctor, Romana, and K9 once got trapped in E-Space when the TARDIS accidentally flew through the CVE.

BEHIND THE SCENES

The 18th season of *Doctor Who* included the *E-Space Trilogy* (*Full Circle*, *State of Decay*, and *Warriors' Gate*, 1980–81), which saw the fourth Doctor briefly trapped in a different universe. He left Romana and K9 behind in E-Space and then returned to our universe with a new companion, Adric.

FIRST APPEARANCE
📺 Full Circle *(1980)*

INHABITANTS
Marshmen and Marshspiders, Great Vampires, Tharils

ABOVE: A Marshman of Alzarius.

LEFT: The Doctor met his companion Adric on Alzarius, in E-Space.

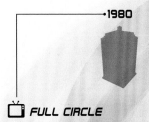

TIMELINE

📺 WARRIORS' GATE

1981

The presence of the slaver ship is causing the void to collapse in on itself. The Doctor frees the Tharils, and Romana and K9 go with them to help end the slave trade. The Doctor and Adric return to N-Space.

📺 FULL CIRCLE

👤 FOURTH DOCTOR

✒️ ANDREW SMITH

The TARDIS is heading to Gallifrey when it passes through the CVE. It lands on Alzarius, a planet that shares coordinates with Gallifrey—but expressed as negative numbers. Initially, the TARDIS viewscreen shows the landscape of its home planet.

1980

📺 WARRIORS' GATE

1981

The slavers are trading in Tharils—naturally time sensitive and once the masters of a vast space empire, but now valuable commodities, as they can be plugged into the navigation systems of starships.

1980

📺 FULL CIRCLE

Alzarius is a warm, forested planet. Years before, a starliner from the planet Terradon had crashed there. When the Doctor, Romana, and K9 visit, they find a full crew endlessly working to repair the ship. It is here that they meet Adric, who will stow away in the TARDIS.

📺 WARRIORS' GATE

👤 FOURTH DOCTOR

✒️ STEPHEN GALLAGHER

1981

After defeating the King Vampire, the Doctor, Romana, Adric, and K9 calculate a possible way out of E-Space: setting the coordinates to zero. They arrive in a white void, empty except for a ruined castle, the Gateway … and a slave ship that has become trapped there.

1980

1980

1980

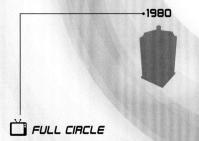

📺 FULL CIRCLE

The planet has a peculiar weather condition—Mistfall—whereby, once a generation, a strange fog manifests and monstrous Marshmen emerge from the water. The Doctor discovers that the original starliner crew all died in the crash, and that the current crew evolved from the Marshmen. Nevertheless, with his help, they launch the starliner and head "home" to Terradon.

📺 STATE OF DECAY

👤 FOURTH DOCTOR

✒️ TERRANCE DICKS

After attempts to locate a way out of E-Space, the TARDIS next lands on a world where most of the population live like medieval peasants, subjects of the Three Who Rule, who dwell in a large metal castle.

📺 STATE OF DECAY

The Doctor is surprised to see the peasants have an ancient computer—evidence the world is regressing technologically. The planet is the refuge of the last of the Great Vampires, ancient enemies of the Time Lords, and the castle is actually a rocket from Earth, drawn through the CVE by the King Vampire.

THE ANTIMATTER UNIVERSE

Since the beginning of time, a second universe has existed side by side with ours—its equal and opposite, its antithesis: a universe of antimatter. All the known laws of physics say that the antimatter universe is a nothingness, a nowhere, a void; that nothing stable can exist there; and that anything from our universe that went there would be annihilated. But the laws of physics are wrong. In fact, the antimatter universe contains unknown forces that would wreak havoc with ours if they came into contact with it. In the antimatter universe, causes cannot be observed—only effects.

HISTORY

The Doctor's first contact with the antimatter universe came when the Time Lords united his first three incarnations to investigate a mysterious energy drain that threatened Gallifrey, as well as the fabric of space and time. The antimatter universe existed close to the singularity of the black hole that Gallifreyan solar engineer Omega created to power the time travel of the early Time Lords. Omega became trapped there but took control of the singularity, learning how to master its vast forces. The Doctor defeated Omega but would go on to face him a number of other times. The Doctor's knowledge of antimatter was vital when he came to Zeta Minor, "the last planet of the known universe," in the year 37166. Zeta Minor was on the boundary of our universe and the universe of antimatter—indeed, the "night" side passed out of our universe.

BEHIND THE SCENES

There's no explicit connection between the antimatter universes in the TV stories *The Three Doctors* (Bob Baker & David Martin, 1972–73) and *Planet of Evil* (Louis Marks, 1975), but they share several characteristics. The Doctor would meet Omega again in the TV story *Arc of Infinity* (Johnny Byrne, 1983), novel *The Infinity Doctors* (Lance Parkin, 1998), and audio drama *Omega* (Nev Fountain, 2003). The book *Zeta Major* (Simon Messingham, 1998) was a sequel to *Planet of Evil*.

FIRST APPEARANCE
The Three Doctors *(1972)*

MONSTERS
Omega, Gel Guards, Ergon, antimatter monsters

OPPOSITE: Professor Sorenson's exposure to antimatter makes him an anti-man.

BELOW: Three Doctors were brought together to fight the threat of Omega.

PARALLEL UNIVERSES

"Sideways in time," there are billions of other universes almost identical to ours, but where history took a different path. The Doctor has encountered a universe where Britain was a fascist Republic,[1] and another where the Republic was democratic but dominated by the Cybus Corporation, creators of the Cybermen.[2] In one, the Arthurian myths were real and the descendants of the Camelot knights fought Morgaine for 1,000 years.[3] In another, the Roman Empire continued, its Iron Legion conquering the whole galaxy.[4] In yet another, the events of *Star Trek* were real, not just an old TV series.[5]

FIRST APPEARANCE
Inferno (1970)

INHABITANTS
Evil doubles of friends and colleagues, Cybus Cybermen, the Iron Legion

HISTORY

There have also been occasions when the timeline of our universe has been changed by powerful beings or the use of time travel. For example, human guerrillas from a Dalek-occupied Earth of the 22nd century once came back to the 20th century and accidentally started the sequence of events that led to the Dalek victory.[6] The Trickster twice changed history by getting to one of the Doctor's friends before he met them: having Sarah Jane Smith die as a schoolgirl, instead of her friend,[7] and having Donna Noble turn right instead of left for a job interview, meaning she never met the Doctor; without her help, he died, and all the subsequent disasters he prevented occurred.[8] In all these cases, the timeline was restored.

LEFT: Morgaine, Battle-Queen of a parallel universe.

BEHIND THE SCENES

Parallel universes have long been a staple of pulp science fiction, and *Doctor Who* has not been afraid to use them. While it's never quite been said in the show, there does seem to be a distinction between parallel universes, which are permanent, and alternate timelines, where the Doctor sees it as his duty to restore the original version of history.

FOOTNOTES
[1] *Inferno* • [2] "Rise of the Cybermen" / "The Age of Steel" • [3] *Battlefield* • [4] *The Iron Legion* • [5] *Assimilation²* • [6] *Day of the Daleks* • [7] "Whatever Happened to Sarah Jane?" • [8] "Turn Left"

TIMELINE

THE EDGE OF DESTRUCTION

FIRST DOCTOR

DAVID WHITAKER

The Doctor and Susan visit Quinnis in the Fourth Universe.

1964

1970

INFERNO

THIRD DOCTOR

DON HOUGHTON

THE FACE OF THE ENEMY (1998)

DAVID A. MCINTEE

The first parallel universe the Doctor visits is very similar to ours, but Britain is a fascist Republic, populated by "evil" versions of his friends and colleagues. This world is destroyed in a vast volcanic eruption when the scientists at the Inferno project crack open the Earth's crust.

1970

1989

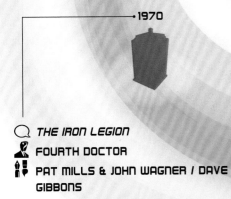

THE IRON LEGION

FOURTH DOCTOR

PAT MILLS & JOHN WAGNER / DAVE GIBBONS

The Doctor is swept to a universe where Rome never fell and has conquered the galaxy by the 20th century, thanks to a brutal robot army, the Iron Legion, led by the eagle-headed robot General Ironicus. This civilization has long benefited from the power of the evil Malevilus, demonic creatures who feed on death.

BATTLEFIELD

SEVENTH DOCTOR

BEN AARONOVITCH

A future incarnation of the Doctor lives as Merlin in another parallel universe, one where King Arthur dies at the Battle of Camlann, but the fight against Morgaine continues for nearly 1,200 years, with knights fighting using powered armor, laser guns, and ornithopters.

2012

ASSIMILATION²

ELEVENTH DOCTOR

SCOTT & DAVID TIPTON, TONY LEE

The Cybermen discover a parallel universe where a similar cyborg race, the Borg, exist. They make contact, and together they begin a conquest of this universe. The Doctor follows them and teams up with Jean-Luc Picard of the starship *Enterprise* to defeat the cybernetic races.

2006

"THE ARMY OF GHOSTS" / "DOOMSDAY"

TENTH DOCTOR

RUSSELL T DAVIES

The universes are separated by the Void, a nothingness that not even the Time Lords can explore. Four Daleks escape the Time War by hiding in the Void, and Rose ends up living in this universe with a mortal copy of the tenth Doctor.

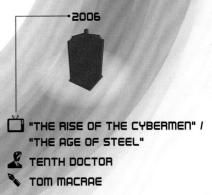

2006

"THE RISE OF THE CYBERMEN" / "THE AGE OF STEEL"

TENTH DOCTOR

TOM MACRAE

In another world, Britain has a President, but the true power is John Lumic of the Cybus Corporation, who is converting people into Cybermen. In this world, Rose Tyler's father has not died and has become rich selling the soft drink Vitex.

THE TIME VORTEX

The Doctor's TARDIS and most other time machines travel through the Time Vortex. This usually resembles a tunnel lined with writhing, ever-changing patterns of energy. There have been references to "paths" within the Vortex,[1] and the Doctor may have hinted at its overall shape by describing it as the "time spiral."[2] Anything entering the Vortex without the correct shielding is killed, destroyed, or at best splintered. There are beings that live in the Vortex and are sustained by its energies, like the Mandragora Helix, the Chronovores, the Vortisaurs, and the Reapers.

BEHIND THE SCENES

The Time Vortex is one of those ideas that ended up as a fact without ever really being established in a specific story. The phrase probably gained currency from Terrance Dicks's influential novelizations of TV stories. Those books coined many terms for things not named in the show. For example, they established the column in the middle of the TARDIS console as the "time rotor" and the device meant to disguise the TARDIS as the "chameleon circuit." While the TV series had always called the TARDIS's main room the "control room," the phrase used in the books—"console room"—has stuck.

HISTORY

On Gallifrey there was a place, possibly a natural feature, the Untempered Schism, where Time Lords could look straight into the Vortex. Young Time Lords were initiated by being taken to it. The Doctor has said that a Time Lord who absorbed the energies of the Time Vortex would become "a vengeful god."[3] This may have temporarily happened to Rose Tyler when she opened up the TARDIS console.[4] Everyone traveling through the Vortex absorbs a little of its energy, and humans who time travel "too much" become "more than human." Amy and Rory conceived a child while the TARDIS was in the Vortex, and she was born with a number of Time Lord abilities as a result.[5]

RIGHT: The TARDIS in the Vortex, a realm which also sustains many strange entities.

FOOTNOTES
[1] ▭ *The Chase* • [2] ▭ *The Sun Makers* • [3] ▭ "The Sound of Drums" • [4] ▭ "The Parting of the Ways" • [5] ▭ "A Good Man Goes to War"

FIRST APPEARANCE
▭ *(seen)* The Chase (1965)
▭ *(named)* Day of the Daleks (1972)

INHABITANTS
Chronovores, Vortisaurs, Reapers

FACT FILE

📺 *THE ENEMY OF THE WORLD*
🔍 *STAR DEATH*
Salamander, would-be dictator of 21st-century Earth, and Fenris, an agent of the Order of the Black Sun, both fell into the Vortex and became trapped floating in time and space.

🔍 *4-D WAR*
Fenris was later retrieved.

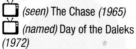

 CITY OF DEATH

In 1979, human scientist Professor Kerensky could create a time machine that could age an egg into a chicken skeleton in moments, but—perhaps because he did not know about the Vortex—this was not true time travel, just the creation of a separate time-space continuum.

TIMELASH

It is possible to travel in time without entering the Vortex—the Kontron Tunnels of Karfel created "time corridors in space."

THE CHASE, THE DALEKS' MASTER PLAN

It's unclear if the Daleks' time corridors used similar techniques, but other time machines they operated— such as the TARDIS-like machines—certainly entered the Vortex.

DAY OF THE DALEKS

The portable time machines used by the Daleks in the 22nd century (when they also operated a "vortex magnetron" that could attract time travelers) could also enter the Vortex.

"THE EMPTY CHILD" / "THE DOCTOR DANCES"

The Time Agents of 51st-century Earth used wristwatch-style Time Vortex Manipulators to travel in time.

THE END OF TIME

At the end of the Last Great Time War, the Time Lords planned the "Ultimate Sanction"—opening a rupture in time that would have destroyed the Time Vortex, and with it, the universe. The Time Lords would have escaped by becoming beings of pure consciousness.

THE FIRST PLANETS AND ANCIENT CIVILIZATIONS

As matter coalesced, stars and galaxies formed, soon followed by the first planets. Life began on some of these worlds. The first humanoid life—ancestors of the Time Lords—evolved on Gallifrey. The early civilizations would become powerful in their own right; later, beings such as the Osirians,[1] Exxilons,[2] and Time Lords would be worshiped as gods. Beings like the Daemons[3] and Light[4] had no qualms about intervening to affect the development of other species. As life developed, so did creatures that fed on life.

FIRST APPEARANCE

📺 *Racnoss: "The Runaway Bride" (2006)*

📺 *Nestenes:* Spearhead from Space *(1970)*

📺 *Great Vampires:* State of Decay *(1980)*

HISTORY

When the universe was smaller and darker, it swarmed with predatory creatures like the Racnoss, Nestenes, and Great Vampires. These were fought by the Fledgling Empires, the first interstellar powers.[5] The early universe was a dangerous, lawless place, until the Time Lords imposed order—not just in the sense of law enforcement (although there were times when they did that, and the Doctor once described them as "galactic ticket inspectors"[6]), but because it was the early Time Lords who locked down the laws of physics we see today. Other early races operated rival sciences, some of which strongly resembled magic.[7] The Time Lords took action against other races' time-travel experiments, which, if they went wrong, had the potential to destroy the universe.[8] The early Time Lords also fought wars against species that were antilife, driving them all to extinction or near extinction. Other ancient civilizations collapsed as a result of their own hubris or as a result of natural disaster.

FOOTNOTES

[1] 📺 *Pyramids of Mars* •
[2] 📺 *Death to the Daleks* •
[3] 📺 *The Daemons* •
[4] 📺 *Ghost Light* • [5] 📺 *"The Runaway Bride"* • [6] 📺 *The Time Warrior* • [7] 📖 *Christmas on a Rational Planet* •
[8] 📺 *The Two Doctors*

LEFT: The Valley of the Gods, on the ancient planet of Xaos.

RIGHT: River Song left a message for the Doctor on Planet One.

COLONY IN SPACE

A genetically engineered race of superbeings on Uxarieus all but died out when radiation from their ultimate weapon poisoned the soil.

DEATH TO THE DALEKS

The Exxilons built an automated city so advanced that it kicked its people out, reducing one of the most advanced races in the universe to Stone Age primitives.

THE HAND OF FEAR

Kastria was ravaged by solar winds, and the scientist Eldrad destroyed the barriers that would have protected his people when King Rokon refused to abdicate in his favor.

CITY OF DEATH

The Jagaroth wiped themselves out in a huge war, and the explosion of their last ship sparked the creation of life on Earth.

THE LIFE BRINGER

The fourth Doctor once saw a being much like the Greek god Prometheus seed a galaxy much like our own with "life spores."

TIME-FLIGHT

The Vardan–Kosnax War devastated whole worlds, including Xeraphas.

THE WARRIOR'S STORY

The oldest planet in our galaxy is Xaos.

THE ONE DOCTOR

Many thought the Jelloids from Bendalos were the first living creatures.

"THE SHAKESPEARE CODE"

The Carrionites developed a word-based science indistinguishable from magic. These witchlike creatures were banished into the Deep Darkness.

"THE PANDORICA OPENS"

The oldest planet in the universe, known as Planet One, has a mysterious inscription carved into one of its diamond cliffs—the first recorded writing. When the Doctor saw it, he recognized it as a message from his girlfriend, River Song.

SECRETS OF THE STARS

The Ancient Lights were beings who controlled worlds using astrology.

"THE GOD COMPLEX"

The planet Tivoli has a civilization that is one of the oldest in the galaxy and has survived by cowardice—surrendering to all conquerors before any damage is done.

GALAXIES

There are countless galaxies in the universe, and they come in all shapes and sizes. Because of the Doctor's love of Earth, most of the places he goes are either in Earth's galaxy or, further in the future, other places human beings have explored or settled.

Andromeda (p. 250) is the nearest galaxy to the Milky Way of a similar shape and size.

Mutter's Spiral (p. 30), the galaxy containing Earth, is the largest galaxy in its region of the universe. It is surrounded by smaller galaxies.

THE DALEKS

Skaro, home planet of the Daleks, is in the Seventh Galaxy (p. 126).

ROGUE PLANET

The rogue planet Skardal originated in the 84th Galaxy.

GALAXY 4

Galaxy Four was the home of the Rills and the Drahvins—the Doctor met them both on a doomed world.

THE DALEKS' MASTER PLAN

In the year 4000, the "Outer Galaxies" united with the Daleks against Earth's galaxy. Their leaders were Trantis of the Tenth Galaxy (largest of the Outer Galaxies), Gearon, Malpha, Sentreal, and Warrien. They reached an arrangement with Zephon of the Fifth Galaxy (presumably the same Galaxy Five that fought the Federation), who brought with him the rulers of another two galaxies, Celation and Beaus.

THE DOMINATORS

The Dominators claimed to be the masters of ten galaxies.

THE LAST SONTARAN

The home world of the Sontarans is in the Melasaran Galaxy.

THE TIME WARRIOR

The Sontaran Lynx once boasted, "there is not a galaxy in the universe which our space fleets have not subjugated."

THE MONSTER OF PELADON

Galaxy Five fought a war with the Galactic Federation of the Milky Way.

"NEW EARTH," "GRIDLOCK"

Five billion years in the future, humanity is based on New Earth, in the M87 Galaxy, which may be the home of the Macra.

THE STAR BEAST

On the other side of the universe is the Wrarth Galaxy, ruled by the Star Council and policed by the bizarre Wrarth Warriors. This galaxy was menaced by the Meeps when that once-peaceful race was affected by the rays of the Black Sun.

THE TWO DOCTORS

Scientists of the Third Zone studied pin galaxies, which only existed for an attosecond.

DELTA AND THE BANNERMEN, DRAGONFIRE

Earth's influence spread to five then 12 galaxies.

TRAGEDY DAY

Humanity reached the Pangloss Galaxy and settled the planet Olleril.

THE ALSO PEOPLE

The People of the Worldsphere live in what they call Home Galaxy.

THE APOCALYPSE ELEMENT

At one time, the Daleks were based in the Seriphia Galaxy (pp. 142–43).

PLANET OF THE OOD

The Second Bountiful Human Empire stretched across three galaxies (the Tri-Galactic) by the 42nd century. The galaxies were Mutter's Spiral, the galaxy containing both Sense-Sphere and Ood-Sphere, and a third.

THE LAST DODO

Other nearby galaxies include M82, M83, and M84.

"THE UNICORN AND THE WASP"

The Silfrax Galaxy was where the hives of the Vespiforms could be found.

THE END OF TIME

The Doctor once named a galaxy "Alison."

"NIGHTMARE IN SILVER"

Far in the future, humanity destroyed the entire Tiberian Galaxy in an effort to eradicate the Cybermen.

Further afield, there are:

CARNIVAL OF MONSTERS

The Acteon Galaxy (p. 252)

THE WEB PLANET

The Isop Galaxy (p. 260).

THE ARMAGEDDON FACTOR

The Helical Galaxy, location of Atrios and Zeos.

THE WELL-MANNERED WAR

The Fostrix Galaxy (location of Barclow and Metralubit) . . .

"KISS KISS, BANG BANG"

. . . and the Vegas Galaxies.

FOUR TO DOOMSDAY

Urbanka was in the Inokshi system in Galaxy RE 1489.

MUTTER'S SPIRAL: NOTABLE FEATURES

The galaxy containing Earth's Solar System has been known by many names, including the Milky Way, Galaxia Kyklos,[1] and the Stellian Galaxy.[2] The galaxy is a spiral galaxy around 150,000 light years across, containing around 150 billion stars. The Time Lords call it Mutter's Spiral,[3] possibly because it is the home of the Mutts, a mutant insect species.[4]

NIGHTMARE OF EDEN

Early in humanity's interstellar exploration, there seems to have been a region called "West Galaxy," with planets such as Azure, Brus, Gidi, Lvan, Ranx, Eden, Vij, Darp, and Zil, three planets in the M37 system, and the region of space known as the Cygnus Gap.

THE TRIAL OF A TIME LORD

The galaxy has spiral arms. The Perseus Arm is home to the planet Mogar and the Black Hole of Tartarus. There are also secondary and tertiary arms.

THE TWO DOCTORS,
DELTA AND THE BANNERMEN

Other features of the galaxy include the Constellation of Canthares, the Hercules Cluster, the Madillon Cluster, and the Softel Nebula. (Some space travelers seem to use "constellation" to mean a region of stars close to each other.)

The galaxy is divided into Quadrants and Sectors by a number of space-faring races (there may not be a standardized system for numbering sectors).

At the center of the galaxy is a supermassive black hole.

On the edge of the galaxy are the rim worlds.

THE GREATEST SHOW IN THE GALAXY

The Psychic Circus, "the Greatest Show in the Galaxy," visited Marpesia, Othrys, the Grand Pagoda on Cinethon, and the Boriatic Wastes. It ended up on Segonax in the Southern Nebula, also the location of Whizz Kid's home planet, Lelex (planet of the Monopods), and Vulpana. The explorer Captain Cook saw the singing squids of Anagonia, Dioscuros, Golobus, the Baleful Plains of Grolon, Iphitus, the Gold Mines of Katakiki, Leophantos, Melagophon, Neogorgon, Periboea, the Bouncing Trees of Upas, and the Architrave of Batgeld's collection of early Ganglion pottery on Fagiro.

THE RIBOS OPERATION

Mutter's Spiral has the Magellanic Clouds, dwarf galaxies that most consider part of the same structure as the main galaxy. These are the location of the Cyrhennic Alliance, whose planets include Cyrrhenis Minima, Freytus, Leviatha, Stapros, and the worlds of the Pontenese and Schlangi. Ribos is in the constellation of Skythra, which is three light centuries from the Magellanic Clouds.

FOOTNOTES
[1] Four to Doomsday • [2] The Trial of a Time Lord •
[3] The Deadly Assasin • [4] The Mutants

MUTTER'S SPIRAL: LOCAL POLITICS

Mutter's Spiral is the place of origin for, among others, the Adipose, Alpha Centauri, Arcturans, Argolin, Axons, Cat-People, Chameleons, Chelonians, Cybermen, Daemons, Draconians, Exxilons, Foamasi, Ice Warriors, Jacondans, Jagaroth, Judoon, Kraals, Kronteps, Krynoids, Legion, Manussans, Medusoids, Mentors, Mogarians, Moroks, Movellans, Nestene, Ogri, Ogrons, Pakhars, Poodles, Pyroviles, Silurians, Skonnons, Sycorax, Terileptils, the Third Zone, Trions, Tzun, Union of Traken, Vegans, Vogans, and Zygons. Reports vary on whether the Daleks and Time Lords come from Mutter's Spiral, but they've certainly been active here (the Dalek Empire shares a border with the Earth and Draconian Empires in the mid-26th century), and spaceships from Earth can reach Karn, near Gallifrey.

HISTORY

Over billions of years, civilizations have risen and fallen. The Sontaran–Rutan War has been fought here for thousands of years—the Rutans once controlled the entire galaxy, until they were beaten back by the Sontarans. In the future, there will be several eras where a human government dominates the Milky Way. The first Earth Empire will begin in the early 26th century and last for around 500 years, becoming ever more corrupt. After that, Earth will join the Galactic Federation, containing many worlds, including former enemies of the human race, such as the Draconians and Ice Warriors. Galaxy-wide laws governing such things as distress signals, trade, extradition between planets, and conduct of warfare exist in documents such as the Shadow Proclamation and Galactic Charter, enforced by races like the Judoon, Megara, and Atraxi. (The Shadow Proclamation is both a codification of galactic laws and the name of the "outer space police" who enforce them, see p. 210.)

OPPOSITE: The tenth Doctor and Donna help resolve a dispute between the Draconians and Ice Warriors.

FIRST APPEARANCE

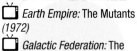

- *Earth Empire:* The Mutants *(1972)*
- *Galactic Federation:* The Curse of Peladon *(1972)*
- *The Sontaran–Rutan War:* The Time Warrior *(1974)*
- *The Shadow Proclamation:* "Rose" *(2005)*

BEHIND THE SCENES

Most of the planets and monsters we've seen in *Doctor Who* are from our Milky Way galaxy. As the series has progressed, especially in media other than TV, we've seen adventures where monsters from older stories have interacted—e.g., in the comic strip *Abslom Daak … Dalek Killer* (Steve Moore, 1980), the human Abslom Daak leads a team including an Ice Warrior and a Draconian who fight the Daleks.

THE SOLAR SYSTEM

OVERVIEW OF THE SOLAR SYSTEM

MARS

EARTH

moon

VENUS

Earth sits at the space-time coordinates 58044684884,[1] or 6309,[2] in Sector 80-23 in the third quadrant,[3] at Galactic North 6° 9077.[4] It orbits the Sun (also known as Sol), and being third planet from the Sun (most of the time), the Time Lords have designated it Sol III in the Mutter's Spiral.[5] The Solar System is the place of origin of the indomitable human race, which billions of years from now, it is said, will have touched every star in the sky.[6]

ABOVE: The Solar System, as seen from the TARDIS in *Logopolis*.

HISTORY

Throughout its history, many of the other planets and moons of the Solar System have seen the rise and fall of other intelligent species, too. Countless aliens have come to the Solar System for countless reasons, both benign and malevolent. While astronomers are always improving their discoveries and definitions, humans consider there are eight planets in their Solar System: Mercury, Venus, Earth, Mars, Jupiter, Saturn, Uranus, Neptune, plus the dwarf planet Pluto. In the ancient past, the Solar System had two additional planets. One was Mondas, twin planet to Earth.[7] The other was the Fifth Planet, which had an orbit where the asteroid belt is now.[8] In the future, the planet Vulcan will be discovered closer to the Sun than Mercury.[9] There is also a planet farther out than Pluto—the human race will call it Cassius;[10] the Daleks call it Omega.[11]

FACT FILE

MERCURY is a hot world, home to bizarre creatures.

VENUS was home to a truly alien race hundreds of millions of years ago, and it will be fully colonized and terraformed by humans in the future.

EARTH was home to the Silurians when mankind was still a primitive ape. In the future it will be called Tellus, Homeworld, Tellurian planet, Ravalox, Terra, Original Terra, Old Old Earth, Original Earth, and Home Planet.

EARTH'S MOON is larger than some planets and has an interesting history.

MARS is a cold, dying world and the ancestral home of the Ice Warriors. It has been visited by a number of other alien races.

JUPITER is a gas giant with several interesting moons.

SATURN'S main feature is its beautiful ring system, but it also has important moons.

URANUS became one of the major human Solar Planets and the source of rare elements.

NEPTUNE, by comparison, seems to be something of a backwater.

PLUTO Mankind will be relocated to Pluto millions of years in the future.

Some have suggested that the mysterious Planet 14, where the second Doctor fought the Cybermen, was a world at the edge of the Solar System.[12]

PLUTO

SATURN

URANUS

NEPTUNE

MERCURY

JUPITER

EUROPA

GANYMEDE

IO

FOOTNOTES
[1] 📺 *The Pirate Planet* • [2] 📺 *Four to Doomsday* •
[3] 📺 *Logopolis* • [4] 📺 *Enlightenment* • [5] 📺 *The Deadly Assassin* • [6] 📺 *"The End of the World"* • [7] 📺 *The Tenth Planet* • [8] 📺 *Image of the Fendahl* • [9] 📺 *The Power of the Daleks* • [10] 📺 *The Sun Makers* • [11] 📖 *The Dalek Book* • [12] 📺 *The Invasion*

THE SUN AND MERCURY

Earth orbits the star Sol (commonly called "the Sun"). The fate of humanity has always depended on the Sun. The earliest humans worshipped it. Millennia from now, solar flares will scour the Earth of almost all life—it will take 10,000 years to recover to the point at which it can sustain a human population. Millions of years from now, Earth will face a catastrophic collision with the Sun. In both cases, the human race will build vast space arks containing carefully selected populations, technology, and artifacts.

HISTORY

The strategy works. Mankind will survive and eventually return to repopulate its home planet. Five billion years from now, though, the Sun will finally expand into a red giant, swallowing up the nearest planets, marking the End of the World (p. 278).

The nearest known planet to the Sun is Mercury, a small and intensely hot world. Humanity sent space probes there to look for water, but it's not known if the planet was ever colonized by people, although Donna Noble claimed the Doctor took her on holiday to Mercury. Even on a world hot enough to melt iron, life can be found. The Daleks knew of the Supermen of Mercury, but they had already left before the earliest Dalek scouts reached the Solar System. In the 19th century, members of the telepathic Indo were marooned there. By the 367th century, there were human mining operations on the planet.

ABOVE RIGHT: Deadly solar flares have ravaged the Earth and left it uninhabitable.

BELOW: A human mining colony was set up on Mercury.

BEHIND THE SCENES

Mercury is the planet in the Solar System we've seen least of in *Doctor Who*. The Sun is a constant presence, of course, but has frequently been a threat to the Earth.

FIRST APPEARANCE
📺 *The Sun:* An Unearthly Child (1963)
🔍 *Mercury:* Hot Stuff! (2011)

LOCATION
The star and (usually) the nearest planet to that star in Earth's Solar System

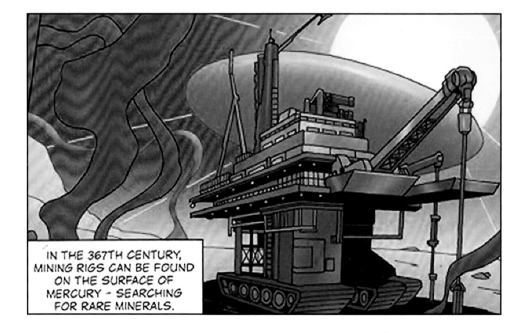

IN THE 367TH CENTURY, MINING RIGS CAN BE FOUND ON THE SURFACE OF MERCURY – SEARCHING FOR RARE MINERALS.

TIMELINE

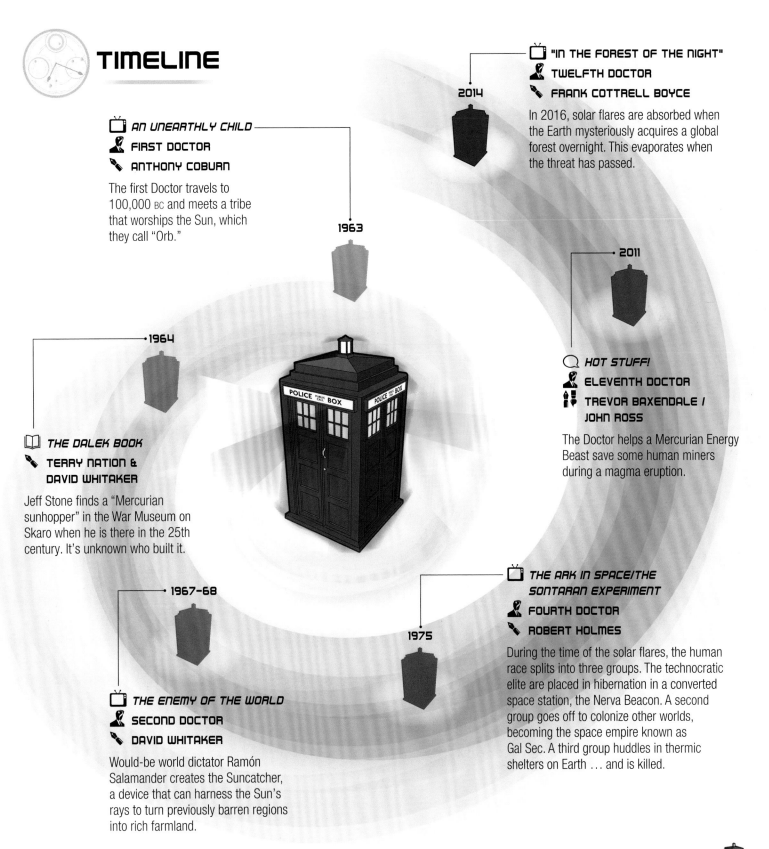

"IN THE FOREST OF THE NIGHT"
TWELFTH DOCTOR
FRANK COTTRELL BOYCE

2014

In 2016, solar flares are absorbed when the Earth mysteriously acquires a global forest overnight. This evaporates when the threat has passed.

AN UNEARTHLY CHILD
FIRST DOCTOR
ANTHONY COBURN

The first Doctor travels to 100,000 BC and meets a tribe that worships the Sun, which they call "Orb."

1963

2011

HOT STUFF!
ELEVENTH DOCTOR
TREVOR BAXENDALE / JOHN ROSS

The Doctor helps a Mercurian Energy Beast save some human miners during a magma eruption.

1964

THE DALEK BOOK
TERRY NATION & DAVID WHITAKER

Jeff Stone finds a "Mercurian sunhopper" in the War Museum on Skaro when he is there in the 25th century. It's unknown who built it.

THE ARK IN SPACE/THE SONTARAN EXPERIMENT
FOURTH DOCTOR
ROBERT HOLMES

1975

During the time of the solar flares, the human race splits into three groups. The technocratic elite are placed in hibernation in a converted space station, the Nerva Beacon. A second group goes off to colonize other worlds, becoming the space empire known as Gal Sec. A third group huddles in thermic shelters on Earth … and is killed.

1967–68

THE ENEMY OF THE WORLD
SECOND DOCTOR
DAVID WHITAKER

Would-be world dictator Ramón Salamander creates the Suncatcher, a device that can harness the Sun's rays to turn previously barren regions into rich farmland.

VULCAN

Since the 19th century, astronomers on Earth had theorized that there was a planet orbiting the Sun closer than Mercury. In the early 21st century, such a planet was discovered and named Vulcan. It's unclear whether Vulcan had always been there, or whether it was a rogue planet recently captured by the Sun's gravity. In any event, incredibly, it was able to support human life, and by 2020 a small group of colonists had set up a base there. The planet had bubbling mercury swamps but a breathable atmosphere, no radiation, and temperatures around 86°F (30°C).

FIRST APPEARANCE
📖 The Dalek Book *(1964)*

INHABITANTS
No native life—marooned Daleks

HISTORY

Vulcan was difficult to reach from Earth, and Governor Hensell's regime was so brutal that it inspired a group of the colonists to form a rebel movement. Earth dispatched an Examiner, but the Governor's men shot him on arrival. The second Doctor discovered the body and was then himself mistaken for the Examiner. The real source of interest on Vulcan was that a scientist, Lesterson, had discovered a space capsule in the swamp. It was retrieved and found to be made of an alien metal that could revolutionize space travel. The capsule was opened, and inside were three Daleks, who activated and declared that they would be the colonists' servants.[1]

OPPOSITE: Vulcan became the resting place for a dormant Dalek capsule.

FOOTNOTE
[1] 📺 *The Power of the Daleks*

FACT FILE

📺 THE POWER OF THE DALEKS
The colonists ignored the Doctor's warnings, keen to take advantage of the Daleks' expertise and labor. The Daleks, of course, had plans of their own. First they needed to lay out power lines to give themselves freedom of movement around the colony.

📽 THE POWER OF THE DALEKS
With that done, the Daleks secretly started up an assembly line in their ship, building a whole army of Dalek casings, homes for Dalek mutants.

📺 THE POWER OF THE DALEKS
The Daleks began to take control of the human colony, exterminating all who resisted. Thankfully, the Doctor was able to mobilize the rebel colonists. Together, they managed to destroy the Daleks' external power supplies, rendering the Daleks immobile once again.

📖 THE DALEK BOOK
Daleks of the year 2400 included Vulcan on their maps of the Solar System.

📺 THE TENTH PLANET
Vulcan must have been discovered after 1986, because in that year Mondas appeared in the Solar System and was designated "the Tenth Planet."

📖 THE TAKING OF PLANET 5
There were references to Vulcan in the Museum of Things That Don't Exist.

📺 "ASYLUM OF THE DALEKS"
A Dalek from Vulcan survived its encounter with the Doctor but was driven insane. It ended up on the Daleks' Asylum Planet.

BEHIND THE SCENES

Vulcan was mentioned in *The Dalek Book*, but its only TV appearance was in the debut story of the second Doctor, *The Power of the Daleks* (1966)—perhaps no coincidence since both were by David Whitaker (with Terry Nation for the former). It is a coincidence, though, that it shares a name with Mr. Spock's home planet in *Star Trek*—that show had only been running a few weeks in the US when *The Power of the Daleks* was written.

VENUS

At the start of the 21st century, the environment on Venus is far too hostile for human life, but by the end of the century, flowers will be cultivated there.[1] Humans had begun to terraform Venus, and by the beginning of the 25th century, the planet had been transformed into an Earthlike world. The Winston Dam supplied all of its electricity. Building it had lowered the sea level, exposing the mineral-rich Churchill Mountains. The planet became an industrial hotbed, with a road network, mines, and refineries. People traveled the planet in hoverskeets and copterjets. The planet had swamps, jungles, and silver grass. The most popular drink was coffeemilk.[2]

HISTORY

Three billion years ago, there was an advanced race of six-legged, four-eyed beings on Venus whose civilization endured for millions of years and at least 25 dynasties, despite the fact that all metals were poisonous to them (they avoided them in their technology). Ancient Venusian animal life included the shanghorn, klak-kluk, and pattifangs.[3] The first Doctor visited this civilization at least twice, while the third Doctor sang Venusian lullabies,[4] was one of the few two-armed beings ever to master the martial art Venusian Aikido (or Venusian Karate,[5]) and mentioned Venusian hopscotch.[6] The Venusians knew for tens of thousands of years that their planet's climate was changing, and that they would die out, and only a few cranks believed there was any way of reversing this effect. Before life on Earth even began, this Venusian civilization had faded from history.[7]

ABOVE RIGHT: *Venusian Lullaby*, by Paul Leonard, visited the ancient Venusian society.

RIGHT: The Daleks launched a vicious attack on Venus as a staging post for an invasion of Earth.

OPPOSITE: Venus is extremely inhospitable for humans.

FIRST APPEARANCE

📖 The Dalek Book *(1964)*

INHABITANTS

Various Venusian civilizations and animals; Dalek invaders

FOOTNOTES

[1] 📺 *The Wheel in Space* • [2] 📖 *The Dalek Book* • [3] 📺 *The Green Death* • [4] 📺 *The Curse of Peladon* • [5] 📺 *Inferno* • [6] 📺 *Death to the Daleks* • [7] 📖 *Venusian Lullaby*

📖 INVASION OF THE DALEKS
(THE DALEK BOOK)

In 2400, the Daleks attacked New Paris, the capital of Venus, enslaving the survivors. Jeff Stone, mineralogist, and his siblings, Andy and Mary, were able to stay free.

📖 THE OIL WELL (THE DALEK BOOK)

The Daleks began building metal roadways across Venus but had difficulty adapting to the moist atmosphere. They were stockpiling resources to use in an invasion of Earth and were in particular need of Venus's vast oil reserves.

📖 THE SECRET OF THE MOUNTAIN
(THE DALEK BOOK)

The Daleks were building 20 war rockets in a secret hangar underneath the Churchill Mountains. The Stone brothers alerted the Space Army, which shot down the rockets. Venus was now free of Daleks.

📺 THE DALEKS' MASTER PLAN

Mavic Chen had a special forces squad that operated from the planet. Mars and Venus had rival sports teams.

📺 GENESIS OF THE DALEKS

The Dalek War against Venus in Space Year 17,000 was halted by the intervention of a fleet of War Rockets from the planet Hyperon. The rockets were made of a metal that was completely resistant to Dalek firepower, and so the Dalek taskforce was utterly destroyed.

🎧 VENUS MANTRAP

The government on Venus was responsible for two artificial moons: Eros and Thanatos. Eros had a reputation for romance; Thanatos was an industrial warhive.

🎧 VOYAGE TO VENUS

In the very distant future, the sixth Doctor took Jago and Litefoot to Venus at a time when Earth was abandoned and the humans of Venus had evolved thick green fur.

BEHIND THE SCENES

The adventures of Jeff Stone fighting the Daleks were told in a series of short stories, comic strips, and text features in the very first *Doctor Who* book, *The Dalek Book* (Terry Nation & David Whitaker). The darker, more alien prehistory of Venus was explored in the 1994 novel *Venusian Lullaby* (Paul Leonard, 1994).

THE YOUNG EARTH

The Earth formed around 4.6 billion years ago as a cloud of matter around the Sun began to coalesce into the various planets. Part of the mix was a Racnoss spacecraft containing the few survivors of that vicious race's war with the Time Lords. It became embedded in the planet.[1] Deep within the crust were pockets of Stahlman's Gas, a great potential heat source, but powerful enough to split the planet apart and capable of producing a substance that could reverse evolution if not carefully controlled.[2]

HISTORY

Life on Earth began 400 million years ago, when a damaged Jagaroth ship, a refugee from a civil war that wiped out the rest of the species, exploded, bathing pools of primordial soup with radiation.[3] Life evolved quickly, emerging from the oceans onto the land. At the same time, aliens and alien technology reached Earth, often damaged or lying dormant. Humans were not the first intelligent life to emerge; 260 million years ago, Permians (animated skeletons with powerful electric fields) hunted 96 percent of life to extinction.[4] The biosphere recovered, and the dinosaur age lasted tens of millions of years. Near the end of that era, the Silurians, intelligent reptile people, evolved and developed an advanced global civilization. They were driven into subterranean hibernation vaults by the arrival of a rogue planet. They expected it to devastate Earth, but in fact it settled into orbit as Earth's moon.

BEHIND THE SCENES

The date given for the beginning of life on Earth—400 million years ago—in *City of Death* (David Agnew, 1979) is far too late. Life began at least 3.8 billion years ago. Various stories have given conflicting accounts of when the Silurian civilization existed. *The Lost Ones* is a story from the 1966 *Doctor Who Annual*. The Permians were heard in the audio story *Land of the Dead* (Stephen Cole, 2000).

FIRST APPEARANCE
📺 *The Silurians:* Doctor Who and the Silurians *(1970)*

INHABITANTS
Racnoss, Primords, Jagaroth, Silurians, Sea Devils, Myrka, Permians, Titanthropes, and Atlanteans

FACT FILE

📺 **DOCTOR WHO AND THE SILURIANS, THE HUNGRY EARTH**

The Silurians lived mainly in hot climates, and there was considerable physical variation between them—even clans who lived as close together as what are now Derbyshire and Wales.

📺 **THE SEA DEVILS**

Under the oceans, the Silurians' "cousins" had a distinct culture of their own. Humans would later call these marine reptile people "Sea Devils."

📺 **DOCTOR WHO AND THE SILURIANS**

Silurians had psychic abilities and technology that allowed them to domesticate dinosaurs. The Silurians had their crops raided by primitive apes—the ancestors of mankind.

📺 **WARRIORS OF THE DEEP,** 🎧 **BLOODTIDE**

The Silurians retreated to their hibernation shelters. The automated systems never revived them, and the surface wasn't devastated to the extent that Silurian scientists had predicted. Instead, the primitive apes evolved to fill the ecological niche, and they also genetically engineered fearsome creatures like the Myrka.

🔍 **TWILIGHT OF THE SILURIANS,** 📖 **BLOOD HEAT**

The Silurians rode tyrannosaurs.

🎧 **LAST OF THE TITANS,** 📖 **THE LOST ONES**

Humans were not the only rival humanoid species to evolve on Earth—at certain points they shared the planet with the Neanderthals and with two races of giants: the Titanthropes and the Sons of the Sun, from the World-State of Atlantis, an aggressive race so advanced they launched thousands of space missions.

FOOTNOTES
[1] 📺 "The Runaway Bride" • [2] 📺 *Inferno* • [3] 📺 *City of Death* • [4] 🎧 *Land of the Dead*

OPPOSITE: *Twilight of the Silurians*—the apes rise against the reptile people.

THIS PAGE: The Silurians' advanced civilization ruled the early Earth.

THE HUMANIAN ERA

The Time Lords have a term, "the Humanian Era," which seems to refer to the period when humans lived on their planet of origin, Earth. We know that 1999 AD falls in the Humanian Era,[1] and it might correspond to what the people of the Ark called "the first segment of Time," encompassing "Nero, the Trojan wars, the Daleks."[2] If it means the period humans lived on Earth, we know something that would meet the scientific definition of human existed 12 million years ago,[3] and that Earth will end in the year 5.5/apple/26, five billion years in the future.[4]

HISTORY

Evolving from apelike creatures in the Eocene (with helpful nudges from various alien visitors), the human race will endure, in one form or another, long after the end of their homeworld—indeed they will be there until the end of the universe … and beyond. Several powerful aliens help the human race to progress, and most are worshipped as gods. The Fendahl helped along evolution; the Daemons destroyed the rival Neanderthals;[5] Scaroth of the Jagaroth taught humans to map the heavens, make fire, and turn the first wheel.[6] Scaroth, the Osirians, the Exxilons, and various renegade Time Lords all inspired ancient building projects like the pyramids and Stonehenge.[7] Earth has been threatened by many alien races, too—some with a desire to enslave or convert the human race; some keen on Earth's abundant resources; and others who, completely indifferent to Earth and humanity, are using the planet as a pawn in some larger struggle.

BEHIND THE SCENES

The phrase "Humanian Era" first appeared in the *Doctor Who* TV movie, on a display on the TARDIS console. The four eras referred to there are the Humanian, Sensorian, Sumaran, and Rassilon. "Sensorian" might somehow be a reference to the Sensorites, the Sumaran Empire appeared in *Snakedance*, and the Rassilon Era applies to Gallifrey.

FOOTNOTES
[1] *Doctor Who: The Movie* • [2] *The Ark* • [3] *Image of the Fendahl* • [4] "The End of the World" • [5] *The Daemons* • [6] *City of Death* • [7] *Pyramids of Mars, Death to the Daleks, The Time Meddler*

LEFT & OPPOSITE: The first segment of time included the Daleks, Nero, and the Trojan War.

FACT FILE

📺 *THE REIGN OF TERROR*

The Earth is the Doctor's favorite planet, and he has said that his very favorite period in history is the French Revolution.

📺 *THE WAR GAMES*

The second Doctor told the Time Lords at his trial that Earth seemed "more vulnerable" to alien aggression than other planets. His people exiled the Doctor to Earth in the late 20th century because he had "repeatedly broken our most important law of noninterference in the affairs of other planets."

📖 *THE BURNING TO ESCAPE VELOCITY*

At the end of one Time War, an amnesiac eighth Doctor spent over 100 years living on Earth, a period that spanned the whole 20th century.

📺 *"THE CHRISTMAS INVASION,"*
📖 *JUST WAR,*
📖 *REMEMBRANCE OF THE DALEKS, AND*
📺 *THE INVASION (RESPECTIVELY)*

Earth's governments set up secret organizations to monitor alien threats: Torchwood, LONGBOW, the ICMG, UNIT, and several others.

📺 *"ALIENS IN LONDON"*

Mankind officially became aware of aliens in the late 20th and early 21st centuries. Invasions by races such as the Ice Warriors, Daleks, and Cybermen were just too public to cover up. In the event, though, most people's first contact with aliens was an incident when the Slitheen steered a spacecraft containing a Space Pig into Big Ben in 2006.

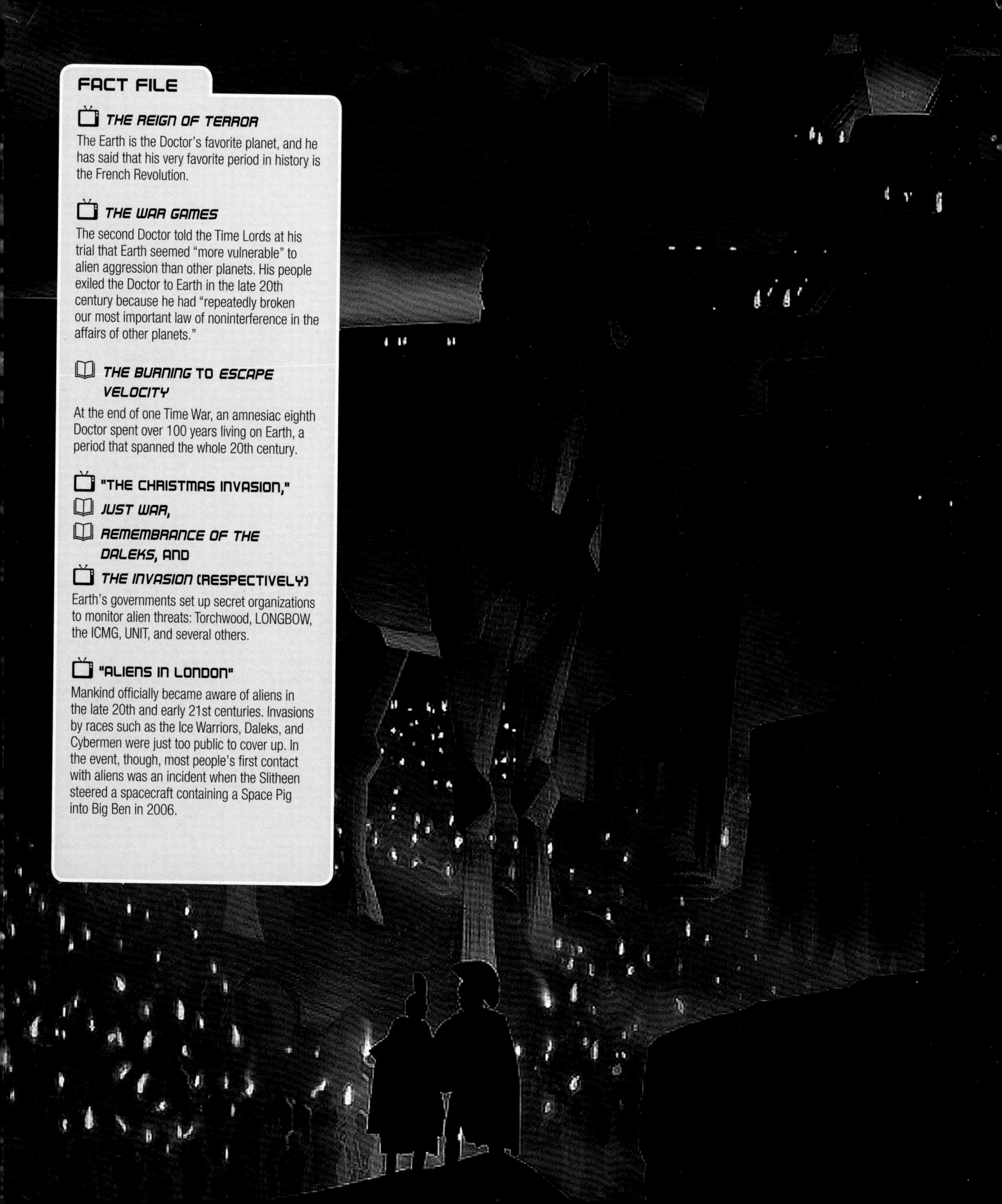

OLD EARTH

INHABITANTS

Haemovores, humans, and posthumans

Far, far into the future, the human race will spread out beyond the Earth and to the edges of the universe. The fortunes of our planet of origin will change and evolve, until the inevitable end. Empires will rise and fall, great knowledge will be won and lost. There will be long eras of peace and devastating wars. Solar flares and other activity will blast the surface, forcing the human race to evacuate in space arks. At times the world will be a beautiful garden; at others the surface will be covered by one giant city. Seas will dry up, continents will rise and fall, deserts will appear where there were once jungles and ice caps—and vice versa.

BEHIND THE SCENES

We've seen space arks in the TV stories *The Ark* (Paul Erickson & Leslie Scott, 1966), *The Ark in Space* (Robert Homes, 1975), *Frontios* (Christopher H. Bidmead, 1984), and "The Beast Below" (Steven Moffat, 2010)—they all seem to be escaping different catastrophes facing the Earth.

HISTORY

All things must pass. Billions of years from now, the National Trust will restore Earth to a "Classic" configuration of continents, but the human race will have moved on. Five billion years from now, the Sun is due to expand, obliterating the Earth and the rest of the inner planets. The end of the world proved to be a great excuse for a party, and it was the first place the ninth Doctor took Rose Tyler in the TARDIS.

LEFT: The dying Earth spawned the vampiric, leechlike Haemovores.

ABOVE: The venerable Face of Boe was there to see the End of the World.

TIMELINE

📖 **THE COMING OF THE TERRAPHILES**

🎗 **ELEVENTH DOCTOR**

✎ **MICHAEL MOORCOCK**

2010

Around the year 51,000 is the era of the Terraphiles (p. 106).

📺 **THE ARK IN SPACE / THE SONTARAN EXPERIMENT**

🎗 **FOURTH DOCTOR**

✎ **ROBERT HOLMES / BOB BAKER & DAVID MARTIN**

Many centuries from now, Earth will be ravaged by solar flares. The human race builds space arks. Ten thousand years after the solar flares, the planet will be recolonized.

1975

1977

📺 **"THE END OF THE WORLD"**

🎗 **NINTH DOCTOR**

✎ **RUSSELL T DAVIES**

By the year 12,005, the New Roman Empire has risen on Earth. Five billion years from now, the elite of the universe come to the space station Platform One to see the Earth's final destruction. At this time there is only one "purebred" human alive, Cassandra—and repeated plastic surgery has reduced her to a large blanket of skin. The universe is full of descendants of humanity.

2005

📺 **THE TALONS OF WENG-CHIANG/THE INVISIBLE ENEMY**

🎗 **FOURTH DOCTOR**

✎ **ROBERT HOLMES, BOB BAKER, DAVID MARTIN**

Around the year 5000, there will be a new Ice Age. World War Six will narrowly be averted. Mankind will plan the Great Breakout, leaving the Solar System once again.

1989

📺 **THE CURSE OF FENRIC**

🎗 **SEVENTH DOCTOR**

✎ **IAN BRIGGS**

Half a million years in the future, Earth is now a polluted wasteland, and the last living creature is the vampiric Great Haemovore.

1986

1977

📺 **THE SUN MAKERS**

🎗 **FOURTH DOCTOR**

✎ **ROBERT HOLMES**

Millions of years from now, when Earth's mineral wealth is exhausted, the Company will move mankind to Mars and then Pluto, and ruthlessly exploit their labor. By the time the Doctor defeats the Company, Earth will have had long enough to regenerate its natural resources.

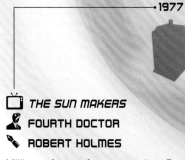

1980

📖 **K9 AND THE MISSING PLANET**

✎ **DAVID MARTIN**

At some point, the whole planet will be an arms factory known as Tellus.

📺 **THE TRIAL OF A TIME LORD**

🎗 **SIXTH DOCTOR**

✎ **ROBERT HOLMES**

To protect their secrets, the Time Lords move the Earth light years across space, where it becomes known as Ravalox. The Doctor arrives on Ravalox—and is framed by the Time Lord High Council to prevent the affair from coming to light.

THE MOON

Earth's Moon seems like a constant companion and has shone in the night's sky for the whole of human history. However, it has not always orbited the Earth. It used to be a rogue planet before it entered the Solar System and was captured by Earth's gravity. Its arrival 100 million years ago was what forced the great Silurian civilization into underground hibernation shelters. The arrival of the Moon may also have been the event that propelled Mondas from its orbit (see p. 152).

HISTORY

As the nearest celestial body to the Earth, the Moon was the obvious target for the first missions to another world. Moonshots were pretty routine by the mid-1980s.[1] It also made a good base for aliens planning to invade. The proximity of the Moon to Earth made it the logical staging post for the Cybermen as they sought to conquer mankind. The Cybermen operated at least one base on the Moon[2] and also hid their fleet on the dark side. At least four attempts to invade Earth used the Moon—the Cyber Fleet was finally destroyed in 1988.[3] The Daleks also operated from the dark side of the Moon.[4]

INHABITANTS
None known; visited by Cybermen, Daleks, and the Lords of the Ether

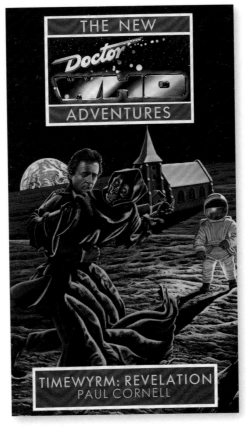

THE NEW
Doctor WHO
ADVENTURES

TIMEWYRM: REVELATION
PAUL CORNELL

ABOVE: We think of the Moon as a permanent presence in the night sky, but we're wrong.

LEFT: The seventh Doctor dances with Death on the surface of the Moon.

BEHIND THE SCENES

Doctor Who began before man had landed on the Moon—*The Dalek Book* (Terry Nation & David Whitaker, 1964) predicted the first landing would be in 1971; the 1965 comic strip *Moon Landing* (Neville Main) guessed July 1970. Stories made while the *Apollo* missions were underway depicted moonshots as being routine in the near future. As real life caught up, these stories were quietly forgotten.

FOOTNOTES
[1] 📺 *The Tenth Planet* • [2] 📺 *The Invasion, Attack of the Cybermen* • [3] 📺 *Silver Nemesis* • [4] 📖 *The Disintegrator*, 📺 *"Victory of the Daleks"*

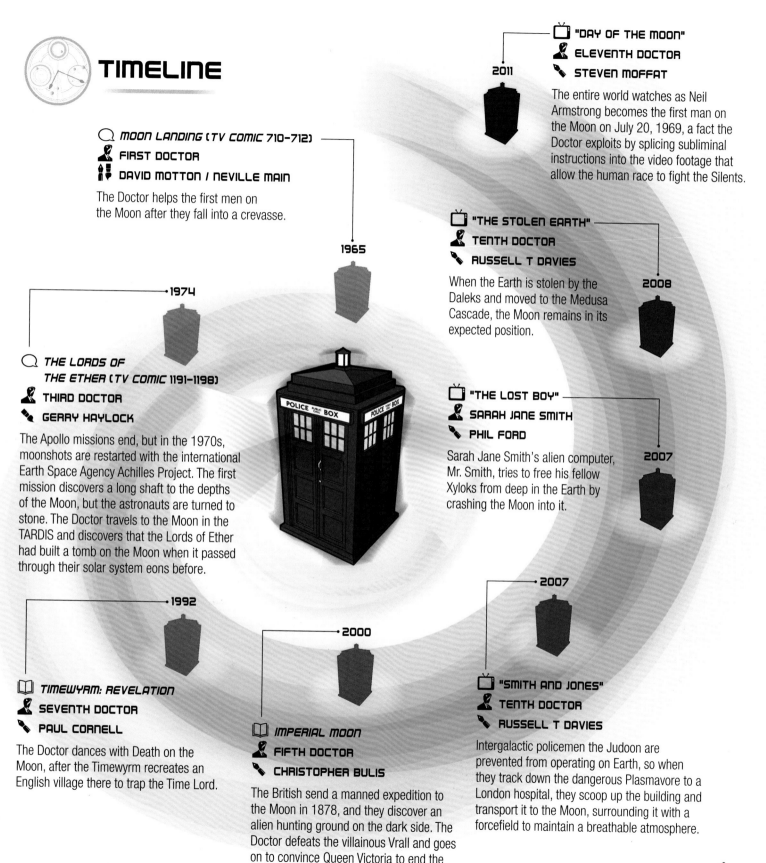

TIMELINE

"DAY OF THE MOON"
ELEVENTH DOCTOR
STEVEN MOFFAT

2011

The entire world watches as Neil Armstrong becomes the first man on the Moon on July 20, 1969, a fact the Doctor exploits by splicing subliminal instructions into the video footage that allow the human race to fight the Silents.

MOON LANDING (TV COMIC 710-712)
FIRST DOCTOR
DAVID MOTTON / NEVILLE MAIN

The Doctor helps the first men on the Moon after they fall into a crevasse.

1965

"THE STOLEN EARTH"
TENTH DOCTOR
RUSSELL T DAVIES

When the Earth is stolen by the Daleks and moved to the Medusa Cascade, the Moon remains in its expected position.

2008

1974

THE LORDS OF THE ETHER (TV COMIC 1191-1198)
THIRD DOCTOR
GERRY HAYLOCK

The Apollo missions end, but in the 1970s, moonshots are restarted with the international Earth Space Agency Achilles Project. The first mission discovers a long shaft to the depths of the Moon, but the astronauts are turned to stone. The Doctor travels to the Moon in the TARDIS and discovers that the Lords of Ether had built a tomb on the Moon when it passed through their solar system eons before.

"THE LOST BOY"
SARAH JANE SMITH
PHIL FORD

Sarah Jane Smith's alien computer, Mr. Smith, tries to free his fellow Xyloks from deep in the Earth by crashing the Moon into it.

2007

1992

2000

2007

TIMEWYRM: REVELATION
SEVENTH DOCTOR
PAUL CORNELL

The Doctor dances with Death on the Moon, after the Timewyrm recreates an English village there to trap the Time Lord.

IMPERIAL MOON
FIFTH DOCTOR
CHRISTOPHER BULIS

The British send a manned expedition to the Moon in 1878, and they discover an alien hunting ground on the dark side. The Doctor defeats the villainous Vrall and goes on to convince Queen Victoria to end the space program.

"SMITH AND JONES"
TENTH DOCTOR
RUSSELL T DAVIES

Intergalactic policemen the Judoon are prevented from operating on Earth, so when they track down the dangerous Plasmavore to a London hospital, they scoop up the building and transport it to the Moon, surrounding it with a forcefield to maintain a breathable atmosphere.

THE COLONIZATION OF THE MOON

The 21st century saw a renewed interest in the Moon. Early in the century, there were secret missions to establish the first moonbases. The next few decades saw other moonbases established, but these tended to be small-scale and perhaps privately operated, rather than part of extensive government projects. The human race had gotten no farther than the Moon when the Travel-Mat network was invented. The teleportation system was coordinated from a base on the Moon, which was reached by Travel-Mat itself. This moonbase was not huge, but it provided a comfortable posting for the Travel-Mat technicians.[1]

HISTORY

Humanity then turned inward during the middle of the 21st century as it faced environmental and political chaos: climate change, ozone layer collapse, the oil apocalypse. The space program was all but abandoned. Eventually, though, the governments of the Earth realized that problems on Earth could be solved by mining materials and energy in space, and when space travel resumed, NASA undertook Project Pit Stop, setting up a refueling base on the Moon.

Adelaide Brooke met Ed Gold when they both worked on the project. Brooke would go on to be the first woman to land on Mars, and she would successfully campaign to colonize Mars before the Moon (p. 60).

ABOVE: 2015 saw Moon Village One invaded by the Lunar Strangers.

BELOW: The Travel-Mat global network was controlled from a London HQ, but run from a moonbase.

FIRST APPEARANCE
🖵 (early moonbase)
The Seeds of Death (1969)

STATUS
Destroyed (see p. 55)

FOOTNOTE
[1] 🖵 The Seeds of Death

TIMELINE

🔍 THE LUNAR STRANGERS
👤 FIFTH DOCTOR
✎ GARETH ROBERTS

Moon Village One sees the arrival of the bovine aliens Ravnok and Vartex, who seek to retrieve the treasure they had buried on the site the moonbase has been built on. They attempt to destroy the base, but the Doctor is able to stop them. The "treasure" is cheese—a valuable commodity on their home planet, Dryra.

2009

📺 "THE DEATH OF THE DOCTOR"
👤 ELEVENTH DOCTOR
✎ RUSSELL T DAVIES

Liz Shaw sends a message to say that she is unable to get back to Earth from the moonbase in time to attend the Doctor's funeral.

1994

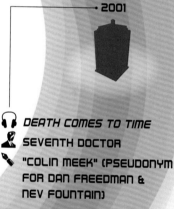

2001

🎧 DEATH COMES TO TIME
👤 SEVENTH DOCTOR
✎ "COLIN MEEK" (PSEUDONYM FOR DAN FREEDMAN & NEV FOUNTAIN)

The Brigadier launches a counterattack from UNIT's moonbase after the Canisian fleet arrives to invade Earth.

1997

📖 ETERNITY WEEPS
👤 SEVENTH DOCTOR
✎ JIM MORTIMORE

A structure that is older than life on the Earth, the Cthalctose Museum, is discovered by human astronauts.

1997

📖 ETERNITY WEEPS

Tranquility Base is built by UNIT to study the Cthalctose Museum in the late 20th century, and the Doctor's former companion, Liz Shaw, works there for a while.

NEW MOON

By the middle of the 21st century, human space exploration had all but ended. The Earth faced a period of political instability caused by a population explosion, a collapsing environment, and dwindling natural resources. There were recessions, riots, wars, and revolutions. And then an unexplained increase in the Moon's gravity drowned coastal cities on Earth, the greatest natural disaster in history.

FIRST APPEARANCE
(by inference) The Moonbase (1967)
(confirmed) "Kill the Moon" (2014)

INHABITANTS
None; colonized by humans

HISTORY

In 2049, a space shuttle from a museum was pressed into service and filled with nuclear bombs, then sent on a suicide mission to destroy whatever was affecting the Moon. The twelfth Doctor arrived on the scene and discovered that the Moon had been a giant alien egg—when it hatched, the resultant display inspired the human race to look up and to travel to the stars. The alien laid a new egg.[1] Only a year or so after the new Moon hatched, the international community set up the Moonbase to house the Gravitron, a device that could affect ocean tides on Earth, controlling the weather and making the climate predictable. The system worked well for 20 years. In 2070, the Cybermen infiltrated the Moonbase, seeking to devastate the Earth and invade in the aftermath, but the second Doctor was on hand to save the day, and the Gravitron remained in service.

OPPOSITE: The Cybermen used the Moon as a staging post for their invasions of Earth.

ABOVE RIGHT: The twelfth Doctor watches as the Moon hatches into a beautiful creature.

BEHIND THE SCENES

Following the revelation in the TV story "Kill the Moon" (Peter Harness, 2014), stories such as *The Moonbase* (Kit Pedlar, 1967) and *Frontier in Space* (Malcolm Hulke, 1973) must now be set on the newly hatched Moon.

FACT FILE

THE DALEK INVASION OF EARTH
When the Daleks invaded Earth in 2157, some humans were able to survive on the Moon colonies.

FRONTIER IN SPACE
By the time of the Earth Empire, there was a prison colony on the Moon. Starting as a place to lock up political dissidents, it soon became a jail for criminals.

WORMWOOD
The time-traveling organization Threshold maintained a base on the Moon for much of human history, where they plotted to usurp the Time Lords. Millennia in the future, Threshold are defeated and the Moon is destroyed.

"THE LONG GAME"
By the time of the Fourth Great and Bountiful Human Empire, the Earth has five moons. The original Moon still has its prison colony.

"THE WATERS OF MARS"
Humanity began Project Pit Stop, using the Moon as a refueling station for missions out to the planets.

"LET'S KILL HITLER," "CLOSING TIME"
River Song earned her doctorate at Luna University on the Moon in the 51st century.

FOOTNOTE
[1] "Kill the Moon"

ANCIENT MARS

The fourth planet from the Sun produced a proud and enduring civilization of reptilian humanoids. They are an ancient race: the Martian equivalent of the Industrial Revolution took place while Earth was in the Pliocene.

HISTORY

We know little about Mars in this golden age. We know that at some point Mars was visited by the Osirians, the powerful and ancient alien race that inspired the legends of the Egyptian gods on Earth. The Martians worshipped the same gods. Pyramids were built on Mars, and one was built to house the immobile Sutekh, destroyer of worlds. The Martians also faced "the Flood," an intelligent virus that infected and possessed larger creatures. They defeated it, although a colony survived locked in a glacier. Then, 12 million years ago, everything changed. The Fendahl, a form of antilife that had evolved on the Fifth Planet of the Solar System, arrived on Mars, swiftly reducing it to the barren, desert world familiar to us today.

BEHIND THE SCENES

Pyramids of Mars (Robert Holmes, 1975) had the fourth Doctor and Sarah visit Mars without mentioning the Ice Warriors. The TV story *Image of the Fendahl* (Chris Boucher, 1977) explains that Mars was left a dead world by the Fendahl. Books such as *GodEngine* helped connect the dots.

ABOVE: Mars has long been known as the planet of war.

RIGHT: The Ice Lords were the aristocratic masters of Mars.

FIRST APPEARANCE
📺 The Ice Warriors *(1967)*

INHABITANTS
Ice Warriors, Fendahl, Osirians, and the Flood

MOONS
Phobos and Deimos

TIMELINE

🎧 **THE JUDGEMENT OF ISSKAR**

👤 FIFTH DOCTOR

✏ SIMON GUERRIER

2009

The Doctor visits the Martian civilization at its height and finds an honorable race that hunts but does not wage wars. The Martians have built impressive pyramids and canals but the planet's ecology is damaged and life on Mars will inevitably become untenable.

🎧 **THE LORDS OF THE RED PLANET**
(RELEASED 2013)

👤 SECOND DOCTOR

✏ BRIAN HAYLES

The only remaining Martian city is Gandor, which is underground and near the source of the Life Drink, a nutrient-rich foodstuff. The genetic engineer Quandril has created an intelligent race, the Evolutionaries, from the armored Saurians that were able to survive on the harsh surface.

1968

1968

🎧 **THE LORDS OF THE RED PLANET**
✏ **BRIAN HAYLES &**
JOHN DORNEY

The Doctor visits and realizes he had been present at the dawn of the Ice Warriors.

2001

🎧 **RED DAWN**

👤 FIFTH DOCTOR

✏ JUSTIN RICHARDS

The legendary Lord Izdal stands outside at Red Dawn, when the ultraviolet radiation on Mars is most lethal, sacrificing himself as a dramatic way of demonstrating how serious the environmental collapse has become. His death spurs the Ice Warriors into action.

1996

📖 **GODENGINE**

👤 SEVENTH DOCTOR

✏ CRAIG HINTON

Some Martians go into hibernation on Mars, others on the Martian moons, and still others begin looking toward other worlds.

DYING MARS

Mars was a dying world, but the Ice Warriors were tough and resourceful, and they managed to eke out an existence for many thousands of years. When Earth fell into its Ice Age 100,000 years ago, the Martians became interested in colonizing the planet, although a lack of resources prevented them from launching a full-scale occupation.

HISTORY

A Martian ship commanded by Varga crashed into a glacier during the first Ice Age and remained frozen until the Second Ice Age, around the year 5000. Grand Marshal Skaldak, Sovereign of the Tharseesian Caste, Vanquisher of the Phobos Heresy, and Commander of the Nix-Thassis Fleet, was the greatest Martian warrior. He traveled to Earth 5,000 years ago but also became trapped in the ice until a Russian submarine crew found him in 1983.

By the late 20th century, humans were exploring the Solar System, making Mars missions a priority. The British launched 13 manned Mars Probes in the 1970s, discovering a planet with a thin but breathable atmosphere … and inhabitants. To prevent interplanetary war, this discovery was covered up, and most people forgot the British had even landed there. It was a cold war that neither side expected to hold forever. A number of other alien threats had made their home on Mars.

LOCATION
Fourth planet from the Sun

INHABITANTS
Ice Warriors

ABOVE: As Mars died, its people looked to Earth for their survival.

LEFT: The eighth Doctor fought off a Martian Invasion.

TIMELINE

RED DAWN

FIFTH DOCTOR

JUSTIN RICHARDS

2000

Early in the 21st century the American Ares mission to Mars also disturbs a Martian tomb. The Doctor is able to ensure that cool heads prevail, helped by the sacrifice of the moderate Lord Zzaal.

THE AMBASSADORS OF DEATH

THIRD DOCTOR

DAVID WHITAKER

The Doctor helps broker a peace between Earth and the highly radioactive alien ambassadors whom British astronauts had encountered on Mars.

1970

1997

THE DYING DAYS

EIGHTH DOCTOR

LANCE PARKIN

Twenty years after the first missions to Mars, Britain launches Mars 97, a mission that disturbs an ancient Martian tomb. The astronauts are killed by the Ice Warriors, who then annex the UK, deposing Queen Elizabeth II and installing the Ice Lord Xznaal in her place. It takes the Doctor, Brigadier Lethbridge-Stewart, and Bernice Summerfield organizing a counterrevolution to set things straight. It is this very public defense of the realm that finally sees the Brigadier promoted to General.

1983

4-DIMENSIONAL VISTAS

FIFTH DOCTOR

STEVE PARKHOUSE / MICK AUSTIN

The Doctor foils the scheme of the renegade Time Lord the Monk, who has teamed up with the Ice Warriors to build a giant sonic cannon that is creating divergences in the timeline.

POLICE BOX

1986

CRISIS IN SPACE

SIXTH DOCTOR

MICHAEL HOLT

The Doctor foils a plot from his old enemy Garth Hadeez, "the Genghis Khan of the Galaxy," and his cruel wife, Queen Tyrannica, who have assembled an army of Golons, robots, and maggots on Mars and plan to launch a black hole disguised as the moon Phobos at Earth.

MISSIONS TO MARS

By the late 20th century, the Ice Warriors had been reduced to a few isolated clans, eking out a subterranean existence. Oblivious to their existence for the most part, the space agencies of Earth started exploring Mars and its two moons, Phobos and Deimos, using both manned and unmanned missions. Other alien races were arriving on Mars, almost always with sinister intent.

HISTORY

At this point, human missions to Mars were very limited, and no attempt was made to establish a permanent base there. Humans had turned their back on space travel for a period (p. 52). However, a new age of exploration was then ushered in by people like Adelaide Brooke, who became the first woman on Mars in 2042. She returned from the Red Planet and was able to muster support for a permanent colony there.

RIGHT & ABOVE: Mars was an obvious target for human exploration.

BIG FINISH

PAUL McGANN IN

DOCTOR WHO

MEMORY LANE

WITH INDIA FISHER AS CHARLEY
AND CONRAD WESTMAAS AS C'RIZZ

 **TIMELINE**

 "THE WATERS OF MARS"
👤 TENTH DOCTOR
✎ RUSSELL T DAVIES & PHIL FORD

2009

Adelaide Brooke leads the mission that establishes Bowie Base One over a subterranean glacier on July 1, 2058. The nine astronauts try to establish whether a permanent settlement will be possible. They free an ancient Martian virus, the Flood, and must sacrifice themselves to prevent it from spreading to Earth. Rather than killing the space program, the loss of Brooke spurs humanity to redouble its efforts.

📖 **SOLDIERS FROM ZOLTA**
👤 THIRD DOCTOR
✎ RON SMETHURST

The Zoltans save the lone astronaut on a mission to Mars. The aliens are keen to colonize Mars, and there is a great deal of pro-Zoltan sentiment on Earth. Feeling the Zoltans are too good to be true, the Doctor discovers that they plan to invade the Earth with insect soldiers. The Zoltans flee the Solar System.

1970

2006

🎧 **MEMORY LANE**
👤 EIGHTH DOCTOR
✎ EDDIE ROBSON

The second decade of the 21st century sees the Commonwealth Space Programme launch the *Led Zeppelin II* manned mission to Phobos, one of the moons of Mars.

1972

📖 **DARK INTRUDERS**
👤 THIRD DOCTOR
✎ UNKNOWN

A Mars capsule splashes down in the Pacific. The Doctor, Jo, and the Brigadier are on the USS *Pohontas*, which is there to retrieve them. The Doctor examines the capsule and finds plant dust from Minos.

   The Minoans are old, ruthless enemies of the Doctor, brain stealers with an unstable molecular makeup; they must have been on Mars and infiltrated the bodies of the astronauts. The Doctor lets the astronauts near him, then defeats the Minoans inside them in a battle of wills.

2005

📺 **"THE CHRISTMAS INVASION"**
👤 TENTH DOCTOR
✎ RUSSELL T DAVIES

The *Guinevere I* unmanned probe to Mars doesn't get to the Red Planet, but it does provoke a reaction from a passing Sycorax spacecraft, which attacks the Earth on Christmas Day, 2006. The newly regenerated Doctor wins the day … and to his horror, Torchwood destroys the ship.

1976

🔍 **COUNTER-ROTATION**
👤 FOURTH DOCTOR
✎ JOHN CANNING

The Doctor defeats the Scartigs—aliens who can survive in space with personal forcefields—who are planning to use Mars as a beachhead to attack Earth.

THIS PAGE: UN forces engaging the Ice Warriors on Mars.

THE THOUSAND DAY WAR

As mankind's technology advanced, and Mars's resources continued to dwindle, war between Earth and Mars became all but inevitable. The Ice Warriors launched the first strikes. They captured the base on the Moon that controlled the Earth's Travel-Mat teleportation network and used it to spread a deadly fungus.[1] That plan was thwarted, so in 2086 the Martians simply diverted the course of an asteroid and destroyed Paris. Humanity's response was swift and massive: the United Nations launched a full-scale military assault on Mars. The battle raged for just under three years.[2]

HISTORY

President Achebe ordered an orbital assault, and a team led by Yembe Lethbridge-Stewart braved massive losses but established a Stunnel, a teleportation bridge that allowed Earth's military to travel instantly to the slopes of Olympus Mons on Mars. Even with that bridgehead secured, it was a hard fight. Nuclear weapons were used, and human soldiers were given genetic and cyborg implants. The Ice Warriors were brutal, skilled opponents, fighting for their homeland, but nevertheless it was a one-sided fight.[3] The only Martian victory was at Viis Claar, where the Ice Lord Abrasaar killed 15,000 Earthmen ... but lost 10,000 of his own men in the action. Then, after nearly three Earth years, the Ice Warriors vanished. UN forces were baffled and suspected a trap. Unknown to them, all but a few Martians had evacuated their planet and had set out to build a new homeworld out beyond Arcturus.[4]

BEHIND THE SCENES

Transit (Ben Aaronovitch, 1992) explored the aftermath of TV story *The Seeds of Death* (Brian Hayles & Terrance Dicks, 1968), inflected by the then-recent Gulf War and the cyberpunk movement. In his 1996 book *GodEngine*, Craig Hinton picked up on events in *Transit* and told a more traditional action-adventure story.

FIRST APPEARANCE
📖 Transit *(1992)*

INHABITANTS
UNIT and Ice Warriors

FACT FILE

📖 *TRANSIT*

A memorial forest is planted at Achebe Gorge—one tree for each of the 450,000 humans who'd died on Mars.

📖 *GODENGINE*

The Martians settle on Nova Martia, establishing other colonies such as Cluut-ett-Pictar. They have no contact with the human race for many centuries.

📖 *FEAR ITSELF,*
   BEIGE PLANET MARS

Mankind colonizes Mars. Wal-Mart build the first trading post. A network of cities is built with names like Sheffield, Ddeb, and Picard, linked by railways and canals.

📖 *TRANSIT*

Yembe Lethbridge-Stewart is the great-great-great-great grandson of the Doctor's old friend Brigadier Alistair Gordon Lethbridge-Stewart. Yembe has a daughter named Kadiatu.

📖 *TRANSIT*

The World Government builds a new Travel-Mat network, the Sol Transit System, which allows people to teleport to and from every planet and moon in the Solar System.

📖 *TRANSIT*

The seventh Doctor meets Kadiatu on Earth a generation after the Thousand Day War, when the human race has rapidly colonized the Solar System, but the psychological scars of the war still remain. .

FOOTNOTES
[1] 📺 *The Seeds of Death* • [2 & 3] 📖 *Transit* • [4] 📖 *GodEngine*

HUMAN MARS

Once the Ice Warriors had left Mars, it was ripe for human colonization. Teleport links between Earth and Mars had been set up during the Thousand Day War and made the process swift and straightforward. Soon there was a thriving human presence on the Red Planet, and terraforming efforts began. The first two cities to be established were Jacksonville and Arcadia Planitia.

HISTORY

The Daleks invaded Mars at the same time as the Dalek Invasion of Earth of 2157. The Ice Lord Falaxyr of Mars contacted the Daleks and offered them the GodEngine, an Osirian weapon that could destroy whole planets and stars. In return, he asked for Ice Warrior sovereignty. The Daleks were eventually defeated when a virus ate through their electrical cables. Mars remained a target for the Daleks for thousands of years—they conquered Mars in three hours in 2400. It was one of the four Solar Planets that they planned to attack as part of their Master Plan. They invaded again in the 55th century.

BELOW & ABOVE: The ninth Doctor took Rose to Mars.

BEHIND THE SCENES

The aftermath of the Thousand Day War was explored in the books *Transit* (Ben Aaronovitch, 1993) and *GodEngine* (Craig Hinton, 1996). *GodEngine* built on a brief mention of the Dalek Invasion of Mars in the TV story *Genesis of the Daleks* (Terry Nation, 1975).

BY THE EARLY 22ND CENTURY, *MARS* HAS BEEN CLEANED UP, DUSTED OFF, AND TURNED INTO A *LEISURE PLANET.* SOMEWHERE FOR THE *RICH* TO SAIL ABOUT AND DRINK *COCKTAILS.*

SPEAKIN' OF WHICH, I COULD *MURDER* A *GRAPEFRUIT JUICE...*

HOW CAN WE *BREATHE?*

ARTIFICIAL AIR. IN FACT, I THINK I CAN *ADJUST IT...*

TIMELINE

2010

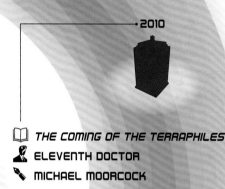

🎧 **DEIMOS / THE RESURRECTION OF MARS**

🎙 **EIGHTH DOCTOR**

✏ **JONATHAN MORRIS**

An Ionizer is set up on Deimos to warm Mars by the 26th century. The Monk wakes the Ice Warriors, who have been hibernating on Deimos. The Doctor causes a chain reaction that turns Deimos into a miniature sun—wiping out the Ice Warriors and allowing Mars to be terraformed.

🎭 **THE CURSE OF THE DALEKS**

✏ **DAVID WHITAKER & TERRY NATION**

By the 22nd century, there are plenty of people on Venus and not many on Mars. For seven years, Harry Sline exploits this, tricking Venusians into moving to Mars, where they became slaves.

1965

2010

📖 **THE COMING OF THE TERRAPHILES**

👤 **ELEVENTH DOCTOR**

✏ **MICHAEL MOORCOCK**

Mars, which has featured so prominently in the literature of Earth, is of great interest to the Terraphiles (p. 106). They rename the planet Barsoom, after the Edgar Rice Burroughs stories, although the original planet Mars was destroyed when Real Phobos crashed into Old Barsoom.

1965

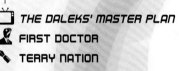

📺 **THE DALEKS' MASTER PLAN**

👤 **FIRST DOCTOR**

✏ **TERRY NATION**

Bret Vyon is born on Mars Colony 16 in the late 39th century.

1969

1992

📺 **THE SPACE PIRATES**

👤 **SECOND DOCTOR**

✏ **ROBERT HOLMES**

Some of the earliest patrol ships that go into deep space have "Martian missiles," presumably manufactured on Mars itself.

📖 **LOVE AND WAR**

👤 **SEVENTH DOCTOR**

✏ **PAUL CORNELL**

The Doctor's companion, Bernice Summerfield, makes her reputation excavating the tombs of the rulers of Mars, known as the "Fields of Death." She also writes a book about the area, *Down Among the Dead Men*.

2005

🔍 **THE CRUEL SEA**

👤 **NINTH DOCTOR**

✏ **ROBERT SHEARMAN**

The Doctor takes Rose to Mars in the 22nd century, when it is a leisure planet for the mega-rich. They spend time on a luxury yacht, but a dormant Martian virus has been revived by the terraforming process and made the sea sentient and able to take human form.

HUMAN EXPLORATION OF THE SOLAR SYSTEM

In the late 21st century, with the Amazon rainforest all but gone, with mass extinctions of animal life, and as global warming—and efforts to correct it—caused the Great Cataclysm on Earth, the human race began colonizing the Solar System.[1] Under the auspices of International Space Command, ion jet rockets powered between the planets. Space stations were established as research and supply facilities, serviced by robotic cargo rockets.[2] The Solar Transit System eventually linked every planet and moon.[3]

HISTORY

Within 100 years, every available planet and moon had some sort of human settlement, and there were networks of space stations and regular rocket routes. From there, mankind would make the leap to the stars. The Ice Warriors demonstrated how humanity had made a mistake by putting all of its eggs in one basket. Earth's environment was on the verge of collapse, which was leading to political instability. Space travel was reintroduced, and ion rockets began exploring the Solar System.[4] There were disasters and hardships in space, and Earth had not solved its old problems. A new cold war developed, corporations grew ever more powerful, and new technologies created new threats. But mankind was finally looking outward.

RIGHT: Proffressor Eldred's ion rockets were destined to explore the Solar System.

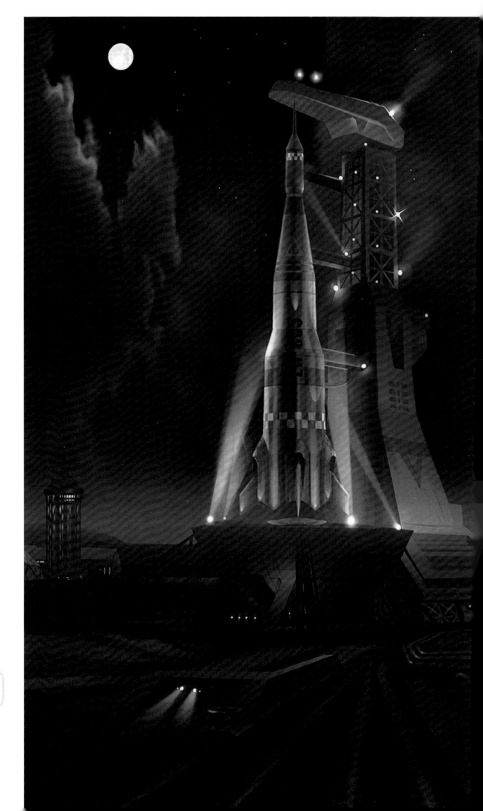

FOOTNOTES
[1] 📺 *Aeolian* • [2] 📺 *The Wheel in Space* • [3] 📖 *Transit* • [4] 📺 *The Seeds of Death*

TIMELINE

THE WHEEL IN SPACE
SECOND DOCTOR
DAVID WHITAKER

The Space Wheels are constructed—
large space stations that are both
astronomical monitoring centers and
waystations for ships going into deep
space. Phoenix IV cargo rockets with
robot crews keep everything supplied.

1968

2009

"THE WATERS OF MARS"

The Doctor arrives at Bowie Base One
on November 21, 2059, the night the
history books said it was destroyed in
a catastrophic explosion, taking the life
of Adelaide Brooke. This will inspire
humanity to follow her lead—to
take risks.

2008

THE GREAT SPACE ELEVATOR
SECOND DOCTOR
JONATHAN MORRIS

The construction of a Space Elevator in Sumatra
means that payloads can be sent into space for a
fraction of the cost of using rockets. The Doctor
prevents an energy being from taking control of
the Elevator soon after it opens.

2009

"THE WATERS OF MARS"
TENTH DOCTOR
RUSSELL T DAVIES & PHIL FORD

Before long, there are refueling stations on
the Moon, and Adelaide Brooke becomes
the first woman to land on Mars.

THE ASTEROID BELT AND THE FIFTH PLANET

Between Mars and Jupiter lies the asteroid belt, a region dense with rocks ranging from the size of a pebble to the size of a small moon. Scientists speculated it was formed when a planet broke up, and this proved to be so: 12 million years ago, the Fifth Planet existed around 107 million miles (172 million km) from Earth. It was broken up by the Time Lords.[1]

FIRST APPEARANCE
Image of the Fendahl

CURRENT STATUS
Shattered remnants of Fifth Planet

HISTORY

By the Humanian Era, the asteroid belt is rich in the minerals and other resources vital to early space expeditions. Bases are established on the larger asteroids, and mining operations begin.

The asteroid belt can be a hazardous place to navigate. Legends say that early space travelers from Earth were guided through it by Star Whales.[2] Some Ice Warriors who fled their home planet of Mars went to hibernate deep in the asteroid belt. In the year 5000, the asteroid belt was full of pioneers preparing for the Great Breakout, when mankind would colonize the whole galaxy. It was also the location of the Bi-Al Foundation, the Centre for Alien Biomorphology—Asteroid K4067 at vector 1-9, quadrant 3743800.

LEFT: The Fendahleen devoured all life on Mars, and would have done the same to Earth.

FOOTNOTES
[1] *Image of the Fendahl* • [2] "The Beast Below"

TIMELINE

2010

IMAGE OF THE FENDAHL
FOURTH DOCTOR
CHRIS BOUCHER

The Fifth Planet is home to the Fendahleen, hideous gestalt creatures like giant leeches, who feed insatiably on all life. Their planet is destroyed by the Time Lords, who see them as a threat to the entire universe. They then place the planet in a time loop, concealing its existence. The Fendahl core, a skull, survives and makes its way to Earth, where it lies undisturbed until the 1970s.

1977

THE BOUNTY OF CERES
FIRST DOCTOR
IAN POTTER

The Doctor, Vicki, and Steven face Thorn, a miner working at Cobalt Corporation's mostly automated facility on Ceres, who, out of jealousy and boredom, has begun killing his co-workers.

2010

"THE SIRENS OF CERES"
K9
DEBORAH PARSONS

A civilization evolves on one of the larger asteroids, Ceres. A stratified society is created when the Masters use the metal cerulium to control the Scribes. The Cerulians are unaware that another asteroid is on a collision course with their planet. A few pieces of cerulium are propelled to Earth by the explosion. The repressive government of the mid-21st century is keen to use the substance to pacify the population.

1977

THE INVISIBLE ENEMY
FOURTH DOCTOR
BOB BAKER & DAVID MARTIN

The Doctor is infected by the Nucleus, a virus that is attempting to enter the macro-world (p. 73). Leela takes him to the Bi-Al Foundation, experts in alien diseases, in an attempt to find a cure.

JUPITER AND ITS MOONS

Jupiter is the largest planet in the Solar System. It is a gas giant with well over a dozen moons, many of which would qualify as planets in their own right if they orbited the Sun. Those moons are soon colonized by human explorers—their government, the Jupiter Axis, is granted independence by 2329. As with the other Solar planets, Jupiter and its moons supported alien civilizations in the distant past.

BEHIND THE SCENES

When *Revenge of the Cybermen* was made in 1975, astronomers thought Jupiter had 12 moons, but since then many more have been discovered. In 2005, the book *To the Slaughter* offered an explanation for this anomaly.

HISTORY

Jupiter has been a persistent target of the Daleks, although exactly what fascinates them about the place remains slightly mysterious. In 2400 the Daleks wiped out the primitive natives of Jupiter's moons in their invasion of the Solar System.[1] Then, 1,600 years later, the Daleks named it as one of the top targets of their Master Plan (pp. 138–39).[2] By 4177, they had conquered and terraformed Jupiter, transforming it into an ocean world with 17 continents. It became the battleground for a major engagement between the spacefleets of two Dalek factions, the Alliance Daleks and Enemy Daleks.[3]

THE NEW ADVENTURES

SO VILE A SIN

BEN AARONOVITCH AND KATE ORMAN

TOP RIGHT: Jupiter and its Moons will become a center of human political power.

ABOVE RIGHT: The Forrester family were prominent nobles in the feudal 30th century.

LEFT: Icecanoes were predicted by *Doctor Who* before scientists discovered real instances of them on some of Jupiter's moons.

FOOTNOTES
[1] *The Dalek Book* • [2] *The Daleks' Master Plan* • [3] *Dalek Empire III*

FIRST APPEARANCE
📖 The Dalek Book *(1964)*

STATUS
By the 42nd century, terraformed and habitable by humans

TIMELINE

THE JUPITER CONJUNCTION
FIFTH DOCTOR
EDDIE ROBSON

2012

The Doctor believes that cloud creatures from Jupiter, the Jovians, are long extinct. In fact, in 2329 they team up with the Jupiter Axis, the human colonies that are in a tense standoff with Earth. One group of Jovians are, unknown to the colonists, planning to invade Earth.

LAIR OF THE ZARBI SUPREMO
FIRST DOCTOR
WALTER HOWARTH

In the late 20th century, the Zarbi Supremo moves Vortis from the Isop Galaxy (p. 260) to the orbit of Jupiter as part of a plan to conquer Earth.

1965

2007

VALHALLA
SEVENTH DOCTOR
MARC PLATT

Valhalla, the capital city of Callisto, is the site of a busy trading post set up during the gas rush, which has fallen on hard times. It is attacked by giant termites—descendants of ones genetically engineered to explore the depths of the moon.

1975

REVENGE OF THE CYBERMEN
FOURTH DOCTOR
GERRY DAVIS

Nerva Beacon is set up near Jupiter to warn shipping of navigational hazards. After the Cyber War, Jupiter gains a new moon, which humans name Neophobus. They do not know this is Voga, and that the Vogans are hiding from revenge attacks by the Cybermen (p. 158).

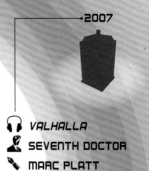

2005

1975

1996

TO THE SLAUGHTER
EIGHTH DOCTOR
STEPHEN COLE

All but 12 of Jupiter's moons are removed by the human race as part of a spring cleaning of the Solar System.

THE ANDROID INVASION
FOURTH DOCTOR
TERRY NATION

The British astronaut Guy Crayford finds himself in orbit around Jupiter when his experimental space freighter malfunctions. He is rescued by the warlike Kraals.

SO VILE A SIN
SEVENTH DOCTOR
BEN AARONOVITCH & KATE ORMAN

The Doctor's companion, Roz Forrester, is a noblewoman whose family members are barons of Io, one of Jupiter's moons. Their ancestral home is a castle there, surrounded by forest, beneath a vast dome.

1

SATURN AND TITAN

The most obvious feature of the gas giant Saturn is its beautiful system of rings. Their origins are somewhat controversial. When humans colonized Titan, they discovered evidence of an ancient Dalek attempt to explore Saturn from a base on that moon and speculated that Daleks were responsible for the formation of the rings.[1] The third Doctor met ancient astronauts from Nakron who had slept on Earth's seabed since the time of the dinosaurs and who believed their planet had broken up to form the rings.[2]

HISTORY

The most detailed account of the rings credits the ArkHive, a supercomputer built as a repository of knowledge by a dying civilization, which ended up destroying an ice moon of Saturn while attempting to build a time machine, creating the rings in the process.[3] (The Doctor discovered the existence of the ArkHive, and prevented it from building a second time machine, which would have failed and wiped out the Solar System.)

For human explorers, as with Jupiter, the moons of Saturn provided valuable resources such as water, organic chemicals, and metals.

The second Doctor visited the Wheel of Ice, a bernalium mining colony that encircled the moon Mnemosyne in the late 21st century. At that time, there was a methane extraction plant on Titan, as well as other facilities. Saturn's orbit was also home to some of the first humans born away from Earth.

RIGHT: The second Doctor uncovered the secret of Saturn's rings in *The Wheel of Ice*.

BELOW: The third Doctor, Jo, and the Brigadier meet astronauts from Nakron.

BEHIND THE SCENES

Three prose stories give three conflicting accounts of the formation of Saturn's rings. *The Wheel of Ice* (Stephen Baxter, 2012) is the only one with an eyewitness account, rather than mere supposition.

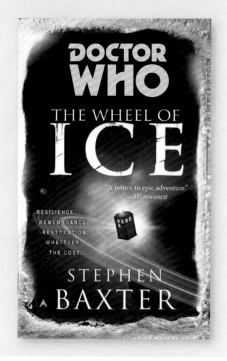

LOCATION
Sixth planet from the Sun

INHABITANTS
ArkHive, Nakronites, and unknown monsters

FOOTNOTES
[1] *The Dalek Outer Space Book* • [2] *Old Father Saturn* •
[3] *The Wheel of Ice*

TIMELINE

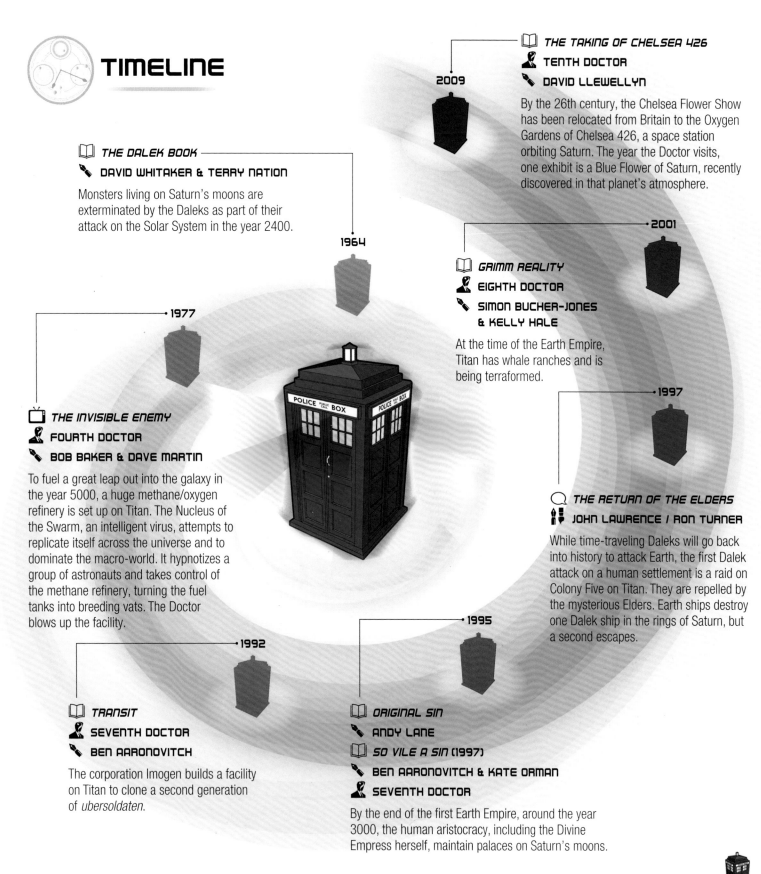

THE TAKING OF CHELSEA 426

👤 TENTH DOCTOR

✎ DAVID LLEWELLYN

2009

By the 26th century, the Chelsea Flower Show has been relocated from Britain to the Oxygen Gardens of Chelsea 426, a space station orbiting Saturn. The year the Doctor visits, one exhibit is a Blue Flower of Saturn, recently discovered in that planet's atmosphere.

THE DALEK BOOK

✎ DAVID WHITAKER & TERRY NATION

Monsters living on Saturn's moons are exterminated by the Daleks as part of their attack on the Solar System in the year 2400.

1964

2001

GRIMM REALITY

👤 EIGHTH DOCTOR

✎ SIMON BUCHER-JONES & KELLY HALE

At the time of the Earth Empire, Titan has whale ranches and is being terraformed.

1977

📺 **THE INVISIBLE ENEMY**

👤 FOURTH DOCTOR

✎ BOB BAKER & DAVE MARTIN

To fuel a great leap out into the galaxy in the year 5000, a huge methane/oxygen refinery is set up on Titan. The Nucleus of the Swarm, an intelligent virus, attempts to replicate itself across the universe and to dominate the macro-world. It hypnotizes a group of astronauts and takes control of the methane refinery, turning the fuel tanks into breeding vats. The Doctor blows up the facility.

1997

💬 **THE RETURN OF THE ELDERS**

👥 JOHN LAWRENCE / RON TURNER

While time-traveling Daleks will go back into history to attack Earth, the first Dalek attack on a human settlement is a raid on Colony Five on Titan. They are repelled by the mysterious Elders. Earth ships destroy one Dalek ship in the rings of Saturn, but a second escapes.

1992

TRANSIT

👤 SEVENTH DOCTOR

✎ BEN AARONOVITCH

The corporation Imogen builds a facility on Titan to clone a second generation of *ubersoldaten*.

1995

ORIGINAL SIN

✎ ANDY LANE

SO VILE A SIN (1997)

✎ BEN AARONOVITCH & KATE ORMAN

👤 SEVENTH DOCTOR

By the end of the first Earth Empire, around the year 3000, the human aristocracy, including the Divine Empress herself, maintain palaces on Saturn's moons.

URANUS AND NEPTUNE

The seventh and eighth planets of the Solar System are both gas giants, smaller than Jupiter or Saturn, with fewer moons. Uranus was colonized by humans and at one point was a powerful force in Solar politics. In the early 27th century the planets of the Solar System are, in order of importance: Earth, Mars, Venus, Saturn, Pluto (a dwarf planet), Mercury, Uranus, Jupiter, and Neptune.[1] By 4000, Uranus is so important that some consider it one of the "Big Four," with Earth, Mars, and Venus.[2]

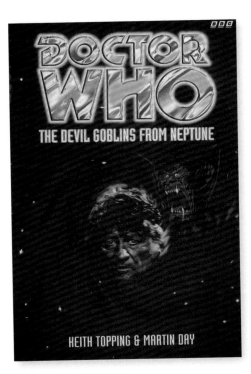

ABOVE: The third Doctor faced the ferocious Waro, from a moon of Neptune.

TOP RIGHT: The planet Neptune remains mostly mysterious.

RIGHT: The Time Destructor was fueled by taranium mined on Uranus.

HISTORY

Uranus achieves this prominence perhaps because it is a source of valuable resources, including the "rarest mineral in the universe," taranium, which is only found there.[3] On the other hand, we know very little about Neptune, which may suggest that it never achieved much significance. Neptune's moon Triton was home to the vicious Waro, who hated all other life forms. The size of human children, and able to fly with the aid of artificial wings, they had come into conflict with the Nedenah, aliens from another solar system who were (one of) the races responsible for sightings of flying saucers on Earth.[4]

LOCATION
The seventh and eighth planets

INHABITANTS
Waro (on Triton)

BEHIND THE SCENES

A Knight of the Order of Oberon appeared in TV's *Revelation of the Daleks* (Eric Saward, 1985), but Craig Hinton's novel *GodEngine* (1996) established their home was Oberon, Uranus's moon, and confirmed they were descendants of the Adjudicators, introduced in the TV story *Colony in Space* (Malcolm Hulke, 1971) but developed in the New Adventures novels, starting with *Original Sin* (Andy Lane, 1995).

FOOTNOTES
[1] 📖 *The Dalek World* • [2] 📖 *The Dalek Outer Space Book* • [3] 📺 *The Daleks' Master Plan* • [4] 📖 *The Devil Goblins from Neptune*

 **TIMELINE**

📺 **"THE WATERS OF MARS"**

2009

👤 TENTH DOCTOR

✎ RUSSELL T DAVIES & PHIL FORD

Unmanned shuttles fly to Neptune in the 2040s.

📖 **THE DALEK BOOK**

✎ DAVID WHITAKER & TERRY NATION

Phelan Kelly nearly starts a galactic war when he ferries Martians on holiday cruises to Uranus. His grandson, the entrepreneurial space explorer Sean Kelly, brings the secret of water-breathing from the Neptunii for a ship full of flower bulbs.

1964

1997

📖 **THE DEVIL-GOBLINS FROM NEPTUNE**

👤 THIRD DOCTOR

✎ KEITH TOPPING & MARTIN DAY

The British space program in the 1970s sends unmanned missions to Neptune. The goblinlike Waro, natives of Neptune's moon Triton, send telepathic signals to control humans on Earth and then move to secure Earth's supplies of cobalt.

1966

📖 **THE DALEK OUTER SPACE BOOK**

✎ TERRY NATION & BRAD ASHTON

The Daleks suffer a massive defeat in the 40th century when their fleet is repelled from the artificial colonies of Uranus by supersonic waves.

1996

1985

📺 **REVELATION OF THE DALEKS**

👤 SIXTH DOCTOR

✎ ERIC SAWARD

Many centuries later, the Adjudicators have become the Knights of the Grand Order of Oberon, a rather old-fashioned group with odd codes of chivalry and a reputation for brutal violence.

📖 **GODENGINE**

👤 SEVENTH DOCTOR

✎ CRAIG HINTON

A powerful interplanetary police force, the Bureau of Adjudicators, is established on Oberon, one of the moons of Uranus. Oberon serves as a secret human military stronghold during the Dalek Invasion of Earth and the rest of the Solar System in the mid-22nd century.

PLUTO AND CASSIUS

Farthest from the Sun are two planets so small and distant that human astronomers only discover them in the 20th century. The dwarf planet of the Solar System (previously referred to as the ninth planet) is Pluto, and any visitor can expect to find a tiny, cold, dark world. There is a planet farther out than Pluto, called Cassius, discovered by astronomers in 1994.[1] Very little is known about it, except that it was the site of the Battle of Cassius at some point before the 26th century, fought between Earth forces and the Daleks.[2] The Daleks knew about the outermost planet, and they called it Omega.[3]

HISTORY

When the Doctor visits Pluto, many millions of years in the future, he is astonished to find 300 million humans living there, packed in six vast Megropolises, each with its own "sun," an orbiting fusion satellite. This is due, fittingly enough, to plutocrats—the Usurians, parasitic fungi who run the Company, an industrial conglomerate that doesn't just tax the population to death, but also charges death duties. The Company has moved the human race from Mars, and then to Pluto. Pluto is nearly exhausted, so rather than pay to move their workforce again, they are planning to switch off the suns and leave them to their fate.

RIGHT: The Doctor went to Pluto long before New Horizons photographed it in 2015.

BELOW: The voracious Black Hunger originated on Pluto.

FIRST APPEARANCE
📺 The Sun Makers *(1977)*

STATUS
A dwarf planet

FOOTNOTES
[1] *The Sun Makers*, 📖 *Iceberg* • [2] 📖 *Love and War* •
[3] 📖 *The Dalek Book*

TIMELINE

📺 THE SUN MAKERS
👤 FOURTH DOCTOR
✒ ROBERT HOLMES

The Doctor, Leela, and K9 help organize resistance to the Company on Pluto. The Doctor introduces rampant inflation to the economic system, and the Usurians abandon the planet. Earth has recovered enough that the human race could repopulate it.

1977

2010

📺 "BLACK HUNGER"
👤 K9
✒ CHRIS ROACHE

In the mid-21st century, Pluto is the home to omnivorous microbes that, when spliced with yeast, become a practically unstoppable eating machine, the Black Hunger.

1992

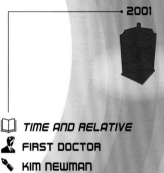

📖 TRANSIT
👤 SEVENTH DOCTOR
✒ BEN AARONOVITCH

Lowell Depot on Pluto is the outermost stop on the Sol Transit System.

2001

📖 TIME AND RELATIVE
👤 FIRST DOCTOR
✒ KIM NEWMAN

The Doctor takes The Cold, an ancient ice sentience that had revived and rampaged through the London of 1963, to Pluto in the distant future, where it can exist without harming others.

1996

1998

📖 GODENGINE
👤 SEVENTH DOCTOR
✒ CRAIG HINTON

The native Plutonians are crystal men, exterminated during the Dalek invasion of the Solar System in 2157.

📖 PLACEBO EFFECT
👤 EIGHTH DOCTOR
✒ GARY RUSSELL

Micawber's World, an artificial leisure planet, is built between Pluto and Cassius in the late 40th century; it hosts the Olympic Games in 3999.

EARTH'S COLONIES IN SPACE

MANKIND SPREADS TO THE STARS

📺 "THE WATERS OF MARS"

The Doctor told Adelaide Brooke, "You began a journey that takes the human race all the way out to the stars. It begins with you, and then your granddaughter, you inspire her, so that in 30 years Susie Fontana Brooke is the pilot of the first lightspeed ship to Proxima Centauri. And then everywhere, with her children, and her children's children forging the way. To the Dragon Star, the Celestial Belt of the Winter Queen, the Map of the Watersnake Wormholes. One day a Brooke will even fall in love with a Tandonian prince; that's the start of a whole new species. But everything starts with you, Adelaide."

🎭 THE CURSE OF THE DALEKS

If it wasn't for the research chemist Philip Clements, space travel would have been impossible. He both revolutionized food packaging and invented compressed water.

📺 THE SENSORITES

Early interstellar missions traveled slower than lightspeed, and the crews were put in hibernation, sleeping through their journey— often for years or decades. It was not

📺 THE SPACE PIRATES

The first to head into deep space were prospectors. Milo Clancey was typical of early prospectors—the LIZ 79, his spaceship, was a "C-class" freighter that remained in service for 40 years. Ships were made of tillium and powered with a thermonuclear pile. Clancey would stake a claim on an asteroid, extract the minerals, then send it home in a "floater"—a slow, unmanned vessel. When humanity reached the Fourth Sector, they discovered planets there rich in "argonite," an indestructible metal that was used in the construction of a new generation of spaceships. Clancey's old partner, Dom Issigri, founded the Issigri Mining Company (IMC), which stripmined the entire planet Ta in ten years.

BELOW: Earth patrol ships were soon policing the space lanes.

📖 THE COMING OF THE TERRAPHILES

Nuke-burning cadmium-damped spacebuckets, "nukers," were the first ships used to conquer the stars.

📖 THE PIT

Pioneer stations were set up—huge bases in deep space that could refuel and restock colony ships.

📺 NIGHTMARE OF EDEN

There was a Galactic Recession that, among other things, saw the company Galactic Salvage and Insurance go bankrupt.

📖 LUCIFER RISING

By the early 22nd century, the Adjudicators were well established and had dealt with the Kroagnon Affair, vraxoin raids over Azure, the Macra Case, and the Vega Debacle.

EARLY COLONIES

FIRST APPEARANCE

📺 *Human survey teams: The Sensorites (1964)*

In the 22nd century, mankind began establishing footholds on other worlds. Earth at the time was facing overpopulation, ecological collapse, and political instability, and the multinational conglomerates held most of the power. It was the corporations that launched the Century Program—sending dozens of colony ships out to suitable planets. A Galactic Recession early in the century led to cost cutting, and many ships and colonies lacked even basic support from Earth. Some of these would become lost colonies (see p. 108).

HISTORY

An exchangeable currency, the "credit," was introduced. New minerals and other resources led to advances in technology but also fierce disputes over ownership rights. It was discovered that planets toward the center of the Galaxy ("hubwards") tended to be better suited to colonization than the ones at the edge of the galaxy (the "rimworlds").

Survey teams, usually made up of just a handful of people, were sent to worlds with conditions that supported human life. They often encountered indigenous life forms or other hazards. If a survey team reported that a planet was suitable for colonization, typically a small group of settlers would arrive. Centuries later, the descendants of the first families to arrive were often politically important (for example on Kaldor, see p. 94). At first, though, life was usually harsh … and most planets had hazards and opportunities the initial survey had missed.

BEHIND THE SCENES

A number of stories have mentioned the "first" colony planet Earth, settled outside our Solar System, but we've seen different names and circumstances given.

LEFT: The jungle world of Deva Loka contained an ancient evil the colonists weren't prepared for.

TIMELINE

1998

📺 *NIGHTMARE OF EDEN*

👤 FOURTH DOCTOR

✒️ BOB BAKER

Two spacecraft merge into one following a freak hyperspace accident—one a passenger liner bound for Azure, the other a scientific research vessel. Animal specimens escape from the science vessel and begin killing passengers. The Doctor uncovers a vraxoin smuggling ring that has been operating under the cover of a zoological survey.

1979

📖 *KURSAAL*

👤 EIGHTH DOCTOR

✒️ PETER ANGHELIDES

The Doctor and Sam arrive on Saturnia Regna to visit the famed theme park but arrive decades early, when construction has just begun. The Gray Corporation, which has bought the planet, has unearthed a Jax Cathedral, an alien structure containing a virus that animates dead bodies. The head of Gray Corp, Maximillian Gray, has become a werewolflike creature, having been exposed to the virus while still alive.

1982

📺 *KINDA*

👤 FIFTH DOCTOR

✒️ CHRIS BAILEY

The idyllic forest world of Deva Loka is home to the Kinda, a tribe that lives in harmony with nature, communicates telepathically, and harbors the Mara—a creature of fear and evil that dwells in the subconscious. The colonial survey team sent to the planet proves psychologically incapable of adapting to the Mara's twisting, tricksterlike nature.

1994

📖 *LUCIFER RISING*

👤 SEVENTH DOCTOR

✒️ ANDY LANE & JIM MORTIMORE

Human corporations match the capitalist races the Cimliss, Usurians, and Okk in ruthlessness. The government-run Eden Project, 280 light years from Earth, seeks to mine a high-mass element from the gas giant Lucifer in order to create a powerful energy source. At the first sign of success, the Interplanetary Mining Corporation (IMC) arrives to annex the planet for the company. The angelic natives quarantine the world.

COMMERCE PLANETS

FIRST APPEARANCE

📺 *Trading colony: Dragonfire (1987)*

Trade between worlds is a vital part of galactic life. Some planets have unique substances or technologies that other planets are willing to pay for. Minerals and supplies that are rare in some places are common in others. Space travelers need fuel and provisions. The routes between major worlds are well traveled, so they attract a lot of trade. In more remote places, trading posts are set up that become local monopolies. The galactic economy is very sophisticated, and some planets specialize in financial services. The economy can also be fickle—this century's boom town can be next century's ghost town.

HISTORY

We've rarely seen the Doctor stocking up with supplies, although he does occasionally run out of the elements needed to operate the TARDIS. His main purpose for visiting trading posts is that they're a good source of information from the travelers and traders who pass through them. The eleventh Doctor and River Song were both fond of one of these institutions: the Maldovarium in the Belt, run by the blue-skinned Dorium Maldovar—a well-connected, well-informed entrepreneur.

BELOW: The Bank of Karabraxos was meant to be impregnable—the Doctor proved otherwise.

TIMELINE

DRAGONFIRE

SEVENTH DOCTOR

IAN BRIGGS

The Iceworld trading colony is located on Svartos, a planet with one side in perpetual sunlight and the other in darkness. It was set up by Kane, a criminal exiled from Proammon who can only exist in extremely cold temperatures and is kept on Svartos by a Biomechanoid dragon jailer. He has maintained a small army and run the colony as a dictator for 3,000 years. He is creating a cryogenically frozen army and plotting a return to Proammon, as soon as he has found a way to kill the dragon.

1987

2014

"TIME HEIST"

TWELFTH DOCTOR

STEVE THOMPSON & STEVEN MOFFAT

The Bank of Karabraxos is famously secure. Not only is it physically impressive—from the outside, it is a pyramid the size of a mountain, but it stretches deep underground—but Madame Karabraxos retains the services of the Teller, a telepathic creature who can sniff guilt on any would-be threat to the institution. The super-rich of the universe lodge their wealth at the bank. The planet it is based on, though, is vulnerable to solar storms. The Doctor is given the job of breaking into the bank, a seemingly impossible task.

2008

"TURN LEFT"

TENTH DOCTOR

RUSSELL T DAVIES

Shan Shen is a human colony, the location of a bustling market visited by the Doctor and Donna. The colonists we see appear to be of Chinese descent. A ringed world, and several other planets or moons, are visible in the sky, even in daylight.

LEISURE PLANETS

Almost as soon as mankind can reach other planets, human tourists flock to visit them. By 2116, cruise liners with 900 passengers are taking hyperspace routes to planets like Azure.[1] Planets with particular natural beauty or exotic landscapes are often popular destinations. K9 has a catalog of holiday destinations and their attractions, which ends with Yegros Alpha (atavistic therapy on a primitive asteroid), Zaakros (the galaxy's largest flora collection), and Zeen Four (historical reenactments).[2]

HISTORY

The Doctor often tries to take his companions somewhere beautiful and relaxing. He would seem to prefer tranquil breaks in natural surroundings—the third Doctor promised to take Sarah Jane to Florana,[3] a planet made beautiful by the Chelonians,[4] and the fifth Doctor loved the Eye of Orion (p. 163). He's not above luxury, though: he reveled in recreations of the *Titanic*[5] and the *Orient Express*.[6] Presumably many of his holidays are uneventful, a chance to unwind.

We have never seen one, though, that hasn't ended in some form of disaster, even when he's managed to steer the TARDIS to the planet he was planning to visit.

FIRST APPEARANCE
The Leisure Hive *(1980)*

RIGHT: The Argolin were an exotic, beautiful race.

FOOTNOTES
[1] *Nightmare of Eden* • [2] *The Leisure Hive* • [3] *Death to the Daleks* • [4] *The Hungry Bomb* • [5] *"Voyage of the Damned"* • [6] *"Mummy on the Orient Express"*

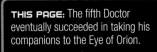

ESTABLISHED COLONIES

Some colony planets quickly came to thrive, developing huge populations in big cities, and many of these planets grew rich exploiting a natural resource. Often they were the only source for a rare mineral or other substance, but this reliance on one product led to rather homogenous societies that were highly vulnerable to changes in demand for what they produced.

HISTORY

Established colony planets seemed prone to misrule; either authorities on Earth turned a blind eye to problems, or planets were too far away for effective oversight. As colonies grow, they often acquire a corrupt leader or dynasty of leaders. They often harbor terrible secrets, such as alien infiltration. Human colonists commonly treat any native population of the planets they settle as second-class citizens, drive them out, or attempt to wipe them out.

FIRST APPEARANCE

📺 *Human colonists:* The Sensorites *(1964)*

STATUS

The Doctor makes it his business to topple corrupt regimes

LEFT: The third Doctor and his companion encounter aliens on a colony world.

FACT FILE

📺 THE MACRA TERROR

The Colony on an unnamed world was based on the principle of "healthy happiness" and resembled a holiday camp; it was run by the Pilot, who conditioned the population with catchy tunes and enforced group fun. The people worked hard, mining gas. Beyond the Colony, the planet was a clay pit lined with refineries and pipelines. The humans were unaware that they were harvesting the gas for the giant crablike Macra.

📺 THE POWER OF KROLL

When humans arrived on the Earthlike Delta Magna, they shipped the green-skinned indigenous population to the planet's third moon. The "Swampies" began to worship Kroll, a giant being they believed slept in the swamp. Hundreds of years later, Delta Magna was getting crowded. The humans then learned that the swamps of the third moon were rich in methane feedstock, a source of protein, and once again shoved the Swampies aside to set up refineries.

📺 THE HAPPINESS PATROL

Terra Alpha was ruled by the dictator Helen A, who set up a thousand factories and set human "drones" to work, classifying everyone carefully by allocating them a letter grade. The small native Pipe People fled underground. Terra Alpha produced sweets, under the aegis of the Candyman, a robot constructed from sugars. People were happy there—under pain of death, enforced by Helen A's police force, the Happiness Patrol.

📺 "A CHRISTMAS CAROL"

The Sardick family ruled a colony world and grew rich as loansharks, using cryogenically frozen people as security for the loans. They also built a device to control the Cloud Belt over the planet, a dense, electrically charged region where fish and sharks could swim.

DELLAH AND THE BRAXIATEL COLLECTION

The seventh Doctor's longest-serving companion, Bernice Summerfield, is an archaeology professor from the 26th century, specializing in both Earth history 1963–89 and the history of the Martian race (see p. 56). After she left the Doctor, she returned to her native time zone—give or take a few decades—and took up an academic position at St. Oscar's University on the planet Dellah, a planet closer to the Galactic Hub than Earth, near the Shakya Constellation.

BEHIND THE SCENES

First appearing in the book *Love and War* (Paul Cornell, 1992), Benny proved extremely popular with readers of the New Adventures novels published by Virgin Books in the 1990s and went on to become the main character of the range when Virgin lost the *Doctor Who* license. Her series of audio adventures have been running since 1998, released by Big Finish, with Lisa Bowerman in the title role.

HISTORY

The galaxy was recovering from the Galactic Wars. In quick succession, humanity fought the Cybermen, Draconians, Daleks, and many other hostile races. The war had disrupted trade routes, radicalized the politics of many worlds, and left behind many old soldiers and dangerous weapons. The universities served the purpose the monasteries had in the so-called Dark Ages: They were beacons of light.

When forced to leave Dellah, Bernice was given a job at the Braxiatel Collection, an art gallery housing 40 percent of the Wonders of the Galaxy (brainchild of Irving Braxiatel, a renegade Time Lord and older brother of the Doctor). She helped set up the collection in a new home on the asteroid KS159. Besides serving as a base of operations, this was also the site of an attack by the fascist human organization the Fifth Axis and their masters the Daleks, and by the powerful Deindum, beings from the far future.

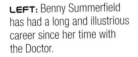

LEFT: Benny Summerfield has had a long and illustrious career since her time with the Doctor.

RIGHT: Professor Bernice Summerfield, and Wolsey.

FIRST APPEARANCE

📺 *Braxiatel Collection (mentioned):* City of **Death** (1979)

📖 *Dellah (mentioned):* Cold Fusion (1996)

STATUS

Both Dellah and asteroid KS159 mysteriously vanished

TIMELINE

THE DYING DAYS / OH NO IT ISN'T

EIGHTH DOCTOR, BERNICE SUMMERFIELD

LANCE PARKIN / PAUL CORNELL

The Doctor drops Benny (and Wolsey the cat) off on Dellah, and she is soon assigned to an expedition to Perfecton. Their ship is hit by a missile that transforms the vessel into a pantomime realm where she is Dick Whittington and Wolsey becomes a talking, human-sized creature.

1997

2006

PANACEA

ALAN BARNES

Braxiatel tries to trade the remnants of the Braxiatel Collection to the fixer Mephistopheles Arkadian in a bid to secure peace for Gallifrey.

2000

THE DEAD MEN DIARIES

BERNICE SUMMERFIELD

PAUL CORNELL (ED.)

Benny takes up her post at the Braxiatel Collection as the Fifth Axis begins annexing planets.

1999

WHERE ANGELS FEAR / TWILIGHT OF THE GODS

BERNICE SUMMERFIELD

REBECCA LEVENE & SIMON WINSTONE / MARK CLAPHAM & JON DE BURGH MILLER

Beings thought to be the exiled gods of the Worldsphere (p. 268) crash on Dellah, transforming it into a world ravaged by fanaticism. The Time Lords feel threatened by this and begin considering a strike against the Worldsphere. Benny discovers that the gods are the Ferutu, a race of Time Lords from a parallel universe. She manages to warp Dellah into their dimension, trapping them.

DIDO

Dido is a sandy planet that's accessible by Earth spaceships in the 25th century, but it is far enough off the beaten track that it takes "a long time" to reach it, and ships can only find it if they have a signal from the surface to lock onto.

FIRST APPEARANCE
The Rescue *(1965)*

LOCATION
Between Earth and Astra

INHABITANTS
Dido people, Sand Beasts

STATUS
Reduced population, rebuilding

HISTORY

It gets dark early on Dido. The local population closely resembles human beings, but with telepathic powers; there are "merely a hundred" inhabitants, although they refer to their settlement as "the city." The native life forms—creatures such as the Sand Beasts—are placid. The Dido people have an advanced technology, including powerful handheld construction rays, and a society that performs ceremonies honoring life.

The first Doctor visited Dido very early in his travels at least once, and got to know the people there very well. Shortly after the Doctor had said his farewells to his granddaughter Susan, the TARDIS accidentally ended up back on Dido. It was here that he would meet a new companion, Vicki. This visit to Dido, though, would be far from peaceful …

BEHIND THE SCENES

The Doctor's first visit to Dido occurred before the TV series started—he says that he's back "after all these years." Later stories suggested he went there on official Time Lord business, but possibly after he fled Gallifrey with Susan. The Doctor calls the locals "Dido people" at one point, while reference books have used either "Didoi" or (more commonly) "Didonians."

LEFT: Koquillion menaced Vicki while waiting for a rescue ship to arrive.

TIMELINE

1965

THE RESCUE

FIRST DOCTOR

DAVID WHITAKER

In 2493 the *UK-201*, a small ship from Earth, is bound for the planet Astra. Among the passengers are Vicki, a young girl whose mother has recently died; her father, who has accepted a new job on Astra; and a man named Bennett, who murders a member of the crew.

1965

THE RESCUE

Before details of his crime can be radioed to Astra, the *UK-201* crashes on Dido. The crew is rescued by the Dido people. Bennett sees his chance—he kills the Dido people and the crew in an explosion and then crawls back to the ship, convincing Vicki that he has survived, but has lost the use of his legs.

THE MIND OF EVIL

THIRD DOCTOR

DON HOUGHTON

Koquillion makes such an impression on the Doctor that the third Doctor remembers him when a mind parasite exposes him to his deepest fears—along with a Dalek, Cyberman, Zarbi, Ice Lord, Sensorite, War Machine, and Silurian.

1971

1965

THE RESCUE

The Doctor comes to realize what Bennett's plan is. Two Dido people appear, terrifying Bennett and causing him to fall to his death. Vicki joins the Doctor on his travels.

1965

THE RESCUE

To add to the deception, Bennett dons alien ceremonial robes and menaces Vicki as "Koquillion," a fearsome alien. Vicki tends to the "wounded" Bennett, sends a distress signal to Earth, and makes a pet out of a Sand Beast, whom she names Sandy.

KALDOR

The deep deserts of one human colony world are rich with rare metals like keefan, zelanite, and lucanol. The minerals are whipped up by huge storms and harvested by storm miners—large wheeled vehicles with giant scoops at the front that trundle out into the desert for years at a time, manned by a handful of humans living in luxury, dependent on robot servants. The wealth of the world is divided up among the influential Founding Families, who scheme against each other in an endless whirl of politics and intrigue.

HISTORY

The fourth Doctor and Leela landed on Storm Mine 4 and were suspected of a series of murders that were taking place. Members of the Storm Mine crew were being killed off, one by one. The victims were being strangled, but the humans were unable to think the unthinkable: that the robot servants were rising against their masters. They had been reprogrammed by Taren Capel, an engineer raised by robots who wanted to see them freed from what he saw as slavery. The Doctor exposed Taren Capel and flooded the room he was in with helium gas, which raised the pitch of the revolutionary's voice, rendering it unrecognizable to the robots relying on his voice commands. The robots then strangled him.

FACT FILE

📺 THE ROBOTS OF DEATH

There are three types of robot: non-speaking black-and-silver Dums, who are only capable of menial tasks; pale-green-and-silver Vocs, who can speak and perform more complicated duties; and silver Super-Vocs, who can hold conversations with humans and are also sophisticated enough to coordinate and plan the running of an entire storm miner.

📺 THE ROBOTS OF DEATH

The robots are uncannily human, but there are enough differences between robot and human body language that humans can automatically discriminate between them. Fear of robots—usually as a result of being disconcerted by these differences—is a known mental illness, "robophobia," also known as Grimwade's Syndrome. Obviously, all Storm Mine personnel are screened for this.

🗨 CRISIS ON KALDOR

Later, a fourth category of robot, the Ultra-Voc, is introduced. By this time, at least some of the storm miner vehicles are operated without any human crew.

🎧 ROBOPHOBIA

As the company who builds the robots has a lucrative trade selling them to other planets, the events on Storm Mine 4 are hushed up. The Doctor first encountered his companion Liv Chenka, a native of Kaldor, on a robot transport ship.

FIRST APPEARANCE
The Robots of Death *(1977)*

STATUS
World consumed by the Fendahleen

LEFT: The inner workings of a Storm Mine vehicle show a vast refinery and tiny living quarters.

BELOW: Crisis on Kaldor, as a new type of robot causes trouble.

KALDOR CITY

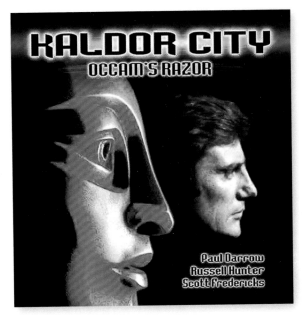

KALDOR CITY
OCCAM'S RAZOR

Paul Darrow
Russell Hunter
Scott Fredericks

A city of 8 million people and 14 million robots, Kaldor City is the hub of a planet grown rich from the proceeds of storm mining. The rich live in grand apartments and palaces, where they are attended to by robot servants. The poor are confined to the sewerpits, crime-infested ghettos where they are granted very few opportunities. The planet is a former Earth colony but had survived in isolation for centuries.

HISTORY

Several years after the Storm Mine 4 incident, one of the survivors, Uvanov, was promoted and became one of the topmasters of the Company. Uvanov was keen to end Kaldor's isolation and develop interstellar trade. He faced resistance from many within the elite, and the whole city faced a terrorist campaign led by robot rights activists. Ultimately, there was a far greater threat lurking in plain sight …

ABOVE: Paul Darrow on the cover of the first *Kaldor City* release.

BELOW: The political machinations of Kaldor City were just as intricate as a chess game.

BEHIND THE SCENES

The world first seen in *The Robots of Death* (Chris Boucher, 1977) was fleshed out in the novel *Corpse Marker* and the *Kaldor City* audio play series, using a number of characters created by Boucher for both *Doctor Who* and the BBC science-fiction series *Blake's 7*.

FIRST APPEARANCE
📺 (named) **The Robots of Death** (1977)
🔊 (seen) **Crisis on Kaldor** (1981)

STATUS
Absorbed into the Fendahl gestalt

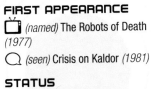

TIMELINE

📖 *CORPSE MARKER*
🎗 FOURTH DOCTOR
✎ CHRIS BOUCHER

Other board members are suspicious of Uvanov because he isn't a member of one of the Founding Families. Uvanov cements his power when his enemies try to introduce cyborg workers, which go haywire. In the aftermath, he is appointed Firstmaster Chairholder.

1999

2002–04

🎧 *HIDDEN PERSUADERS* (2002) / *TAREN CAPEL* (2003) / *CHECKMATE* (2003) / *STORM MINE* (2004) / *THE PRISONER* (2003) (ALL FROM *KALDOR CITY* SERIES)

✎ JIM SMITH & FIONA MOORE / ALAN STEVENS X 2 / DANIEL O'MAHONY / ALAN STEVENS & FIONA MOORE

Paulus discovers a skull in the desert that he believes to be a relic of Taren Capel. Carnell flees, sensing that the society is being manipulated by something immensely powerful. Robots begin revolting, although Iago is able to get them to stand down. Uvanov faces a boardroom revolt, but the planet faces a far more serious problem. The skull Paulus discovered was not that of Taren Capel; it was that of the Fendahl (p. 56). The Fendahl conquers the planet, absorbing everyone into its gestalt. Kaston Iago manages to retain a vestige of individuality and struggles to escape the gestalt.

2001

🎧 *OCCAM'S RAZOR*
✎ ALAN STEVENS & JIM SMITH

A number of Firstmasters are murdered, and suspicion falls on the notorious assassin Kaston Iago, who has recently taken up residence in Kaldor City. Uvanov trusts the opinion of his psychostrategist Carnell that Iago is innocent and hires him as a security consultant—just as Carnell and Iago predicted he would.

2002

🎧 *DEATH'S HEAD*
✎ CHRIS BOUCHER

Another survivor of Storm Mine 4, Poul, becomes "Paulus," leader of an anti-robot terrorist organization, the Church of Taren Capel. Uvanov manages to get agents into the organization … and uses it to eliminate some of his political rivals.

RIBOS

Ribos's elliptical orbit gave it two 32-year seasons, "Sun Time" and "Ice Time." *Bartholomew's Planetary Gazetteer* described it as a Class 3 Society. Technology, fashions, and architecture were reminiscent of mid-19th-century Russia, with some simple electrical devices, such as lighting and alarms. Shur, the capital, had some luxuries, but during Ice Time other towns were cut off completely. Ribosians were oblivious to life elsewhere. They were superstitious, backward, believing the world was flat, stars were ice crystals, and that the Ice Gods lived in ancient catacombs below Shur.

FIRST APPEARANCE
The Ribos Operation *(1978)*

INHABITANTS
Humans, Shrivenzale

STATUS
Backwater, glimmers of a renaissance

HISTORY

The natives, then, had no idea they were in the Constellation of Skythra, three light centuries from the Magellanic Clouds, or that their galactic coordinates were 4940. They were unaware that Ribos was a protectorate of the Greater Cyrrhenic Empire, also known as the Alliance. Planets of the Alliance included the planets Cyrrhenis Minima (116 parsecs from Ribos, at coordinates 4180), Mirabilis Minor, Stapros, and Levithia. The civilization was policed by Alliance Security, with disputes ending up in the High Court. Worlds in Alliance territory were still being surveyed by organizations like the Magellanic Mining Conglomerate. Communication was made via hypercable. Close by were the shipyards of the Pontenese and the mercenaries, the Schlanghi.

BEHIND THE SCENES

The first and only appearance of Ribos was in the debut story of the 16th season. This was also the story that introduced Romana, the new version of K9, the Guardians, and kicked off a season-long story arc in which the Doctor tracked down the six segments of the Key to Time.

LEFT: The costume Garron wore to blend in on Ribos.

RIGHT: The Time Lady Romana joined the Doctor, and their first adventure was on Ribos.

TIMELINE

THE RIBOS OPERATION
FOURTH DOCTOR
ROBERT HOLMES

The Graff Vynda-K is Royal Prince of the Greater Cyrrhenic Empire and Emperor of Levithia. He leaves to fight for the Alliance in the Frontier Wars on worlds including Skaar, the Freytus Labyrinth, and Crestus Minor. He is a brutal tyrant, though, and in his absence his half-brother is installed as ruler. The Graff Vynda-K seeks revenge against his people.

1978

1978

THE RIBOS OPERATION

The Doctor, Romana, and K9 arrive on Ribos looking for the first segment of the Key to Time. They meet Garron and thwart the Graff's dreams of glory. The small lump of jethryk Garron used to fool the Graff is the first segment of the Key to Time, and the Doctor picks Garron's pocket to acquire it.

THE RIBOS OPERATION

The Graff seeks a base of operations to build an army, which he knows will be a lifetime's work. Garron claims to represent the owners of Ribos and offers the planet to him for ten million opeks. He leaves a fake mineralogical survey where the Graff can see it, which states that the planet is rich in jethryk, the most valuable element in the universe—a blue crystal that powered battle fleets.

1978

1978

1978

THE RIBOS OPERATION

Garron flees Earth for the Cyrhennic Alliance after a failed attempt to sell the Sydney Opera House to an Arab. He quickly becomes known to Alliance Security after he sells the planet Mirabilis Minor to three different buyers. He marks out the Graff Vynda-K for his latest con.

THE SIRIUS SYSTEM

Sirius is a bright star—actually a binary star—less than nine light years from Earth. As a near neighbor, it was one of the earliest solar systems to be colonized, and a number of its planets have interesting features. The Sirius system is clearly wealthy and important enough to be granted special status by Earth.

HISTORY

The twin planets of Androzani Major and Androzani Minor are important. Androzani Major is an Earthlike world that's nominally democratic, with a President, but where true power lies with the Sirius Conglomeration, a company with massive mining interests— and the political influence to use unpaid criminals as workers. They also control the trade in spectrox, a rare substance found on Minor—a smaller world, one that's muddy and all but uninhabited. They face resistance from Sharaz Jek and his army of androids.

FIRST APPEARANCE
(mentioned) Frontier in Space (1973)

INHABITANTS
Humans, androids, spectrox bats, the Varlon Empire, the Kith, snegs

STATUS
Prospering

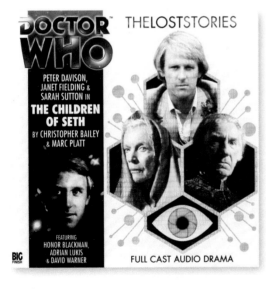

DOCTOR WHO
THELOSTSTORIES

PETER DAVISON, JANET FIELDING & SARAH SUTTON IN
THE CHILDREN OF SETH
BY CHRISTOPHER BAILEY & MARC PLATT

FEATURING
HONOR BLACKMAN, ADRIAN LUKIS & DAVID WARNER

BIG

FULL CAST AUDIO DRAMA

LEFT: The Sirius system became the heart of a powerful empire.

RIGHT: Beneath the surface of Androzani Minor lurks the Magma Beast.

TIMELINE

2013

📻 **STARLIGHT ROBBERY**
👤 **SEVENTH DOCTOR**
✒️ **MATT FITTON**

The A-rated Galactic Credit Bank is based on Sirius IX.

📺 **FRONTIER IN SPACE**
👤 **THIRD DOCTOR**
✒️ **MALCOLM HULKE**

By 2540, Sirius has a degree of autonomy within the Earth Empire as a Dominion. The Master passes himself off as a Commissioner from Sirius IV and attempts to extradite the Doctor and Jo from Earth on the false charge of making an unauthorized landing on Sirius III.

1973

🎧 **MAX WARP**

The Sirius Exhibition Station hosts the Inter-G Cruiser Show, where new spacecraft are exhibited. It is in orbit around Sirius Alpha, a planet with at least four moons.

2008

1979

📺 **CITY OF DEATH**
👤 **FOURTH DOCTOR**
✒️ **"DAVID AGNEW" (PSEUDONYM FOR DAVID FISHER, DOUGLAS ADAMS & GRAHAM WILLIAMS)**

Sirius V is the home of the Academia Stellaris, an art gallery Romana rates as at least on a par with the Louvre.

🎧 **MAX WARP**
👤 **EIGHTH DOCTOR**
✒️ **JONATHAN MORRIS**

When the Varlon Empire tries to establish itself in Sirius, it ends up in a war with the Kith, a race of sentient sponges from a neighboring system.

2008

1984

1984

1985

🎧 **THE CHILDREN OF SETH (RELEASED 2011)**
👤 **FIFTH DOCTOR**
✒️ **CHRISTOPHER BAILEY & MARC PLATT**

The Sirius Archipelago is home to a sector-wide human empire that creates a fictional enemy, Seth, to justify its explansion. Androids, outlawed by the empire, attempt a coup.

📺 **THE CAVES OF ANDROZANI**
👤 **FIFTH DOCTOR**
✒️ **ROBERT HOLMES**

The Sirius Conglomerate is run from Androzani Major, and its chairman, Morgus, is "the richest man in the five planets." Presumably, this means Androzani is in the Sirius system.

📺 **THE CAVES OF ANDROZANI**

Morgus's wealth is based on mining and exploitation of other natural resources, but one key to his fortune is that he has the monopoly on spectrox, a substance that can dramatically extend human lifespans, found only on Major's twin planet, Androzani Minor.

SOLOS

Solos was an unspoiled, temperate world, and the humanlike Solonians were farmers and hunters. Then, in the 25th century, ships from the Earth Empire arrived on Solos intent on mining thaesium, a radioactive crystal fuel. A nitrogen isotope that reacted to sunlight released gases that meant Earthmen needed oxymasks to survive on the surface for more than a few minutes, so they forced the natives to become thaesium miners. After 500 years, the planet was a slagheap on top of stripped-out caves. The Marshal, its colonial master, ruled Solos from his Skybase, segregating the natives from the "Overlords."

FIRST APPEARANCE
The Mutants *(1972)*

LOCATION
The Nebula of Cyclops

STATUS
Rebuilding, home of angelic beings

HISTORY

The Earthmen faced serious problems, though. Earth was collapsing and could no longer afford its Empire. Planets were being given independence, and an Administrator arrived at Skybase to announce that the Empire would grant freedom to Solos. He arrived as a plague was spreading that was transforming the Solonians into powerful insectoid creatures, the Mutts. The Marshal, facing a return to Earth and a low-grade career in the Records Bureau, decided he could kill two birds with one stone: by altering the atmosphere of Solos, he could make the world a garden paradise—and kill off all the Solonians. It was a situation so precarious it demanded a rare intervention from the Time Lords ...

BEHIND THE SCENES

The Mutants (Bob Baker & David Martin) was a barely veiled allegory for apartheid policies. One of the monsters from this story, a Mutt, reappeared briefly at the beginning of *The Brain of Morbius* (Terrance Dicks & Robert Holmes, 1976), and the Doctor said it was from the Nebula of Cyclops.

LEFT: The radioactive mines beneath Solos harbored more than just the hordes of Mutts.

TIMELINE

THE MUTANTS
THIRD DOCTOR
BOB BAKER & DAVID MARTIN

The Doctor has been exiled to Earth by the Time Lords and rarely has use of his TARDIS. The situation on Solos is important enough that his people send him on a mission to deliver a message pod that will only open for its intended recipient.

1972

THE MUTANTS

Like a butterfly emerging from a chrysalis, when exposed to thaesium radiation, the rebel leader Ky is transformed into an angelic being. He destroys the Marshal. The Earth authorities grant Solos full independence.

1972

1972

THE MUTANTS

Inside the message pod are ancient tablets from Solos explaining that the planet takes 2,000 years to orbit its sun. The whole human occupation of Solos has only lasted for "spring," and the planet is now entering "summer." The mutations are a natural part of this cycle; they mutate to adapt to the climate at the start of each 500-year "season."

1972

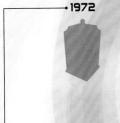

THE MUTANTS

The Doctor and his assistant, Jo Grant, arrive on the Skybase to find segregated teleport booths and humans terrified by the threat of a plague on the surface that is causing the Solonians to mutate.

1972

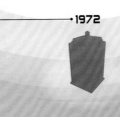

THE MUTANTS

The message pod is meant for the rebel leader Ky, who has been fighting the evil Marshal. The Marshal is conducting atmospheric experiments that many believe are causing the mutations.

TARA

Tara is a world with a temperate climate and Earthlike gravity and atmosphere, 12 parsecs from Earth. What we've seen of the planet is that it is divided up into feudal domains, forests and parkland for hunting, and rivers for fishing. Features include the lands of Prince Reynart, and the domains of Thorvald, Mortgarde, and Freya. Close by is the Castle Gracht—ancestral home of Count Grendel of Gracht. The Royal Kings of Tara have great faith in astrology and in the state religion, led by the Archimandrite. The currency is the gold piece.

HISTORY

Tara, though, is not a primitive world. The Tarans have sophisticated electronics; they have devices that can read the alpha waves of a person's brain. Their weapons include rapiers that carry a burning electric charge and crossbows that fire bolts of energy. Their most distinctive technology, though, is androids that—when functioning normally—are almost impossible to tell apart from real human beings. These had been developed 200 years before the Doctor first visited the planet, when a plague wiped out 90 percent of the population. Repairing androids was not an honorable profession; it was work for the peasantry.

BEHIND THE SCENES

The Androids of Tara (David Fisher, 1978) was the fourth story of the *Key to Time* saga. The Taran Wood Beast is generally felt to be one of the less successful *Doctor Who* monster designs.

FIRST APPEARANCE
The Androids of Tara *(1978)*

INHABITANTS
Tarans, horses, androids, Taran Wood Beasts

LEFT: It's easy to see why Romana would be terrified of this Wood Beast.

THIS PAGE: Grand Castle Gracht.

THE ERA OF THE TERRAPHILES

By 51,007 there are billions of worlds in the Galactic Union, but humans are hungry for more. Great corporations terraform worlds and theme them to eras of human history and works of literature. The wealthy can live like Ancient Romans, Native Americans, or as if in a Jane Austen or Alan Moore book. After a comet strike and nuclear winter, Earth is an abandoned snowball in the Oort Clouds of Orion. Very few of its relics survive, so recreations mingle fact and fiction, but their love of Earth's heritage means that the people of this era are known as the Terraphiles.

FIRST APPEARANCE

📖 The Coming of the Terraphiles (2010)

CURRENT STATUS

Vibrant interstellar civilization c.50,000 ad

HISTORY

Thanks to the invention of color pool drive by O'Bean the Younger, humanity has spread across the Mutter's Spiral, to the dwarf galaxies surrounding it (see p. 30), and into other space-time continua. Lord Renark of the Rim led much of the human race out of our universe—to where, no one knows—and they never returned. The conjecture is that they went to "Renark's Multiverse" or "Renark's Dilemma."

Peaceful periods and dark ages came and went in cycles, and there were 12 intergalactic wars. Humans exploring the multiverse found the Second Aether, a liminal state "between … everything: Matter and Antimatter, Law and Chaos, Life and Death, Reason and Romance." Miracles were performed there, feats impossible to science and magic, and entities there included Spammer Gain and the Original Insect.

RIGHT: Renowned author Michael Moorcock wrote *The Coming of the Terraphiles.*

OPPOSITE: The eleventh Doctor and Amy visited the era of the Terraphiles.

BEHIND THE SCENES

Michael Moorcock's novel *The Coming of the Terraphiles* gleefully established a whole new era of future history for the Doctor Who universe, while including names familiar from his own earlier work, like Cornelius and O'Bean.

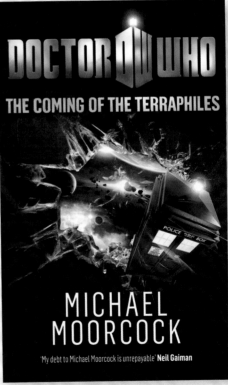

DOCTOR WHO

THE COMING OF THE TERRAPHILES

MICHAEL MOORCOCK

'My debt to Michael Moorcock is unrepayable' **Neil Gaiman**

FACT FILE

📺 THE ANDROIDS OF TARA

The main city of Tara—also called Tara—surrounds a large palace, where the Royal King and his court normally reside. The palace has a throne room dominated by a large clock marked with astrological symbols. There are tunnels underneath the city, built at the time of the plague so the royal court could leave the palace without becoming contaminated. They lead to secret passages in the palace—including one that leads to right behind the throne.

📺 THE ANDROIDS OF TARA

Prince Reynart, rightful heir to the throne of Tara, maintains hunting grounds, including an impressive Hunting Lodge.

📺 THE ANDROIDS OF TARA

Castle Gracht is about eight leagues from the Hunting Lodge. It is a large structure, centuries old, and able to withstand a siege for over two years. It is surrounded by a moat and contains an advanced laboratory.

📺 THE ANDROIDS OF TARA

The Pavilion of the Summer Winds is a beautiful wooden structure in the grounds of Castle Gracht.

📺 THE ANDROIDS OF TARA

The fauna of Tara is friendly—except for the Beasts that Count Grendel keeps in the wood for hunting. The Taran nobility ride horses.

📺 THE ANDROIDS OF TARA

The TARDIS has records of Tara detailed enough to tell Romana about this year's fashions.

FACT FILE

EarthMakers, run by the Tarbutton family, is the largest terraforming company. The second largest, TerraForma, run by the Banning-Cannons, specializes in Medieval and Edwardian English versions of Earth, the PeersTM.

The Terraphiles play sports such as broadswording (with swords wider than they are long) and Arrers, a combination of darts, archery, and cricket.

Other worlds include the beautiful worlds of Calypso V—Venice, Ur XVII, and New Venus—as well as the howling terraces of Arcturus-and-Arcturus, Cygnus 34, Loondoon (home of many fashion houses), New North Whales, and Old Barsoom.

While revisiting this era, the eleventh Doctor became aware General Frank/Freddie Force and his Antimatter Men were trying to take control of the black hole at the center of the galaxy. He joined a cruise ship heading to Miggea, a planet that orbits between universes.

Captain Cornelius, an old rival and acquaintance of the Doctor, was also aware of the problem—dark tides threatened the existence of the multiverse. The Doctor and Cornelius secured the Arrow of Law, an artifact from the Realm of Law that restored the cosmic balance.

LOST COLONIES

FIRST APPEARANCE

Lost colony: **The Chase** *(1965)*

The universe is large, and spacecraft go missing. Most lost ships must simply be destroyed, either by accident or contact with some malevolent force. Others are able to send out a rescue signal, which is quickly detected.[1] Some ships, though, end up marooned on alien worlds. A proportion of those have crews with the necessary skills and supplies to carve out a life on what are necessarily remote and often very hostile worlds.

HISTORY

Over time, Earth is gradually forgotten. Life on a spaceship is usually regimented, hierarchical, and specialized, and as lost colonists build their new community, the social structure is often retained in some form. Surviving artifacts offer clues to their origins, but they often do not understand these. There's also a clear pattern of atavism— human societies taking on earlier ways of life, from hunter-gatherers to feudalism and early industrial societies.

The Doctor has visited many such worlds. For example, on Mechanus, robots maintain a vast city, in preparation (they say) for human colonists.[2] The rulers of Metebelis III came from Earth after the starship they were on crashed there: They were the evolved descendants of spiders from a human vessel.[3] The planet Tara bears all the hallmarks of a lost human colony.[4] The medieval peasants of an unnamed world in E-Space are the descendants of the crew of the *Hydrax*.[5]

OPPOSITE: Leela shows the fourth Doctor the face of her tribe's mad god.

RIGHT: Steven Taylor became marooned on the hostile jungle colony of Mechanus.

FACT FILE

THE FACE OF EVIL

A hostile jungle planet is the home of two societies: the Sevateem, who live in the jungle as a tribe of warriors, with a heavily ritualistic society that worships the god Xoanon; and the Tesh, who live in the mountains and have psychic powers. Both are descendants of the crew of an Earth ship; the division between the "Survey Team" who explored the planet and the "Techs" who remained onboard are retained in the names of their tribes.

TRAGEDY DAY

The people of Olleril, a world in the Pristatrek Galaxy, are humans who have rebuilt their society from the clues found in the only books to survive their ship's crashing: *The Collins Guide to the Twentieth Century*, *One of Us* by Hugo Young, *Manufacturing Consent*, and *The Smash Hits Yearbook*. Olleril society is almost as ridiculous and unequal as the 1990s Britain that inspired it. One highlight is the annual Tragedy Day festival, when the rich are moved to donate as much as 0.0000001 percent of their wealth to the poor.

FOOTNOTES
[1] *The Rescue* • [2] *The Chase* • [3] *Planet of the Spiders* • [4] *The Androids of Tara* • [5] *State of Decay*

PLANETS OF ORIGIN

TIME LORD PLANETS

RIGHT: A warrior who would fight the Time War was born on Karn from the ashes of the eighth Doctor.

KASTERBOROUS

Gallifrey, the Time Lords' home planet, was in the Kasterborous constellation—"the Shining World of the Seven Systems," which may indicate how many stars it had.[1] A ceremonial dais on Gallifrey showed what looked like a solar system with six worlds, two in the same orbit [2]—possibly the planets Gallifrey; Karn; the gas giant Polarfrey; Kasterborous the Fibster (a large asteroid); an unnamed fifth; plus Gallifrey's copper-colored moon, Pazithi Gallifreya.[3] Maren of the Sisterhood of Karn also spoke of "the five planets."[4] The Doctor once referred to Gallifrey's "second sun," implying it was a binary system (or that the Time Lords had replaced the first).[5]

HISTORY

Gallifrey's coordinates were 10-0-11-0-0 x 0-2.[6] A Time Lord once told the Doctor he'd traveled 29,000 light years to Earth.[7] The Time Lords knew of the Mutts,[8] so they may have lived close to Solos, and spaceships from Earth could reach Karn[9]—this all suggests that Kasterborous was in Earth's galaxy. The Doctor has said Gallifrey was 250,000 light years away from Earth, on the other side of the galaxy.[10] Races we know have traveled to Gallifrey or Karn under their own power include the Vardans (whose home planet was at Vector 3052, Alpha 7, 14th Span), Sontarans,[11] Birastop, Hoothi,[12] Rutans,[13] and the Daleks.[14] Gallifrey was destroyed in a Time War with a mysterious enemy,[15] but the eighth Doctor apparently restored it, only for it to be lost again on the last day of the Last Great Time War.[16]

BEHIND THE SCENES

Since 1975, Kasterborous has been mentioned on-screen in *Attack of the Cybermen* (Paula Moore, 1985), "Voyage of the Damned" (Russell T Davies, 2007), "The Day of the Doctor" (Steven Moffat, 2013), and "Death in Heaven" (Moffat, 2014). As elsewhere in *Doctor Who*, "constellation" seems to mean a group of stars close together, rather than—as in astronomy—a pattern formed in a particular planet's night sky, of stars that are varying distances away.

FIRST APPEARANCE
Pyramids of Mars *(1975)*

INHABITANTS
Time Lords, Sisterhood of Karn, possibly the Mutts

FACT FILE

DOCTOR WHO AND THE SEVEN KEYS TO DOOMSDAY
The Doctor and his companions Jenny and Jimmy once prevented the Daleks and Clawrantulars from assembling the Seven Keys of Doomsday on the planet Karn.

THE BRAIN OF MORBIUS
Karn was actually the greatest hazard to spacefarers in the area—to protect the Elixir of Life, the Sisterhood of Karn used their telekinetic powers to dash passing spaceships into a rocky plain, which became a graveyard of ships. In the recent past, the planet was the base of operations for Morbius, a Time Lord who raised an army to conquer the universe but was defeated.

LUNGBARROW
Millions of years ago, Karn was an old Gallifreyan colony planet. The supporters of the Pythia, mostly women, fled there with the secret of immortality when their leader was deposed by Rassilon.

THE INVASION OF TIME
The Time Lords monitored space traffic around their planet but were protected by powerful Transduction Barriers that blocked any unwanted visitors—even those with their own TARDIS.

SHADA
The Time Lords maintained a prison asteroid, Shada, where they imprisoned both alien and Time Lord criminals.

THE TRIAL OF A TIME LORD
The Time Lords also operated a large space station, the location of the Doctor's second trial.

THE INFINITY DOCTORS
In the distant future, there is a mysterious organization called the Children of Kasterborous, presumably spiritual or actual descendants of the Time Lords.

FOOTNOTES
[1] "The Sound of Drums" • [2] *The Invasion of Time* • [3] *Lungbarrow* [4, 9 & 12] *The Brain of Morbius* • [5] "Gridlock" • [6] *Pyramids of Mars* • [7] *Terror of the Autons* • [8] *The Mutants* • [9 & 12] "The Night of the Doctor" • [10] *Doctor Who: The Movie* • [11] *The Invasion of Time* • [13] *The Infinity Doctors* • [14] "The Day of the Doctor" • [15] *The Ancestor Cell* • [16] "Dalek"

ANCIENT GALLIFREY

One of the oldest civilizations in the universe, Time Lord society survived for millions[1]—perhaps a billion—years.[2] It began when a humanoid race, a powerful, somewhat savage species with an instinctive sensitivity to time, evolved on Gallifrey. The Gallifreyans could see the future, and they learned how to build simple time machines. They explored the universe and were gods at a time when the galaxy was full of beings like gods.[3]

INHABITANTS
The Time Lords, Rassilon, the Pythia, the Minyans

HISTORY

The Time Lords, as we know them, were born thanks to the legendary leader, Rassilon, who developed time travel, bodily regeneration, the Looms from which Time Lord bodies were spun, and the Matrix—a supercomputer that preserved all the knowledge of the Time Lords, including the memories of the dead. In their early history, the Time Lords tried to encourage the development of some races ... a policy that went disastrously wrong. The peoples of Minyos and Micen Island wiped themselves out using technology the Time Lords had supplied. The Time Lords of Gallifrey vowed that from that point on, they would observe the universe and never intervene.

ABOVE: Omega's ship was lost at the dawn of Time Lord history.

OPPOSITE: The only known image of the mysterious other Time Lord who helped Rassilon and Omega.

BEHIND THE SCENES

Rassilon was first mentioned in the TV story *The Deadly Assassin* (Robert Holmes, 1976), and so many subsequent stories introduced artifacts "of Rassilon" that it became something of a joke in the series (the rudest perhaps being the fourth Doctor's use of the mild expletive "Rassilon's Rod!"). The TV story *Underworld* (Bob Baker & David Martin, 1978) and audio drama *Death Comes to Time* (Colin Meek, 2002) explored the origins of the Time Lords' noninterference policy.

FACT FILE

📺 **THE THREE DOCTORS**

Omega was lost, believed to be killed, detonating a star that became a supernova and black hole, which would power all Time Lord technology, including TARDISes.

📺 **THE FIVE DOCTORS**

Early Gallifreyans kidnapped creatures from across time and space and set them in gladiatorial combat in an area of Gallifrey known as the Death Zone.

📺 **THE FIVE DOCTORS**

Rassilon discovered the secret of bodily regeneration. Eventually, he was entombed in a Tower in the Death Zone. He did not die; he slept, having discovered the secret of perpetual regeneration—true immortality.

🔍 **4-D WAR**

The Order of the Black Sun sent missions to the dawn of the Time Lords and retaliated against a Time Lord attack that had not yet happened, from the Time Lords' point of view. The Time Lords had never even heard of the Order. This was the first Time War.

📺 **REMEMBRANCE OF THE DALEKS**

Rassilon developed time travel with the stellar engineer Omega and a mysterious third person, known to legend as "the Other."

📖 **TIME'S CRUCIBLE, LUNGBARROW**

Before Rassilon, Gallifrey was ruled by the Pythia, a line of women who could see the future. The last Pythia was deposed by Rassilon, architect of modern Time Lord society. She cursed the race with sterility, but Rassilon simply invented the Looms, machines where new Gallifreyans were woven.

📺 **STATE OF DECAY, IMAGE OF THE FENDAHL, "THE RUNAWAY BRIDE"**

Rassilon became Lord High President. Early in their history, the Time Lords fought great wars against the Vampires; the Racnoss; the Fendahl; and other vile, monstrous races.

FOOTNOTES
[1] 📺 *The Deadly Assassin* • [2] 📺 "The End of Time" •
[3] 📖 *Time's Crucible*

THE GEOGRAPHY OF GALLIFREY

The Time Lords lived in the Capitol, sealed inside a dome on the continent Wild Endeavour;[1] anything outside this was called "Outer Gallifrey."[2] Gallifrey had an orange sky, silver-leafed trees,[3] and mostly desert terrain. When the War Doctor needed a remote place to operate the Moment superweapon, he used a barn here.[4] Gallifrey was also quite mountainous, with peaks including Solace and Solitude (near the Capitol[5]), Mount Cadon (the tallest, home of the Prydonian Academy), Mount Perdition, and Mount Lung.[6]

HISTORY

The Capitol was the center of Time Lord society. It dated from the time of Rassilon, but in those days wasn't enclosed.[7] At the center of the Capitol was the Citadel, and at the center of this was the Panopticon, a vast ceremonial chamber.[8] It was here that the Flowers of the Remembrance of the Lost Dead were released.[9] Far below the Panopticon was a monolith connected to the Eye of Harmony, the black hole that provided power to all Gallifreyan technology, including TARDISes.[10]

The Capitol included the chambers of the High and Supreme Councils, the office of the President, the Towers of Canonicity and Likelihood,[11] the Endless Library, the Tomb of the Uncertain Soldier, and the Omega Memorial.[12] The Capitol also housed the Infinity Chamber, from where Time Lords could observe the entire universe, and the Matrix, a repository for all Time Lord knowledge, including memories of the dead.

OPPOSITE: A Time Lord outside the Capitol on Gallifrey.

FOOTNOTES
[1] "Gridlock" • [2] *The Invasion of Time* • [3] *Marco Polo* • [4] "The Day of the Doctor" • [5] "The Sound of Drums" • [6] *Lungbarrow* • [7 & 12] *The Infinity Doctors* • [8 & 10] *The Deadly Assassin* • [9] *Earth and Beyond* • [11] *The Blue Angel*

FIRST APPEARANCE
The War Games *(1969)*

INHABITANTS
Time Lords, other Gallifreyans, alien ambassadors

BEHIND THE SCENES

Although first seen in *The War Games* (Terrance Dicks & Malcolm Hulke, 1969), Gallifrey wasn't named until *The Time Warrior* (Robert Holmes, 1974). Details about the planet have accumulated very gradually, but much of what we know comes from *The Deadly Assassin* (Holmes, 1976). We saw Gallifrey destroyed in the book *The Ancestor Cell* (Peter Anghelides & Stephen Cole, 2000) and TV's "The Day of the Doctor" (Steven Moffat, 2013).

FACT FILE

THE FIVE DOCTORS
The Death Zone of Gallifrey was mountainous but had green vegetation and grasses and a blue sky. Its most notable artificial feature was the Tower of Rassilon, where the founder of Time Lord society existed in undying sleep.

CRISIS IN SPACE
Refugees from over 100 planets, victims of the Great Famine of 2359, were housed in Riff City, a shantytown around the fortress city of Prydon on Gallifrey. The "riffos" were overseen by snakelike Malian guards and fed Promaze, a nasty artificial foodstuff.

THE TIDES OF TIME
Some buildings resembling skyscrapers were actually vast computers.

CAT'S CRADLE, LUNGBARROW
The Time Lord Academy was a large complex in the mountains. Individual colleges also had their own property. The Doctor's family home was Lungbarrow, on the side of Mount Lung, in South Gallifrey. It overlooked the Cadonflood River and was two days' walk from the ancient fortress Rassilon's Rampart. To the East of the Capitol were the Three Minute Cities, one of which was called Olyesti.

THE EIGHT DOCTORS
The poor lived in Low Town, a shantytown that grew up around the base of the Capitol dome.

THE EIGHT DOCTORS
The Capitol was built over far more ancient structures and contained many sections that had been put to other uses or just forgotten over the centuries. Ancient weapons were stored in the Time Vaults, but other valuable artifacts had been left in half-forgotten storerooms or were otherwise gathering dust.

"THE DAY OF THE DOCTOR"
There were other settlements. The second largest was Arcadia, which fell to the Daleks on the last day of the Time War.

MODERN GALLIFREY

For millions of years, Gallifrey's defining characteristic was that nothing changed; 1,000 Time Lords lived in the Capitol, content to live academic lives, monitoring the universe from their Infinity Chambers.[1] They were pledged not to intervene in the wider universe—unless an entity emerged that threatened all life forms or the fabric of time itself. Not every Gallifreyan was a Time Lord; others were students, in the ceremonial Guard, or served their masters as technicians, and there were always a few who left the Dome for a simpler life—either in the deserts of Gallifrey or in retirement on a backwater world.[2]

HISTORY

A generation emerged that challenged the establishment. The Rani was exiled for unethical experiments. The War Chief left to work with alien Warlords. The Monk, Drax, and Madrigor left Gallifrey to profit from crimes it was only possible to commit using a TARDIS. Braxiatel preferred political manipulation and covert diplomatic efforts. The two most important Time Lords of their age, though, were the Doctor and the Master. We have only seen hints of their early life, but they were great friends who saw much that was corrupt about Gallifrey and great potential in the wider universe. The Time Lords' isolationist approach was no longer acceptable—dark forces were gathering. The Doctor and Master found themselves exiled from Time Lord society just as Gallifrey faced its darkest hours. The Time Lords soon became aware that they were facing a threat that could well destroy them…

RIGHT: The renegade Madrigor was known as the Time Thief.

BELOW: It took more than one Doctor to defeat the corrupt Lord President Borusa.

FOOTNOTES
[1] *The Invisible Enemy* • [2] *The Invasion of Time*

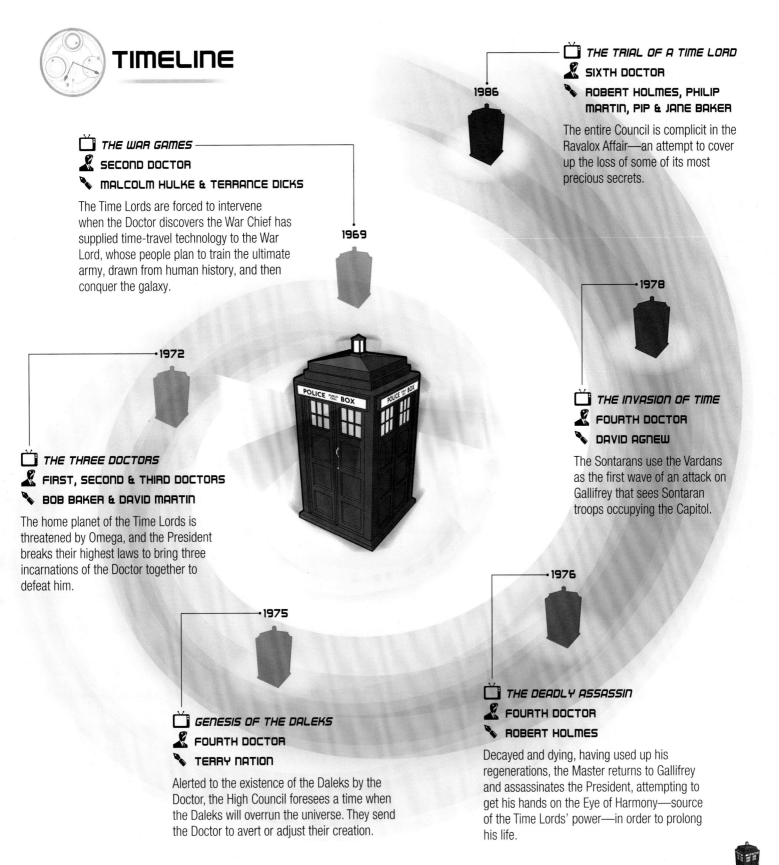

TIMELINE

THE TRIAL OF A TIME LORD
SIXTH DOCTOR
ROBERT HOLMES, PHILIP MARTIN, PIP & JANE BAKER

1986

The entire Council is complicit in the Ravalox Affair—an attempt to cover up the loss of some of its most precious secrets.

THE WAR GAMES
SECOND DOCTOR
MALCOLM HULKE & TERRANCE DICKS

The Time Lords are forced to intervene when the Doctor discovers the War Chief has supplied time-travel technology to the War Lord, whose people plan to train the ultimate army, drawn from human history, and then conquer the galaxy.

1969

1978

THE INVASION OF TIME
FOURTH DOCTOR
DAVID AGNEW

The Sontarans use the Vardans as the first wave of an attack on Gallifrey that sees Sontaran troops occupying the Capitol.

1972

THE THREE DOCTORS
FIRST, SECOND & THIRD DOCTORS
BOB BAKER & DAVID MARTIN

The home planet of the Time Lords is threatened by Omega, and the President breaks their highest laws to bring three incarnations of the Doctor together to defeat him.

1975

1976

GENESIS OF THE DALEKS
FOURTH DOCTOR
TERRY NATION

Alerted to the existence of the Daleks by the Doctor, the High Council foresees a time when the Daleks will overrun the universe. They send the Doctor to avert or adjust their creation.

THE DEADLY ASSASSIN
FOURTH DOCTOR
ROBERT HOLMES

Decayed and dying, having used up his regenerations, the Master returns to Gallifrey and assassinates the President, attempting to get his hands on the Eye of Harmony—source of the Time Lords' power—in order to prolong his life.

THE WAR IN HEAVEN

It was becoming clear that the Time Lords' High Council was utterly corrupt. President Borusa himself was exposed as a power-mad would-be tyrant. By now, some of the new generation of Time Lords had formed a secret society, known as the Faction Paradox, which rebelled against the iconography and staid politics of Gallifrey and reveled in misrule and disruption.

HISTORY

The Time Lords became aware that they were facing a threat that could destroy them. Most assumed it was the Daleks, but there was an unnamed, perhaps unknowable, Enemy to contend with first …

The eighth Doctor started to encounter echoes of a war in his personal future, and hints began amassing that it would end with the Time Lords defeated … and start with his death.

RIGHT: The eighth Doctor's era was overshadowed by the Time War.

BELOW LEFT: The intricacies of the Time War were cataloged in *The Book of the War.*

BELOW: The novel *Alien Bodies* introduced many of the threats that the eighth Doctor would come to face.

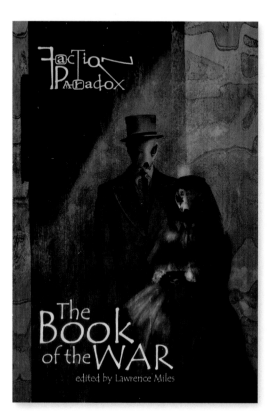

BEHIND THE SCENES

Lawrence Miles masterminded a running thread in the BBC *Doctor Who* novels that hinted at a vast Time War between the Time Lords and an unknown "enemy." In the event, the Doctor was able to avert the war. This is not the same Time War seen later in the TV series.

FIRST APPEARANCE
📖 Alien Bodies *(1997)*

TIMELINE

THE ANCESTOR CELL / THE GALLIFREY CHRONICLES
EIGHTH DOCTOR
STEPHEN COLE & PETER ANGHELIDES / LANCE PARKIN

2000/2005

Nearly 300 years after the war begins, Faction Paradox sends skulltroopers back in time to invade Gallifrey at the start of the war. They conquer Gallifrey—and three minutes, seven seconds later the Doctor destroys the planet, erasing their entire timeline and averting the War in Heaven. Compassion helps the Doctor download the entire contents of the Matrix into his own brain, causing him to lose all his own memories. He wakes in a carriage on Earth, not knowing who he was or how he had got there.

ALIEN BODIES
EIGHTH DOCTOR
LAWRENCE MILES

1997

The Doctor discovers an auction … for his corpse. He will die at the start of a time war. He does not learn who the "enemy" is, but discovers that some Time Lords had been so scared of them they'd become the Celestis, purely conceptual beings who worked through agents. The two sides endlessly traveled back in time to refight every battle they lost. Time started to collapse.

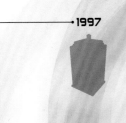

1997

ALIEN BODIES

The Enemy destroyed most Time Lord weapons early on, making the Doctor's biodata extremely valuable. The Doctor steals his own corpse and destroys it.

1999

THE TAKING OF PLANET FIVE
EIGHTH DOCTOR
SIMON BUCHER-JONES & MARK CLAPHAM

The War King, an elderly former renegade with a white beard, is made official head of the Time Lords to lead them in the war. The Time Lords create nine duplicate Gallifreys as backups. They try to free the Fendahl from the timelocked Fifth Planet (p. 68) to fight the Enemy. Instead, the Fendahl Predator eats the Celestis.

1999

INTERFERENCE
EIGHTH DOCTOR
LAWRENCE MILES

Knowing they have lost the War, the Time Lords plan to destroy the Earth in 1996, collapsing the web of time. By now, Time Lords are regenerating into monstrous bodies that are designed for combat. They are performing experiments on TARDISes, which will eventually lead to the creation of Compassion, a human–TARDIS hybrid.

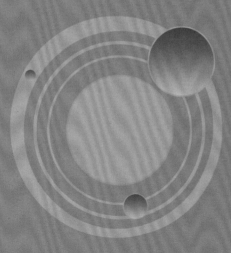

DALEK PLANETS

THE SEVENTH GALAXY

The Daleks come from Skaro, the twelfth planet in a solar system in the Seventh Galaxy,[1] listed in the starcharts of the Movellans as D5-Gamma-Z-Alpha.[2] Dalek missile defenses connected to the sky-spy early-warning system destroy any ship that comes close to Skaro. While Dalek space patrols occasionally capture ships, they will destroy even the smallest probes. There have been times when Earth forces have reached, and even bombed, the surface of Skaro, but all information gleaned by organizations such as the Space Security Service or the Anti-Dalek Force is sensitive military intelligence and is invariably classified Top Secret.

HISTORY

While the Daleks' creator, Davros, believed Skaro was the only planet in the universe capable of supporting life, early Dalek space missions quickly discovered that the Seventh Galaxy was home to a variety of advanced civilizations. Many worlds kept themselves to themselves and valued the centuries of peace their worlds had achieved. They were, then, quite unprepared for the emergence of the Daleks as galactic conquerors. We know little of what happened to these colorful worlds after their initial contact with the forces of the Golden Emperor ... we can only conclude that even those that initially managed to hold out must have soon fallen and become subsumed into the fledgling Dalek Empire.

FIRST APPEARANCE
📺 The Daleks *(1963)*

LOCATION
Deep in hyperspace

BEHIND THE SCENES

The Daleks have had a life beyond *Doctor Who*. *Dalek Annuals* were published from 1964–67 and 1976–79, while a comic strip dedicated to the Daleks ran in *TV Century 21* from 1965–67. There were also books—*Dalek Pocketbook and Space Travellers' Guide* (Terry Nation, ed. 1965), *Doctor Who and the Daleks Omnibus*, and *Dalek Special* (both Nation, 1979). Together, they built up a substantial body of lore about the Daleks and their home planet.

ABOVE RIGHT: The Zeron Council debate the threat to their Seventh Galaxy.

RIGHT: The seventh Doctor examines a Dalek chart of Skaro's solar system.

FOOTNOTES
[1] 📺 *The Daleks* • [2] 📺 *Destiny of the Daleks*

FACT FILE

📖 DOCTOR WHO AND THE DALEKS OMNIBUS

Skaro has three moons. Flidor is a lifeless world rich in a unique blue-gold, used in the construction of the Golden Emperor's travel machine. The Dal scientist Yarvelling was the first man on Flidor.

📖 DOCTOR WHO AND THE DALEKS OMNIBUS

Not even the Daleks know anything about the second moon of Skaro, Omega Mysterium. No space probe or traveler has ever returned from it.

📖 DOCTOR WHO AND THE DALEKS OMNIBUS

Skaro's third moon, Falkus, is actually a giant space station, built by the Daleks and able to think, repair, and defend itself. It contains the seeds of a new race of Daleks, should the originals ever become extinct.

◯ THE AMARYLL CHALLENGE

The nearest planet to Skaro was Alvega, a world of intelligent plants, all of which shared roots with the Controller, a vegetable mass at the core of the world. The Controller ordered that the Dalek invasion should be resisted, but a lone Dalek was able to reach it—destroying the Controller shattered the entire planet.

◯ THE PENTA RAY FACTOR

Soon after destroying Alvega, the Daleks reached Solturis, a world that had developed the deadly Penta Ray but had enjoyed a century of peace. The Daleks were unable to conquer Solturis on the first attempt.

◯ ROGUE PLANET

The uninhabited planet Omega Three was nearly destroyed by the passage of the rogue planet Skardal.

◯ IMPASSE

The Daleks were unable to reach the mineral-rich world of Oric without building a refueling station.

◯ THE DALEKS

The Seventh Galaxy is home to a number of blue-skinned races, including the Krattorians (slave traders), the Monstrons (who use robot soldiers called Engibrains), and the Zerons. The Dals, ancestors of the Daleks, were also blue-skinned.

📖 THE EYELESS

The Seventh Galaxy is also home to the peaceful cityworld of Arcopolis, devastated during the Time War, and the Eyeless, an acquisitive race of glass men with a collective consciousness.

THE GEOGRAPHY OF SKARO

Skaro was once a beautiful world, home of two proud civilizations: Thals and Kaleds.
An all-consuming 1,000-year conflict between those races ravaged the planet (p. 130),
leaving it tilted on its axis, with radioactive soil, poisonous air, and oceans of acid—dead,
apart from the most brutal and bizarre plant and animal life. A very few Thals still manage
to eke out an existence there, but the Kaleds are gone, replaced by their creations:
genetically engineered mutants with devious minds and a mastery of technologies
that give them an unparalleled ability to survive any disaster: THE DALEKS!

FIRST APPEARANCE

📺 The Daleks *(1963)*

LOCATION

*Twelfth planet in a solar system in
the Seventh Galaxy*

INHABITANTS

*Tharons, Dals, Thals, Kaleds,
Daleks, Varga plants, Slyther,
Magnedon, Mutos, and many
bizarre creatures*

STATUS

Ruined and abandoned

HISTORY

Vestiges of the former planet remain. The
mountain ranges and polar ice caps seem
relatively unaffected by conflict. A dense jungle
that once teemed with exotic beasts like the
Magnedon—a metal animal with its own
magnetic field—is perfectly preserved but
petrified following the detonation of a neutron
bomb. Skarosian life survived by mutating—into
the monsters of the Lake of Mutations (such as
two-headed giant Terrorkons and Urvacryls),
Varga plants that breed by converting animal life
into copies of themselves, and the fearsome
Slyther. Arkellis plants can take root in solid metal.
Many centuries after the Thal–Kaled War,
radiation levels on Skaro were so high that even
Time Lords would succumb to radiation sickness
if they didn't take antiradiation pills.

LEFT: Skaro was the site of
some magnificent architecture.

BELOW: Bizarre things exist
beneath Skaro, according to
The Dalek Outer Space Book.

BEHIND THE SCENES

Skaro appeared in the first Daleks
TV story, *The Daleks* (Terry Nation,
1963–64), and has featured in many
Dalek stories since.

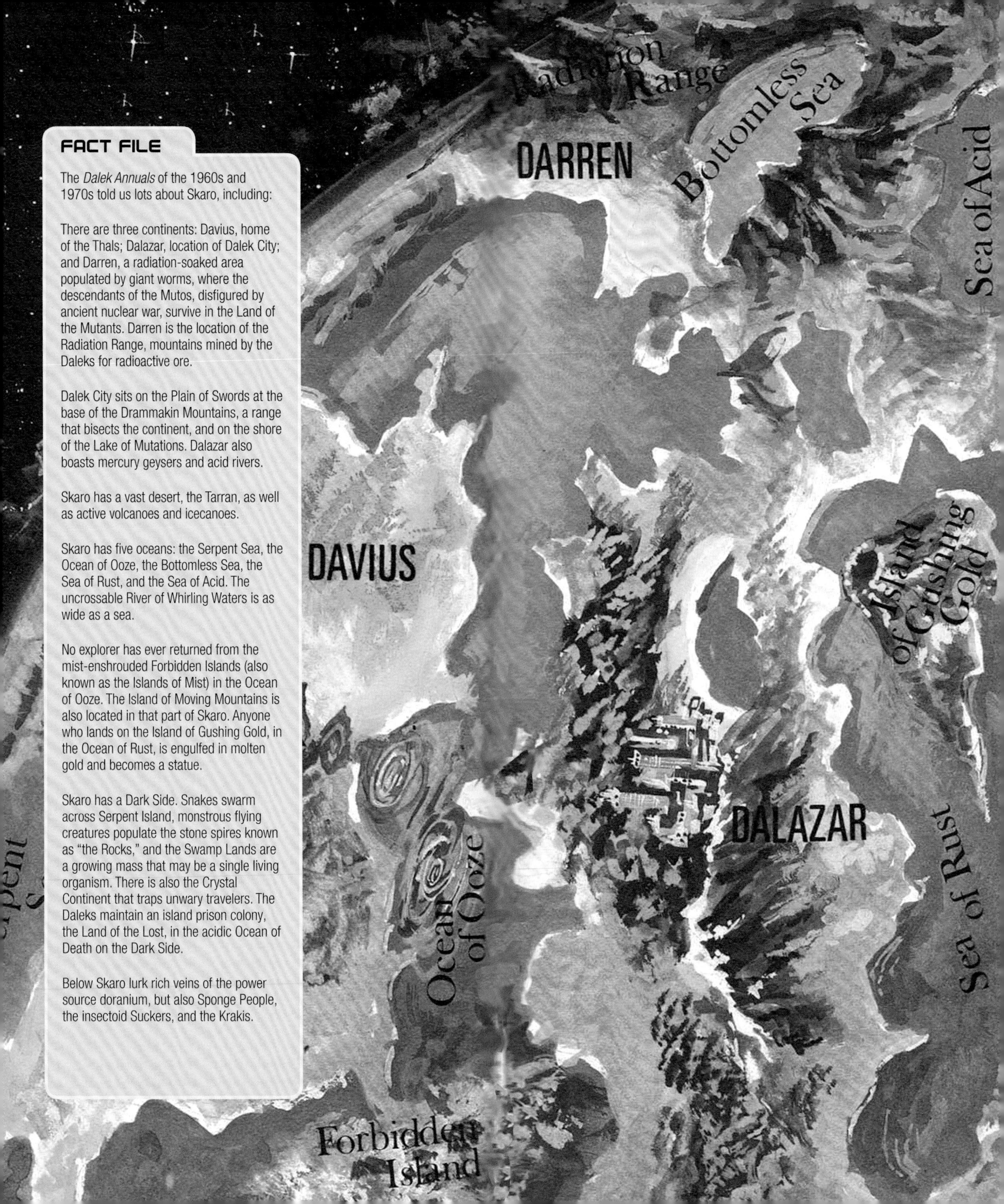

Radiation Range

Bottomless Sea

DARREN

Sea of Acid

DAVIUS

Island of Gushing Gold

DALAZAR

Sea of Rust

Serpent Sea

Ocean of Ooze

Forbidden Island

THE THAL-KALED WAR

Two intelligent species evolved at the same time on Skaro. For millions of years, they were separated—some say by a churning ocean, others by a huge mountain range. The Thals of Davius were a warrior culture. The Kaleds of Dalazar were a race of philosophers. In a startling example of parallel evolution, although their last common ancestor had been living at the time of the simplest marine life, hundreds of millions of years before, both came to outwardly resemble human beings. Conflict between two such proud races was almost inevitable.

FIRST APPEARANCE

📺 The Daleks *(1963)*

LOCATION

Skaro

INHABITANTS

Thals, Kaleds, Davros, Mutos, giant clams … and the Daleks

HISTORY

The war between the Thals and the Kaleds raged for 1,000 years. Nuclear and chemical weapons were used in the early stages. As the war dragged on and on, it consumed the resources of the planet. By the end, both sides resorted to using whatever they could find—soldiers could be found wearing synthetic clothes but using clubs and knives. The survivors huddled in two domed cities, their armies so depleted that "senior" officers were often very young. Both sides sought a weapon capable of breaching the dome of the other city. Skaro's ecosystem was dying, its life mutating into monsters.

BEHIND THE SCENES

Although mentioned in *The Daleks*, the war between the Thals and Daleks was first depicted in *Genesis of the Daleks* (Terry Nation, 1975). The Big Finish audio drama *Davros* (Lance Parkin, 2003) and series *I, Davros* (Gary Hopkins, James Parsons & Andrew Stirling-Brown, Lance Parkin, Scott Alan Woodard, 2006) filled in a great deal of backstory about the creator of the Daleks and the nature of the conflict.

LEFT: The Kaled scientist Davros, flanked by his creation.

OPPOSITE: The final war between the Thals and the Kaleds raged for 1,000 years.

FACT FILE

📺 GENESIS OF THE DALEKS

Davros betrays the Kaleds, showing the Thals how to destroy their enemy's city. He then sends his newly created Daleks to exterminate the Thals. Only a few Thals survive. The Doctor is able to seal the Daleks into the Kaled bunker, where they exterminate their creator.

📺 GENESIS OF THE DALEKS

The Time Lords send the Doctor and his companions back to this point in history to avert the creation of the Daleks. They fail.

📺 GENESIS OF THE DALEKS

Davros comes to realize that the Kaleds will die out. He needs to force evolution along, genetically engineering a successor race, one that will be able to survive on Skaro. Working from his lab in a deep bunker, he develops the first Daleks.

🎧 I, DAVROS

After 1,000 years, it has become clear to both the Thals and the Kaleds that the war is nearly over—there are few survivors on either side, and if one side fails to finish the other off soon, Skaro will become completely uninhabitable.

🎧 I, DAVROS

Davros gains great prestige by inventing powerful weapons. The Kaled Supremo moves against him, but Davros's mother sacrifices her life to reveal the plot to Davros. He blackmails the Supremo into gaining more independence for his Science Division. A Thal shell devastates the Science Division, leaving Davros crippled and utterly dependent on a mobile life-support system.

🎧 I, DAVROS

Davros is born to the Kaled politician Lady Calcula. Kaled politics is Machiavellian and brutal, and Davros wants to turn his talents to science. After a spell of military service, he is assigned to the Scientific Corps.

DALEK CITY

Eventually, the Daleks emerged from the ruins and built a vast, eerily beautiful metal city over the remains of the old Kaled bunker. Known by some as Mensvat Esc-Dalek,[1] or Kaalan,[2] most called it "Dalek City." Under the leadership of the first of their kind, who declared himself Emperor, the Daleks grew in numbers and turned their minds to developing powerful new weapons and exotic machines that demonstrated their mastery of such forces as magnetism and static electricity. Very few non-Daleks who ever saw the inside of Dalek City survived long enough to divulge its secrets.

BORN OUT OF DESTRUCTION, THE DALEK MACHINES CONSTRUCT A NEW AND TERRIBLE CITY.

DALEKS! THE CITY IS NEARLY COMPLETE.

HISTORY

One human who escaped Dalek City was Jeff Stone, hero of the Dalek War on Venus. On a mission to Skaro, he discovered the Dalek War Museum, full of artifacts from their conquests, and a dome celebrating scientific achievements. In the Council Chamber, Dalek elders issued commands to their Empire. A whole section of the City was a "War Office," run by a red War Leader Dalek who coordinated the actions of every Dalek in the universe. Advanced weapons were developed in the Invention Halls. Officers known as Storm Blast Daleks ran Daleks through drills and target practice. The City had vast parade grounds and factories and was powered by nuclear generators that fed electricity into metal floors and highways. At its very center lurked the Dalek Emperor, basking in revitalizing rays and connected to the Daleks' central computer.[3]

FIRST APPEARANCE
The Daleks (1963)

LOCATION
The continent of Dalazar, on Skaro

BEHIND THE SCENES

A number of the Dalek stories of the 1960s, especially in books and comics, featured the Daleks' city. It was often portrayed as abandoned, but since the end of the TV story The Evil of the Daleks (David Whitaker, 1967), it has only been shown as ruined.

ABOVE RIGHT: The early Daleks built and rebuilt a magnificent city.

RIGHT: A Dalek rally deep in Dalek City.

FOOTNOTES
[1] Remembrance of the Daleks • [2] City of the Daleks (video game) • [3] The Dalek Book

TIMELINE

"ASYLUM OF THE DALEKS"

ELEVENTH DOCTOR

STEVEN MOFFAT

2012

The Doctor is lured to the ruins of the City by Dalek sleeper agent Darla. He meets her in a vast statue of a Dalek that looms over shattered buildings, below a sky boiling with clouds of sulfuric acid.

THE DALEKS

FIRST DOCTOR

TERRY NATION

Following the detonation of a neutron bomb that leaves Skaro an all but dead planet, the Daleks retreat underneath their city to protect themselves from the radiation.

1963–64

1967

THE EVIL OF THE DALEKS

SECOND DOCTOR

DAVID WHITAKER

The Doctor is brought here by the Emperor, who hopes to instill the Dalek Factor in humanity. Instead, the Doctor gives some Daleks the Human Factor—disobedience—provoking a civil war that sees the death of the Emperor and Dalek City in flames.

1963–64

THE DALEKS

The Doctor first visits Skaro 500 years later and stumbles across Dalek City. He helps a band of Thals to defeat the Daleks, immobilizing the mutant creatures by destroying the generator powering the Daleks' equipment, including their travel machines.

1965

THE MENACE OF THE MONSTRONS

DAVID WHITAKER / RICHARD JENNINGS

Early in their history, Dalek City is destroyed by a Monstron missile attack. The Daleks defeat the Monstrons and their army of robot Engibrains. Within months, the Dalek City is rebuilt with improved defenses.

1964

THE DALEK BOOK

TERRY NATION & DAVID WHITAKER

Dalek City is built on the shore of the Lake of Mutations, at the foot of a mountain range, on the site of Dalazar, capital city of the Daleks' ancestors.

MECHANUS

Instilled with the belief that they were the supreme beings of the universe, the Daleks constructed vast fleets of flying saucers and attacked every world they learned of. This was the time of the Golden Emperor, who wore an ornate golden casing with a massively enlarged brain case. His second in command was the ruthless Black Dalek. The Daleks spread out from Skaro, eagerly seeking everything, ranging from raw materials to esoteric knowledge.

HISTORY

As the Daleks adjusted to their new role as galactic conquerors, they faced a number of threats, ranging from internal dissent, rust plagues, and invasions of Skaro to counter-insurgency on planets they conquered. The rapid rise of the Daleks alarmed the people of their galaxy, who could do little to contain them. However, they met their match with the Mechanoids, a race of purely robotic creatures from Mechanus who possessed faster, more powerful spacecraft. At their first encounter, the Mechanoids killed the Red Dalek, a senior space commander. This merely spurred the Daleks to create more advanced weapons. The Mechanoids were ruled by the Menoid Master and came from a beautiful stilt city on the jungle planet of Mechanus. Like the plant life of Skaro, some vegetation on Mechanus could move and pursue human prey—particularly the Fungoids.

FIRST APPEARANCE
The Chase *(1965)*

ABOVE RIGHT: The Golden Emperor briefs the Daleks on their new enemy.

RIGHT: The Daleks prepare to do battle in the Mechanoid City.

TIMELINE

📖 BIRTH OF A LEGEND
✏ JUSTIN RICHARDS

The Daleks continue to fight the Mechanoids for many centuries. Finally, the last of the Mechanoids is exterminated on Magella. The Black Dalek responsible for that victory is promoted by the Emperor to become Sec, head of the Cult of Skaro.

2007

📺 THE CHASE
🧑 FIRST DOCTOR
✏ TERRY NATION

At one point, the Mechanoids are confined to their city on Mechanus. They tell the marooned human astronaut Steven Taylor that they were built by humans 50 years ago to prepare Mechanus for colonization. They may be lying or may have forgotten their origins.

1965

1966

🔍 THE ROAD TO CONFLICT
🖊 DAVID WHITAKER / RON TURNER

Centuries later, the human spacecraft *Starmaker* crashes on Skaro. Searching the wreckage, the Emperor discovers the existence and location of the planet Earth.

1965

📺 THE CHASE

Two years after Taylor crashes on Mechanus, the Doctor arrives on the planet, chased by the Daleks. As the Daleks encounter the Mechanoids again, they use an atom divider, and a great fire is started that threatens to consume the Mechanoid City. The Doctor rescues Steven Taylor and leaves the Daleks and Mechanoids to battle it out.

1966

🔍 THE ROGUE PLANET
🖊 DAVID WHITAKER / RON TURNER

A space storm deflects the rogue planet Skardal until it is on collision course with Skaro. The Daleks are able to change its course again and aim it at Mechanus. The advanced Elders of Zeros are very concerned about the brewing war and send a robot agent to destroy Skardal and trick the Mechanoids into thinking the Daleks have done so to save their planet. Hostilities die down for a time.

1966

🔍 IMPASSE
🖊 DAVID WHITAKER / RON TURNER

When the Daleks begin construction of a deep-space refueling station in order to reach the mineral-rich world of Oric, they inadvertently stray into an area of space claimed by the Mechanoids.

1966

🔍 THE ARCHIVES OF PHRYNE
🖊 DAVID WHITAKER / ERIC EDEN

The Daleks invade and subjugate Phryne but fail to secure the fabled Archives of that planet, which would have given them valuable scientific knowledge to use against the Mechanoids.

DALEK PLANETS

The Dalek Empire stretches across many worlds. Everywhere, the pattern is the same: the Daleks destroy all military opposition, exterminate every leader, enslave the survivors, and set them to work in mines and factories. The Daleks have advanced machines that could do this work, yet they delight in making other life forms pick away at the rock, feeding them only a tiny amount of food and watching them drop dead from exhaustion and hunger. The Daleks always find quislings among the local population who are happy to help them in return for some material comfort.

HISTORY

The Daleks always seek rare minerals and environments, often basing a plan around the unique properties of certain substances or places.

For the early part of their history, their casings were quite limited—while on Skaro or inside their spacecraft, Daleks picked up static electricity from the metal floors, but elsewhere they relied on solar power, making them somewhat sluggish by comparison. When they conquered worlds, they would often build metal roadways that allowed them the same freedom of movement they had on their home planet. We see them build roadways on Venus, a jungle planet, and Skaro itself.

ABOVE RIGHT: The seventh Doctor had to use all his guile to fight the Daleks on Kar-Charrat.

ABOVE: The Daleks swiftly build alien structures on worlds they conquer.

FIRST APPEARANCE

📺 The Dalek Invasion of Earth *(1964)*
📖 The Dalek Book *(1964)*

INHABITANTS

Subjugated natives, brutal enforcers, and a tiny number of Daleks

TIMELINE

📺 *PLANET OF THE DALEKS*

👤 THIRD DOCTOR

✒ TERRY NATION

The surface of the planet Spiridon is a jungle inhabited by invisible natives and cursed with lethal plant life that spits a choking venom. The Daleks are keen to learn the secret of invisibility, but their main reason for being on Spiridon is to exploit the icy core of the planet. On Spiridon, ice flows like magma on most worlds, and there are icecanoes instead of volcanoes. The Daleks seek to store a vast army on this world, one that could sweep aside the Earth and Draconian Empires.

1973

2000

🎧 *THE GENOCIDE MACHINE*

👤 SEVENTH DOCTOR

✒ MIKE TUCKER

The Daleks conquer Kar-Charrat, a jungle world on the edge of the galaxy containing a famed repository of galactic knowledge. However, they cannot break through the temporal barrier protecting the library—only a Time Lord can. They place agents on every planet in the sector and go into deep hibernation, awaiting the arrival of a Time Lord.

1985

📺 *REVELATION OF THE DALEKS*

👤 SIXTH DOCTOR

✒ ERIC SAWARD

When the rich and powerful humans of the far future die, their bodies are cryogenically preserved on Necros, awaiting advances in medical technology that could restore them. Davros arrives on the world and begins building an army of Daleks from this genetic material. The Doctor summons the original Daleks, who wipe out Davros's new creations and take him to be tried for his crimes.

THE UNIVERSE IN 4000 AD

Around the year 4000, many intergalactic civilizations vied for power. Under the leadership of Mavic Chen, Guardian of the Solar System, Earth was influential and peace was maintained. The Daleks had not been seen for centuries but were working in secret. To fight them, an elite force was set up: the Space Security Service (SSS). Veteran pilot Colonel Marc Forest was placed in charge. His key agents were Kurt Soren, David Carson, Sara Kingdom, and the android Agent Seven. The SSS was based in a secret mountain HQ and carried gold ID cards, pocket computers, and other gadgets.

HISTORY

The Daleks invaded the constellation of Miros and 70 planets in the ninth galactic system. They brought an army of 5,000 Daleks to a secret city on the jungle planet Kembel. They allied themselves with the rulers of the Outer Galaxies, but their greatest coup was to recruit Mavic Chen, a man who secretly desired to be the first ruler of the entire universe. Using the full resources of the alliance, and Dalek ingenuity, a deadly Time Destructor would be used to conquer Earth's galaxy ... then the Daleks would subjugate the Outer Galaxies themselves. Chen was able to supply the final, most vital, component of the Time Destructor, an emm (archaic term for a "very small amount") of the rare mineral taranium. The Master Plan ended back on Kembel, with the Doctor using the Time Destructor against the Dalek army. Before that, the struggle had been fought on many worlds, and many of the Doctor's allies were killed.

LOCATION

Earth, Skaro, Uranus, Kembel, Desperus, Barzilla, Vara, and many other worlds

BEHIND THE SCENES

The Daleks' Master Plan was an epic 12-episode space opera shown in 1965–66, with a prologue episode— "Mission to the Unknown"—that, uniquely, did not feature the Doctor. We learned more about this era in *The Dalek Outer Space Book* (Terry Nation & Brad Ashton, 1966).

ABOVE RIGHT: The Daleks do battle with the rocketships of the Space Security Service.

RIGHT: The alien delegates of the Outer Galaxies, allies of the Daleks.

TIMELINE

📺 THE DALEKS' MASTER PLAN
✎ DENNIS SPOONER

1966

… which the Daleks pilot back to Kembel, where the Dalek army is assembled and the Time Destructor is ready for testing. The Doctor delays this with a fake piece of taranium and convinces Sara Kingdom that Chen is insane. Now that the other delegates are no longer needed, Chen and the Daleks turn on their allies, imprisoning or killing them. The Doctor activates the Time Destructor, reducing Kembel to a desert planet, destroying the Dalek army, and killing Sara.

📖 THE OUTLAW PLANET
✎ BRAD ASHTON & TERRY NATION

Over eight years, the Daleks occupy the small, uninhabited planets Phergo, Dizmus, and Lagum, planning to use them as bases to launch a simultaneous attack on the "Big Four" planets—Earth, Mars, Venus, and Uranus. SSS forces ambush a Dalek invasion fleet at Barzilla, earning their first victory.

1966

1965

📺 THE DALEKS' MASTER PLAN

The Doctor arrives at Central City on Earth. Chen is already there and sends Sara Kingdom to recover the taranium. She kills Bret Vyon (her brother), but the Doctor and Steven escape. They hide in an experimental chamber, and their molecules are dispersed across the universe to planet Mira. The Daleks arrive but are attacked by the native (invisible) species, the Visians. The Doctor steals the Daleks' spaceship …

1966

📖 SARA KINGDOM: SPACE SECURITY AGENT and SECRET OF THE EMPEROR (THE DALEK OUTER SPACE BOOK)
✎ BRAD ASHTON & TERRY NATION

Sara Kingdom rescues the alloy expert Lomberg from the low-oxygen world of Vara. The colonists of Uranus beat the Daleks back with supersonic waves, and the SSS learns to block brain-tapping signals that have allowed Dalek spies to operate on Earth. This causes unprecedented internal dissent among the Daleks. The Emperor submits to rigorous examination and a new, immobile casing is constructed for him.

1965

📺 THE DALEKS' MASTER PLAN

The Doctor steals the taranium and Chen's ship. The Daleks force it down on Desperus, a desolate prison planet, and Katarina sacrifices herself to save the others from a violent convict.

1965

1965

📺 "MISSION TO THE UNKNOWN"
✎ TERRY NATION

On Kembel, agent Marc Cory stumbles across a meeting where the Dalek Supreme and delegates from seven galaxies are pledging to attack Earth's Solar System, but he is exterminated before he can warn Earth.

📺 THE DALEKS' MASTER PLAN
👤 FIRST DOCTOR
✎ TERRY NATION

The Doctor and his companions, Steven and Katarina, arrive on Kembel six months later and team up with agent Bret Vyon, who is looking for Cory. They find the recorded warning and learn that Chen is a Dalek ally.

SKARO ABANDONED

The Daleks eventually abandoned Skaro, although the reasons why aren't known. Perhaps a Thal counterinsurgency succeeded, or the efforts of human military organizations like the Space Security Service or the Anti-Dalek Force drove them out. Perhaps the expansion of their empire simply moved their center of power away from their planet of origin, or Skaro's environment collapsed beyond even the Daleks' ability to survive there. We also can't discount Dalek infighting; at least one civil war left the Emperor Dalek dead and their city in flames. Whatever the reason, the Daleks left behind a planet that was almost completely dead.

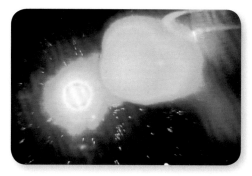

HISTORY

During the war with the Movellans, the Supreme Dalek operated from a huge space fleet, just as the Emperor had at the beginning of their conquests, and just as a later Emperor would lead his forces into battle during the Last Great Time War (p. 144). Since the Time War, the Dalek Parliament has convened in a huge spacecraft. The planet Skaro retained a pull on the Daleks, though. During the war with the Movellans, the Daleks returned there to excavate the corpse of Davros, whom they hoped to revive to provide them with a strategic advantage. The Daleks are fascinated by their own nature, and they are the children of Skaro.

ABOVE RIGHT: The seventh Doctor tricked Davros into destroying Skaro, or so they thought.

BELOW: The eleventh Doctor was lured to the ruins of Dalek City.

LOCATION

Skaro, after the Daleks have all but abandoned their home world

BEHIND THE SCENES

Since we saw the Dalek City burn in *The Evil of the Daleks* (David Whitaker, 1967), we've never seen Daleks based on Skaro, although it has been referred to. Many stories have shown Skaro as a ruined world that the Daleks have abandoned (the stories usually give them a reason for returning to it).

TIMELINE

📺 **"ASYLUM OF THE DALEKS"**

👤 **ELEVENTH DOCTOR**

✏️ **STEVEN MOFFAT**

2012

After the Time War, the Daleks do not occupy Skaro, but they lure the Doctor there as part of their plan to have him and his companions infiltrate the Dalek Asylum planet.

📺 **THE DALEKS**

👤 **FIRST DOCTOR**

✏️ **TERRY NATION**

The Doctor's original visit to Skaro is at a time when a small number of Daleks survive in their city. This is 500 years after a neutron bomb exploded on Skaro. It's possible the Daleks the Doctor meets are those who chose not to join the Golden Emperor on his missions of conquest.

1963-64

1997

📖 **WAR OF THE DALEKS**

👤 **EIGHTH DOCTOR**

✏️ **JOHN PEEL**

The seventh Doctor thought he had tricked Davros into destroying Skaro with the Hand of Omega, but the eighth Doctor learns that time-traveling Daleks have tricked them both into destroying an innocent planet.

1965

🎭 **THE CURSE OF THE DALEKS**

✏️ **DAVID WHITAKER &TERRY NATION**

The Daleks are defeated in a war against the Earth when their power supplies are destroyed. The Daleks remain on Skaro, immobile—that is, until the Earth ship *Starfinder* crashes on Skaro.

1988

📺 **REMEMBRANCE OF THE DALEKS**

👤 **SEVENTH DOCTOR**

✏️ **BEN AARONOVITCH**

Davros usurps that Supreme Dalek and declares himself Emperor. He plans to use the Time Lord artifact, the Hand of Omega, to transform Skaro's sun into a source of unimaginable power. It's unclear if he plans for Skaro to survive this process. The Doctor refers to Davros's plan as a return to their "ancestral seat."

1979

📺 **DESTINY OF THE DALEKS**

👤 **FOURTH DOCTOR**

✏️ **TERRY NATION**

At the time of the war with the Movellans, Skaro is highly radioactive, and there is little evidence of native life besides sparse vegetation and a mutant blob the Doctor discovers. Dalek City has been reduced to rubble.

1985

📺 **REVELATION OF THE DALEKS**

👤 **SIXTH DOCTOR**

✏️ **ERIC SAWARD**

Following the defeat by the Movellans, the new Supreme Dalek does seem to be based on Skaro—that is where the Daleks plan to put Davros on trial after capturing him on Necros.

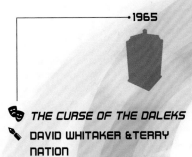

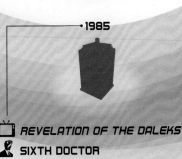

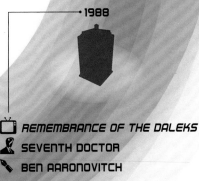

THE APOCALYPSE ELEMENT

The Seriphia Galaxy is four times the size of the Mutter's Spiral, with over 600 billion solar systems. Bizarre crystals (the "Apocalypse Element") were discovered on Etra Prime, an asteroid close to the planet Archetryx, which could focus mental energy to affect the behavior of time. Delegations from many advanced civilizations—including the Time Lords and the Monan Host—arrived on Archetryx and began negotiating a deal to send a scientific expedition to Etra Prime. Disaster struck: Etra Prime vanished, taking 500 top scientists with it.

BELOW: The Daleks were at their most murderous as they plotted to invade Gallifrey.

HISTORY

A year later, 300 bodies riddled with time distortion materialized. The other scientists remained missing, among them the President of the Time Lords: the Doctor's former companion, Romana.

Twenty years later, the sixth Doctor arrived on Archetryx as an intergalactic conference began trying to set limits on temporal manipulation. The Time Lords were involved mainly to assess the capabilities of those with time technology. The Doctor quickly learned that the disappearance of Etra Prime had been devised by the Daleks. He rescued President Romana, who had been degraded as a Dalek slave for 20 years, but soon became embroiled in the Daleks' most destructive scheme yet. Historians believe that "the Etra Prime Incident" was one of the main precursors to the Last Great Time War.

LOCATION
Close to Gallifrey's galaxy

 TIMELINE

2008

The occupation is ended by the Great Catastrophe, the deliberate sabotage of the Daleks' technology, which is so devastating that it kills a Dalek Emperor and plunges civilization into a dark age lasting centuries.

🎧 **THE APOCALYPSE ELEMENT**

👤 **SIXTH DOCTOR**

✏️ **STEPHEN COLE**

Initially, it is thought the Daleks are attempting to sabotage the time treaty being signed by 20 of the greatest powers in space time, including the Time Lords, Monan Host, and Virgoans.

2000

2008

🎧 **DALEK EMPIRE**

✏️ **NICHOLAS BRIGGS**

President Romana vows to contain the Daleks, but the Seriphia Galaxy becomes a major power base for the Dalek Empire. They launch attacks on Mutter's Spiral from here in the sixth millennium, and they conquer Earth's galaxy in 30 years.

2000

🎧 **THE APOCALYPSE ELEMENT**

The Daleks do not merely wish to acquire the rare crystals from Etra Prime; they have specific plans for it. First, though, they destroy Archetryx by smashing Etra Prime into it.

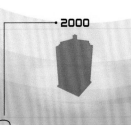

2000

🎧 **THE APOCALYPSE ELEMENT**

The Doctor and Romana are able to harness the power of the Time Lords to repel the Daleks, but the Black Dalek has a contingency plan: the Apocalypse Element is used to reshape the Seriphia Galaxy, removing all life but creating billions of worlds for the Daleks to occupy and exploit unopposed.

2000

🎧 **THE APOCALYPSE ELEMENT**

The Daleks seek to invade Gallifrey. The Doctor sees through the ruse of using a fake Monan Host ship as a Trojan Horse, but the Daleks get a small invasion force through the transduction barriers.

2000

🎧 **THE APOCALYPSE ELEMENT**

The Apocalypse Element can be used to control time. The combined mental energy of the Daleks could prove devastating.

2000

🎧 **THE APOCALYPSE ELEMENT**

The Daleks blackmail the Time Lords into lowering their defenses by threatening the structure of the entire universe. They unleash forces that begin tearing the Seriphia Galaxy apart, a destructive wave that will keep spreading unless the Time Lords intervene.

THE LAST GREAT TIME WAR

The Time Lords had long worried that the Daleks would become supreme beings of the universe. They sent the fourth Doctor back into early Dalek history to avert their creation.[1] The fifth Doctor thwarted a Dalek plot to infiltrate Gallifrey using duplicates of himself and his companions.[2] The Daleks landed a beachhead on Gallifrey during the sixth Doctor's time,[3] and Davros escalated the stakes by securing the Gallifreyan Hand of Omega—the device used by the Time Lords to grant their great powers. The seventh Doctor turned the tables, tricking Davros into destroying the Daleks' home planet, Skaro.[4]

HISTORY

The Last Great Time War—"a war between the Daleks and the Time Lords with the whole of creation at stake"[5]—erupted in the eighth Doctor's time. The Daleks vanished from time and space, massing their fleet in the Time Vortex.[6] The Time Lords resurrected the Master[7] and even Rassilon[8] (p. 116) to fight the Time War. The Daleks recruited their creator, Davros, but in the first year, the Doctor saw Davros die when his command ship flew into the jaws of the Nightmare Child at the Gates of Elysium.[9] Countless planets were devastated, and species were displaced or extinguished. The Master fled the war when the Dalek Emperor took control of the Cruciform, hiding himself in the distant future.[10] The Cult of Skaro fled the war in a Voidship.[11]

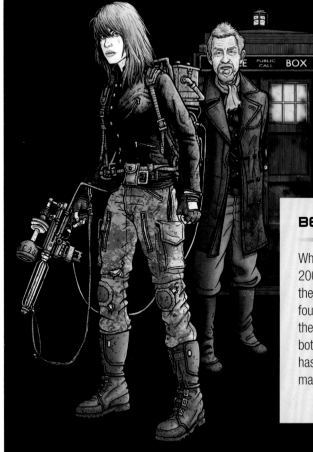

ABOVE & LEFT: The War Doctor was joined, briefly, by a young woman named Cinder.

FIRST APPEARANCE
📺 Genesis of the Daleks *(1975)* or *"The End of the World"* (2005)

STATUS
Timelocked, utterly inaccessible

BEHIND THE SCENES

When the TV series returned in 2005, we gradually learned that the Doctor and the Daleks had fought the ultimate war, and that the Doctor had ended it by wiping both of them out. As the series has progressed, we've learned many more details.

FOOTNOTES
[1] 📺 *Genesis of the Daleks* • [2] 📺 *Resurrection of the Daleks* • [3] 🎧 *The Apocalypse Element* • [4] 📺 *Remembrance of the Daleks* •
[5] 📺 *"The Parting of the Ways"* • [6] 📺 *"Bad Wolf"* • [7&10] 📺 *"Utopia"* • [8] 📺 *"The End of Time"* • [9] 📺 *"Journey's End"* • [11] 📺 *"Doomsday"*

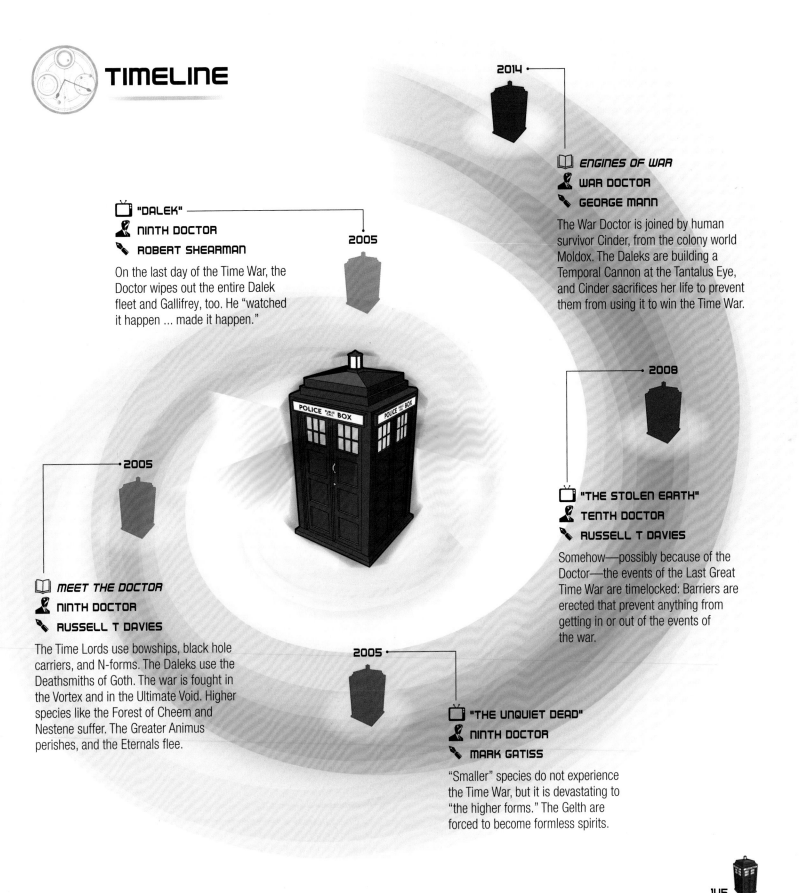

TIMELINE

2014

📖 ENGINES OF WAR

👤 WAR DOCTOR

✏️ GEORGE MANN

The War Doctor is joined by human survivor Cinder, from the colony world Moldox. The Daleks are building a Temporal Cannon at the Tantalus Eye, and Cinder sacrifices her life to prevent them from using it to win the Time War.

📺 "DALEK"

👤 NINTH DOCTOR

✏️ ROBERT SHEARMAN

2005

On the last day of the Time War, the Doctor wipes out the entire Dalek fleet and Gallifrey, too. He "watched it happen ... made it happen."

2008

📺 "THE STOLEN EARTH"

👤 TENTH DOCTOR

✏️ RUSSELL T DAVIES

Somehow—possibly because of the Doctor—the events of the Last Great Time War are timelocked: Barriers are erected that prevent anything from getting in or out of the events of the war.

2005

📖 MEET THE DOCTOR

👤 NINTH DOCTOR

✏️ RUSSELL T DAVIES

The Time Lords use bowships, black hole carriers, and N-forms. The Daleks use the Deathsmiths of Goth. The war is fought in the Vortex and in the Ultimate Void. Higher species like the Forest of Cheem and Nestene suffer. The Greater Animus perishes, and the Eternals flee.

2005

📺 "THE UNQUIET DEAD"

👤 NINTH DOCTOR

✏️ MARK GATISS

"Smaller" species do not experience the Time War, but it is devastating to "the higher forms." The Gelth are forced to become formless spirits.

THIS PAGE: The tenth Doctor and Donna faced the Daleks and Davros, who were intent on collapsing the whole of reality.

OPPOSITE: The Crucible, a space station the size of a planet, was the Daleks' vast center of operations.

THE STOLEN EARTH

A few Daleks survived the Time War. A lone, dormant Dalek was acquired by an American collector of alien artifacts.[1] The Emperor also survived and spent centuries rebuilding his fleet.[2] The Cult of Skaro had hidden in the Void and located the Genesis Ark, a Time Lord prison that held thousands of Daleks.[3] Sec, leader of the Cult of Skaro, had a plan to create human/Dalek hybrids.[4] The Doctor saw to it that the Dalek survivors were destroyed, but one Dalek from the Cult of Skaro survived: Caan.

HISTORY

Caan managed to do the impossible—break the timelock around the Last Great Time War long enough to retrieve Davros, who then created a new Dalek race from the cells of his own body. Caan had been driven insane, but now had the power of prophecy.[5]

The first of the new Daleks became the Supreme Dalek, and under his leadership a New Dalek Empire emerged. Its hub was the Crucible, an artificial planet powered by Z-neutrino energy, and a new fleet of Dalek saucers was constructed. The Daleks began an ambitious plan. They'd learned of the Medusa Cascade, a giant rift in

space and time, during the Time War and calculated that harnessing the forces there would allow them to create a reality bomb: a device that could destroy all non-Dalek life in the universe. They would need to move 27 planets across the universe and into a precise alignment. The last piece of the puzzle was Earth.

BEHIND THE SCENES

David Tennant's last full season included a running subplot in which he learned that several planets had gone missing. In "The Stolen Earth" he discovered that all of these had been hijacked by the Daleks; he defeated the Daleks in "Journey's End" (both Russell T Davies, 2008).

FIRST APPEARANCE

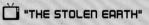 (by inference) "Partners in Crime" (2008)

LOCATION

The Medusa Cascade

FACT FILE

📺 "THE STOLEN EARTH"

The Crucible was a sphere the size of a planet, with large structures emerging from it where the Dalek Fleet docked. It contained a control room, linked to the Vault—a chamber containing both Dalek Caan and Davros's laboratory.

📺 "LAST OF THE TIME LORDS"

The Medusa Cascade had been known to the Time Lords since at least the Doctor's childhood. It was the Doctor who sealed the rift during the Time War.

📺 "LAST OF THE TIME LORDS"

As he traveled the universe, the Doctor became aware that a number of planets had disappeared but didn't connect this to the Daleks.

📺 "PARTNERS IN CRIME"

Adipose 3 was the breeding world of the Adiposian First Family. When it vanished, the Adipose were forced to move farther afield—they selected Earth.

📺 "THE FIRES OF POMPEII"

The Pyrovilles of the volcanic world Pyrovillia faced the same fate—and also came to invade the Earth.

📺 THE PIRATE PLANET

Callufrax Minor was an uninhabited world, possibly related to Calufrax, a planet stripmined and miniaturized 30 years before by the pirate planet Zanak (p. 226).

📺 "LOVE AND MONSTERS"

Clom was in the Isop Galaxy, and was the home of the Abzorbalovians (p. 260). Griffoth was the home planet of the Graske. Strepto was the planet of the Water Hags.

📺 "THE STOLEN EARTH"

Jahoo was an uninhabited world. Little is known about another world taken by the Daleks, Shallacatop.

FOOTNOTES
[1] 📺 "Dalek" • [2] 📺 "The Parting of the Ways" • [3] 📺 "Doomsday" • [4] 📺 "Daleks in Manhattan" / "Evolution of the Daleks" • [5] 📺 "The Stolen Earth" / "Journey's End"

THE DALEKS NOW

FIRST APPEARANCE
New Dalek paradigm:
"Victory of the Daleks" (2010)

LOCATION
The 31st century

Three Daleks escaped the destruction of the Crucible in a ship capable of time travel but very badly damaged. Those Daleks managed to locate a Progenitor containing the material needed to build a new race of Daleks, and with it they created a new Dalek paradigm: five purebred Daleks in state-of-the-art casings who became the officer class of a new Dalek race. The five Daleks were Drone (red), Eternal (yellow), Supreme (white), Scientist (orange), and Strategist (blue). The Daleks forced the eleventh Doctor to let them escape rather than destroy the Earth.[1]

HISTORY

The Daleks returned to their own time, the 31st century, where they multiplied, built space fleets, and took control of many planets. The new Daleks were ruled by a Prime Minister; below him was a Supreme Dalek and a large Parliament, overseeing the Empire from a large spacecraft. The new casings were reserved for ranking Daleks, which included—as with the Daleks of old—Red Daleks and Black Daleks. The vast majority of Daleks we have seen since use the old-style cases, including almost all the Daleks in the Dalek Parliament.

The Daleks restored their Empire and consolidated their power. They operated prison camps from which no one escaped and converted people into Dalek puppets—mind-controlled slaves that were part Dalek machine. The new Daleks are connected by the pathweb, an Internet-like system of communicating and sharing data.[2]

BEHIND THE SCENES

We see the new Daleks in (briefly) "A Good Man Goes to War," then "Asylum of the Daleks," "The Time of the Doctor," and "Into the Dalek." A stage direction in the script for the latter specifies that this is the 31st century, and it seems to be the native time of the Daleks.

FOOTNOTES
1. "Victory of the Daleks" •
2. "Asylum of the Daleks"

ABOVE: The eleventh Doctor witnessed the birth of the new Dalek paradigm.

TIMELINE

2014

🖵 "INTO THE DALEK"
👤 TWELFTH DOCTOR
✎ PHIL FORD & STEVEN MOFFAT

In their native time, the Daleks fight the Combined Galactic Resistance, an alliance of planets—including those of the human race. From what we've seen, the Daleks have little difficulty picking off individual Resistance spacecraft and bases.

2013

🖵 "THE TIME OF THE DOCTOR"
👤 ELEVENTH & TWELFTH DOCTORS
✎ STEVEN MOFFAT

The Daleks are one of the first races to arrive at Trenzalore in response to mysterious transmissions from that world. They are beaten there by the Papal Mainframe, a human religious military organization that creates a forcefield that seals off the planet. Hundreds of spacefaring races flock to the planet. Eventually, only the Daleks and the Doctor are left (p. 244).

🖵 "VICTORY OF THE DALEKS"
👤 ELEVENTH DOCTOR
✎ MARK GATISS

The first act of the new paradigm Daleks is to exterminate the three Daleks who have rescued them—as they have been grown from Davros's cells, they are not considered "pure" Daleks.

2010

2011

🖵 "A GOOD MAN GOES TO WAR"
👤 ELEVENTH DOCTOR
✎ STEVEN MOFFAT

The Doctor traps a white Dalek—perhaps the same individual he'd seen created by the Progenitor—in order to steal information in the Dalek databanks about the Silence.

2012

🖵 "ASYLUM OF THE DALEKS"
👤 ELEVENTH DOCTOR
✎ STEVEN MOFFAT

The Daleks run an asylum for insane members of their own species—including those driven insane after encountering the Doctor. Many of these individuals seem to have somehow survived the Time War. The Dalek Parliament dare not send other Daleks on missions to the Asylum, but they maintain the facility because they admire the purity of the inmates' hatred.

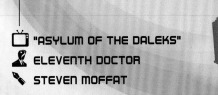

2012

🖵 "ASYLUM OF THE DALEKS"
👤 ELEVENTH DOCTOR
✎ STEVEN MOFFAT

The Asylum is beneath the surface of a mountainous, snowbound planet that is sealed from the universe by an impenetrable force field. An Earth ship crashes there, and although she has been converted into a Dalek, one of the crew is able to hack and compromise the security systems. Fearing a breakout, the Daleks recruit the Doctor, Amy, and Rory to reestablish control. This operation ends with the destruction of the planet.

CYBERMAN PLANETS

CYBERMAN THROUGHOUT HISTORY

MONDAS, C. 1986

DEEP SPACE, DATE UNKNOWN

TELOS, 26th CENTURY

VOORD OF MARINUS. PRE-20th CENTURY

COULD THIS BE AN EARLY CYBERMAN?

CYBERCONTROLLER TELOS, 26th CENTURY

CYBERMATS

CYBERMAT, THE WHEEL, 21st CENTURY

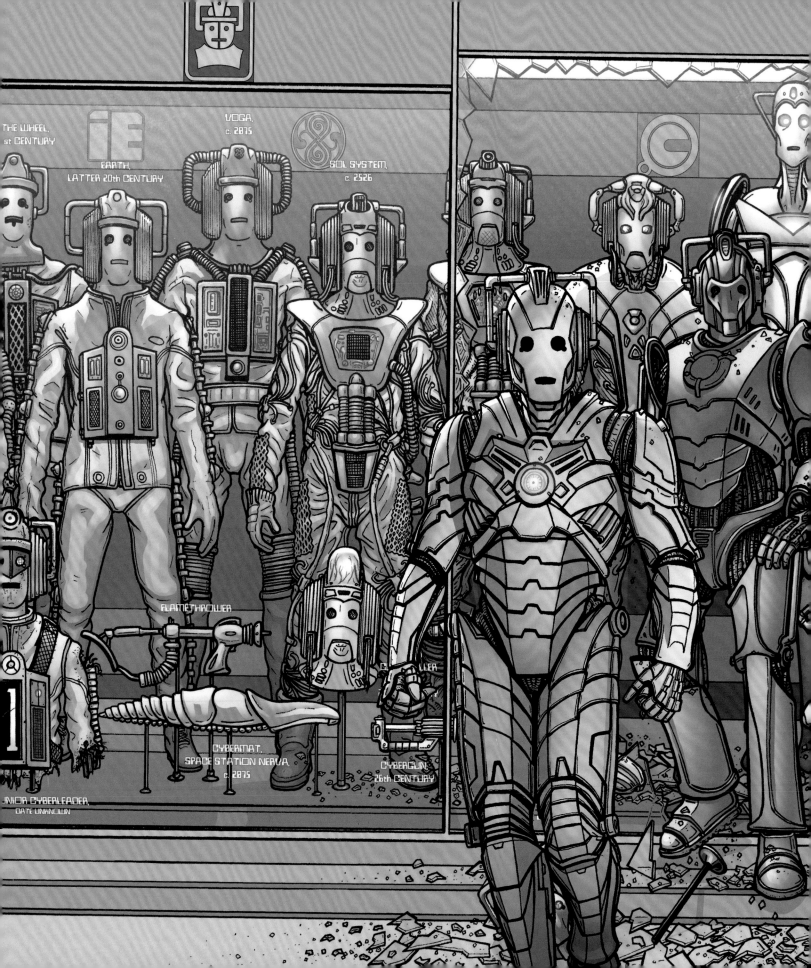

THE WHEEL,
st CENTURY

EARTH,
LATTER 20th CENTURY

VOGA,
c. 2875

SOL SYSTEM,
c. 2526

FLAMETHROWER

CYBERMAT,
SPACE STATION NERVA,
c. 2875

CYBERGUN,
26th CENTURY

JNIOR CYBERLEADER,
DATE UNKNOWN

EARLY MONDAS

Mondas is Earth's twin planet; it even has the same layout of continents. Eons ago, it shared the same orbit.[1] Life evolved there as it did on Earth—a race of Silurian reptile people ruled for millions of years but became extinct, with apemen evolving into human beings and becoming the new dominant species.[2] A civilization of human beings developed at almost the same rate as the one on Earth. Mondas resembled Earth because they were both part of an experiment into planetary development conducted by the ancient, godlike Constructors of Destiny.[3]

FIRST APPEARANCE
The Tenth Planet (1966)

LOCATION
Ancient Solar System

HISTORY

Unlike the Earth, however, Mondas drifted away from the Sun, traveling to the edge of space before returning, and its people were irrevocably changed by the experience. Plunging deeper into space, the Mondasians survived using medical technology, replacing their limbs and organs with mechanical parts. Most people resisted the idea of becoming fully mechanical, although some factions saw it as the only long-term solution. The ruling Committee also moved the population to underground cities.

The Mondasians could have subsisted like that for centuries more ... except Mondas was heading for a new, unstable region of space. The Committee developed cyborgs capable of working on the surface of the planet and perfected the techniques that allowed mass conversion of the population. People were scared and angry at the thought that they would become cyborgs—a problem solved by eliminating all emotions from those who were converted. Mondas now had a logical, efficient society that would do anything to survive: the Cybermen.[4]

BEHIND THE SCENES

We heard an account of the origins of the Cybermen in the TV story *The Tenth Planet* (Kit Pedler & Gerry Davis, 1966), saw the ancient times in the *Doctor Who Magazine* strip *The Cybermen*, and the audio *Spare Parts* showed the last generation of Mondasian humans.

ABOVE LEFT: The people of Mondas eked out a life underground as their planet plunged through space.

TIMELINE

THE WORLD SHAPERS
SIXTH DOCTOR
GRANT MORRISON / JOHN RIDGWAY

Initially, Mondas settles into a new orbit and the world becomes home to a diverse, mostly peaceful human civilization, whose people called their planet Marinus (p. 154).

1987

2002

SPARE PARTS

The Committee that rules Mondas can build a propulsion system to save Mondas, but doing so requires a vast workforce capable of surviving on the surface. Full cyber-conversion is the only practical option.

1987

THE WORLD SHAPERS

Thousands of years later, Marinus is left barren when the Voord steals an alien terraforming device, the Worldshaper.

2002

SPARE PARTS
FIFTH DOCTOR
MARC PLATT

The subterranean civilization comes to strongly resemble that of England in the mid-20th century. They survive for millennia but face a new disaster as Mondas's course propels it toward the chaos of the Cherrybowl Nebula.

1994-96

THE CYBERMEN
ALAN BARNES / ADRIAN SALMON

Mondas, like Earth, was once ruled by the Silurians. Here, though, they convert some apes into cybernetic servants who wipe out their masters, before dying off.

MARINUS

A world visited by the first Doctor, different parts of Marinus were home to quite different cultures. There were mountainous regions with only small villages and savage trappers, and jungles where vicious plant life grew at an accelerated rate. There was the city of Morpho, ruled by the Brain Creatures of Morphoton who kept the population in blissful hypnotic slavery. The city of Millennius was advanced but strictly ruled by the Elders. Marinus was kept in harmony for 700 years by the Conscience of Marinus, a machine that controlled the minds of the population, purging them of violence.

LOCATION

A transformed planet Mondas, eons ago (see p. 152)

INHABITANTS

Voord, Arbitans, Brain Creatures, Fishmen

LEFT: The Daleks and Voord would come to blows.

OPPOSITE: The Doctor's granddaughter Susan is captured by one of the alien Voord.

BELOW: The Conscience was housed in a Pyramid on a desolate island, surrounded by an acid sea.

HISTORY

A group called the Voord learned to resist the effects of the Conscience and sought to take control of the machine to use its abilities to dominate the minds of the entire planet. The Conscience was housed in a well-defended pyramid on an island surrounded by an acid sea, but the Voord were more than capable of reaching their goal. To prevent this, the microkeys of the Conscience were hidden throughout Marinus. The guardian of the Conscience, Arbitan, asked the Doctor and his companions to recover all the keys before the Voord. They achieved this, but the Conscience was destroyed when the head Voord, Yartek, tried to use a fake microkey. The Voord would continue to be a menace.[1]

FOOTNOTE
[1] *The Keys of Marinus*

FACT FILE

📺 THE KEYS OF MARINUS

The Conscience was built 2,000 years before the Doctor's first visit. At first it was used as a justice machine, dispensing perfectly impartial verdicts. Its abilities expanded until it began radiating a force that eliminated criminal and violent urges. Yartek and his followers were able to block the Conscience and rob and cheat without hindrance.

📖 THE FISHMEN OF KANDALINGA

After the Conscience had been destroyed, the human population became known as the Arbitans, and they drove the Voord away. The Voord went on to menace the Fishmen of Kandalinga. Although the Doctor believed Kandalinga was a separate planet, it later transpired that it was a region of Marinus.

🔊 DOCTOR WHO AND THE DALEKS

The Voord formed a truce with the Daleks, and teamed up to launch an Ultkron rocket in order to invade the Earth. The Doctor was able to defeat them.

🔊 THE WORLD SHAPERS

Eventually the Voord transformed Marinus using a Worldshaper, and, thanks to its time-distorting effects, they began their evolution into the Cybermen.

🎧 DOMAIN OF THE VOORD

The Doctor, Ian, Barbara, and Susan aided the Predoran resistance on the ocean planet Hydra, disrupting the Voord telepathic network and defeating the invading Voord leader, Tarlak.

🔊 FOUR DOCTORS

The War Doctor helped Siatak, leader of the alien Voord, down a Dalek saucer on a Marinus that had become an acid desert thanks to the Time War.

MONDAS: 1986

Mondas traveled hundreds of light years away from the Solar System, but the Cybermen were able to build a propulsion unit and use that to bring the planet under their control. Mondas appeared identical to Earth—although upside down. Plunging into interstellar space must have radically altered conditions on the surface, perhaps explaining why the planet appeared cloudless. Eons in the void had drained Mondas of energy. The Cybermen steered their home world toward the one place in the universe where they knew they could be sure of replenishing their resources: Earth, Mondas's twin planet.

HISTORY

In December 1986, human astronomers were astonished by the appearance of "the tenth planet," identical to Earth. The Cybermen moved quickly, landing spacecraft at key military and political sites to disrupt human resistance efforts. The first Doctor was present at one of these—Snowcap Base in Antarctica, which coordinated Earth's space missions. The Cybermen infiltrated the base and took control. Mondas began draining Earth's energy using devices constructed by the Cybermen. In the event, neither the Doctor nor the human race could do anything to stop the Cybermen; they were defeated when the machines draining Earth's energy overloaded, destroying Mondas. Utterly dependent on power from their home planet, the Cybermen on Earth died instantly. The energy drain was enough to wear out the Doctor's first body, so he got himself a new one, his first recorded regeneration.

BEHIND THE SCENES

The first Cybermen we see (*The Tenth Planet*, Gerry Davis & Kit Pedlar, 1966) are rather bulky and primitive compared with later models. This has inspired a number of artists, and there are several stories about "Mondasian" Cybermen, all of which must be set relatively early in Cyber-History. All 1960s TV comic strips featuring the Cybermen used *The Tenth Planet* design.

FACT FILE

📺 THE TENTH PLANET

Cybermen from Mondas were larger, and their cybernetic components were far bulkier than later models. Their hands appeared fully human, and their eyes were visible behind darkened lenses. The Cybermen from Mondas were highly vulnerable to radiation and, unlike every other model of Cybermen we know about, were powered from a central power supply.

◯ THE COMING OF THE CYBERMEN, FLOWER POWER!, CYBER-MOLE, THE CYBER EMPIRE!, MASQUERADE, THE TIME MUSEUM, ESKIMO JOE

The second Doctor fought the Mondasian Cybermen a number of times. He prevented them from destroying Earth from a base on Minot, saved the etymologist Professor Gnat from a Cyberman patrol, toppled a giant statue on Telos, disguised himself as a Cyberman to infiltrate one of their bases, and thwarted the Cybermen in 1970 when they tried to use a Cyber-Mole to steal a Doomsday Bomb.

◯ JUNKYARD DEMON

Far in the future, Flotsam and Jetsam of the Backwater Scrap and Salvage Company recover a Mondasian Cybernaut, an early space explorer. The Cyberman take them to A54, a planet near Arcturus, where a crashed Cyberfleet has been commanded by Zogron. The fourth Doctor arrives and is able to immobilize the Cyberman before the Cyber army is reactivated.

📺 ATTACK OF THE CYBERMEN

In 1985, the sixth Doctor found Cybermen operating on Earth and the Moon, planning to divert Halley's Comet to prevent the destruction of Mondas.

◯ THE GOOD SOLDIER

The seventh Doctor and Ace met an advance party from Mondas in 1954 in the Nevada desert, where they were testing a weapons system.

CYBERMEN MIGRATIONS

Starting in the 1970s, the Cybermen repeatedly tried and failed to conquer Earth for 100 years. Humans became ever more technologically advanced in that time, and a series of defeats almost wiped out the Cybermen. Facing extinction, the only logical step was to abandon the Solar System and regroup. The main force of Cybermen, led by the Cyber-Controller, conquered the planet Telos.[1] The Cybermen went into hiding around the galaxy—for example, Cantus, where they converted the population of the human colony planet, and then entombed them below the surface.[2]

HISTORY

Other groups of Cybermen became nomadic raiders, "the Vikings of Space." As the human race expanded to the stars, the Cybermen preyed on human colony planets and shipping. The Cybermen had "star destroyer" spacecraft, each containing a regiment of troops, and the weapons and equipment needed to conquer a whole planet. These Cybermen were also able to hibernate—one star destroyer was found drifting in the Garazone system but was able to reactivate and become a threat to the surrounding systems.[3] The human race found itself engaged in the Cyber Wars against an opponent that was skilled in lying low and biding its time, but that was remorseless once it emerged.

BEHIND THE SCENES

The Cybermen suffer huge defeats in *The Tenth Planet* (Gerry Davis & Kit Pedlar, 1966), *The Moonbase* (Pedlar, 1967), *The Wheel in Space* (David Whitaker, 1968), *The Invasion* (Derrick Sherwin, 1968), and *Silver Nemesis* (Kevin Clarke, 1988). *The Tomb of the Cybermen* (Davis & Pedlar, 1967) introduces the idea that they are lying dormant following defeat. Several stories have depicted the Cybermen as world conquerors and empire builders.

FIRST APPEARANCE

Tombs: The Tomb of the Cybermen *(1967)*
Cyber Wars: Revenge of the Cybermen *(1975)*

OPPOSITE: The Cybermen abandoned the Moon and fled to Telos.

FACT FILE

REVENGE OF THE CYBERMEN

The Cyber Wars ended in a total defeat for the Cybermen. Their opponents learned that the Cybermen would suffocate if their chest units were clogged with gold dust and so they used the vast reserves of the planet Voga as ammunition in glitterguns. All that remained of the Cybermen were a few scattered ships and their surviving crews.

THROWBACK

Junior Cyber-Leader Kroton, a converted human, was sent to conquer the human world of Mondaran, but his emotions began to return, and he helped the human colonists instead.

DEATHWORLD

The Cybermen fought the Ice Warriors on Yama-10, a planet rich in trisilicate.

EARTHSHOCK

By 2526, representatives from several planets met on Earth to form an alliance to fight the Cybermen, who responded by planting a Cyberbomb on Earth as well as planting an army of Cybermen in the hold of a space freighter bound for Earth. The fifth Doctor was on hand to thwart their attack.

KILLING GROUND

The colony planet Agora became a breeding ground for Cybermen, with the help of human Overseers. They returned every few years to harvest converted colonists. Some of the humans partially converted themselves into the Bronze Knights to fight the invaders.

HUMAN RESOURCES

Before reaching Telos, some Cybermen who survived the destruction of Mondas settled on the jungle planet Lonsis.

FOOTNOTES
[1] *The Tomb of the Cybermen* • [2] *The Crystal of Cantus* • [3] *Sword of Orion*

159

TELOS

A cold, desolate world, Telos was home to the Cryons, a race that could only exist in subzero temperatures and lived in refrigerated cities. The Cybermen conquered the planet, enslaved the Cryons, and forced them to build a vast Tomb—a subterranean complex containing weapons, computers, and an area in which thousands of Cybermen hibernated.[1] Centuries later, archeologists from Earth discovered the Tomb and revived the Cybermen.[2] The mechanical creatures emerged to fight a series of Cyber Wars with Earth and its space colonies.

FIRST APPEARANCE

The Tomb of the Cybermen (1967)

HISTORY

The leader of the Cybermen on Telos was the Cyber-Controller—particularly tall, with a large, semi-exposed brain. When the sixth Doctor revisited Telos, the Cybermen, their Controller, and even the Tomb itself had radically changed their appearance—perhaps suggesting a major technological upgrade had occurred. By the time of that latter visit, the Cybermen had begun using human slave labor that had been half converted into Cybermen. This was the base from which the Cybermen had coordinated their attack on the rest of the galaxy, but they had been heavily defeated. To add to their woes, Cryon resistance fighters managed to sabotage Cyber operations. Thanks to the Cryons, the Doctor, and a space mercenary—Lytton—the entire Cyber Control was destroyed by vastial explosives.

RIGHT: The Cybermen retreated to their Tomb on Telos.

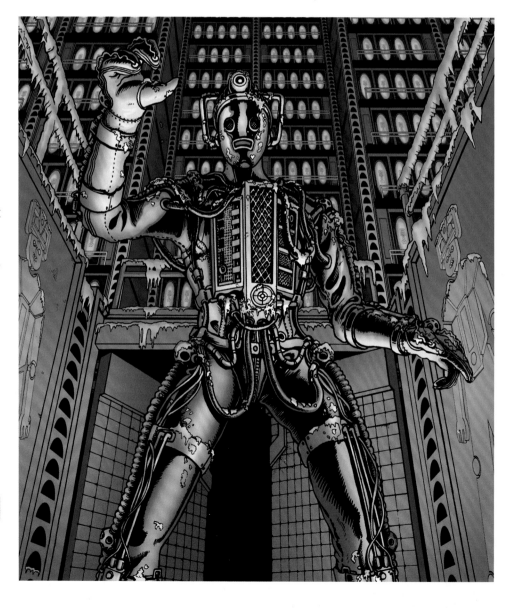

FOOTNOTES

[1] *Attack of the Cybermen* • [2] *The Tomb of the Cybermen*

TIMELINE

THE TOMB OF THE CYBERMEN
SECOND DOCTOR
KIT PEDLAR & GERRY DAVIS

The Cybermen are thought to be extinct. After a series of failed attempts to conquer Earth, they vanish and are not seen for 500 years.

1967

THE TOMB OF THE CYBERMEN

The Brotherhood of Logicians admire the Cybermen, and their leaders, Klieg and Kaftan, sponsor an expedition to Telos, foolishly believing the Cybermen will be interested in an alliance. The Doctor is able to seal the Tomb.

1967

2006

CYBERMAN
NICHOLAS BRIGGS

Telos is eventually destroyed by a meteor strike—but the Tomb survives, drifting in space.

1985

ATTACK OF THE CYBERMEN

The revived Cybermen eventually free themselves but fare badly when they attempt galactic conquest—within a few years, they face total defeat and attempt to change Earth's history. The Doctor defeats them and the Controller is killed.

1985

1968

THE CYBER EMPIRE!
SECOND DOCTOR

The Doctor, John, and Gillian visit Telos at a time when the Cybermen have abducted thousands of Earthmen as slaves, in order to build a huge city and erect a giant gold statue of their Controller. After evading the Cybermen in a hover chariot, they organize the slaves, and the Doctor topples the statue using a minibomb from his utility belt.

ATTACK OF THE CYBERMEN
SIXTH DOCTOR
"PAULA MOORE" (PSEUDONYM FOR PAULA WOOLSEY)

The Cryons are peaceful and advanced enough to know of the Time Lords. Their bodies are crystalline and quickly begin to steam and melt unless kept at subzero temperatures.

ORION

The Constellation of Orion, despite what 21st-century-Earth astronomy says, is a group of stars in close proximity to each other, with a long and varied history. Perhaps most notable, it was the site of the Orion War, fought in the early 26th century, a generation after the first Cyber War. It was sparked when advanced androids on the colony worlds of Orion demanded equal rights to humans. When Earth refused, the androids took control of the Orion Sector and forced humans there to submit to their rule.

HISTORY

Both sides discovered Cyber-technology could help their cause ... neither understood that the Cybermen had their own agenda: mass conversion of humanity into Cybermen and the activation of Cyber-tombs across the galaxy.

In 2503, Earth sent agents to plunder a derelict Cyberman destroyer in the Garazone system. The Cybermen reactivated and planned to overrun the whole sector. The eighth Doctor was on hand and ensured the ship was destroyed in an ion storm. With the Orion androids proving difficult to defeat with Earth technology, the human race tried to involve the Cybermen—either by procuring artifacts, or, in some cases, treacherous humans negotiated deals with the Cybermen themselves. The Cybermen had an elaborate plot to conquer the Earth, but human factions were able to defeat them. The Orion War ended, and androids were granted equal rights.

FIRST APPEARANCE

📺 *Eye of Orion:* The Five Doctors *(1983)*

🎧 *Orion War:* Sword of Orion *(2001)*

📖 *Rigellians:* The Time Trap *(1980)*

RIGHT: The Orion War saw the Cybermen return to the galactic stage after laying dormant for centuries.

TIMELINE

 **DESTINY OF THE DALEKS**

👤 **FOURTH DOCTOR**

✏️ **TERRY NATION**

Betelgeuse, one of the stars of Orion, comes second in a Galactic Olympic Games held around the time of the Dalek–Movellan War.

1979

1980

📖 **THE TIME TRAP**

👤 **K9**

✏️ **DAVID MARTIN**

Rigel, one of the stars of Orion, is home to an advanced race that is on good terms with the Time Lords in the modern era. When their Seventh Fleet vanishes, the High Council of Gallifrey sends K9 to investigate. K9 discovers it is part of a plot of the renegade Time Lord Omegon.

1981

🔍 **BLACK SUN RISING**

✏️ **ALAN MOORE / DAVID LLOYD**

In the ancient days of the Time Lords, the Rigellians are part of the Order of the Black Sun. The Sontarans kill a Black Sun Elder on Desrault as part of a plot to frame the Time Lords.

🎧 **DEATH COMES TO TIME**

👤 **SEVENTH DOCTOR**

✏️ **"COLIN MEEK" (PSEUDONYM FOR DAN FREEDMAN & NEV FOUNTAIN)**

2001

A group of peripatetic Time Lords, the Fraction, build the Temple of the Fourth on Micen Island in the heart of the Great Nebula of Orion to honor those lost when the Time Lords misused their power and killed the entire population.

1996

📖 **RETURN OF THE LIVING DAD**

👤 **SEVENTH DOCTOR**

✏️ **KATE ORMAN**

A generation after the Orion War, the Earth spacefleet is routed by the Daleks at the Battle of Bellatrix. Isaac Summerfield, father of the Doctor's companion, Bernice, apparently flees and is branded a deserter.

1995

📖 **MANAGRA**

👤 **FOURTH DOCTOR**

✏️ **STEPHEN MARLEY**

The Papal Seat of the Catholic Church will move to Betelgeuse by 3278 AD.

1983

📺 **THE FIVE DOCTORS**

👤 **FIFTH DOCTOR**

✏️ **TERRANCE DICKS**

The Eye of Orion is one of the most tranquil places in the universe because of the high bombardment of positive ions in its atmosphere. The Doctor mentions it a couple of times and takes Tegan and Turlough there.

FUTURE CYBER PLANETS

The Cybermen of the future hit upon a tactic they would come to use a number of times, one that was perfectly logical: using time travel to attack Earth in its early history, when humanity had the technological infrastructure to support the Cybermen but lacked the weapons to defeat them. These were desperate moves, and the Doctor was able to counter every strike the Cybermen made. The Time Lords have predicted that the Cybermen will become a race of peaceful philosophers millions of years from now.

HISTORY

There were very few periods in history when the Cybermen were a powerful galactic force. They were born on Mondas as a desperate survival tactic, and a series of defeats on Earth in the 20th and 21st centuries almost wiped them out again. There was a brief blossoming of a Cyber Empire when they emerged from their Tombs but that was dismantled when they suffered crushing defeat at the end of the Cyber War. They will operate powerful legions in the far future but again will be reduced to a handful of surviving ships by the human military. In the far future, the Cybermen will become more technologically advanced than ever but they will still face utter extinction.

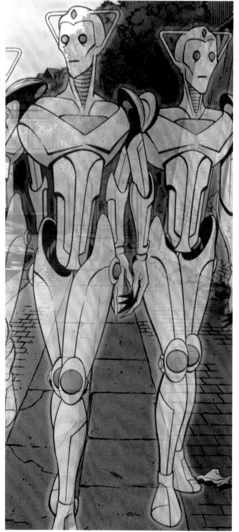

FIRST APPEARANCE
Q The World Shapers
(1987)

STATUS
Finally, peaceful beings of pure logic

ABOVE: The twelfth Doctor.

LEFT: Cybermen from the far future infiltrated London in 2005.

FAR LEFT: The twelfth Doctor faces a resurgent force of Cybermen.

TIMELINE

🎧 REAL TIME
👤 SIXTH DOCTOR
✎ GARY RUSSELL

The Doctor and Evelyn discover a time machine on the desert planet Chronos. The inhabitants use it to travel to the future, where their planet is a hospitable waterworld … and the hiding place of the last surviving Cyber Controller. The Cybermen use the time machine to infect Earth's past with a technovirus that converts people to Cybermen.

2002

🎧 THE GIRL WHO NEVER WAS
👤 EIGHTH DOCTOR
✎ ALAN BARNES

2007

Time-traveling Cybermen from the very distant future become stranded on the abandoned Earth of 500,002 AD but manage to translocate a WW2 ship, the SS *Batavia*, to their time zone. They intended to send the ship back full of equipment to convert humans.

2002

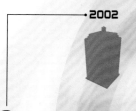

🎧 REAL TIME

Earth's history changes, but the Doctor is able to trigger a temporal blast that ages the Cybermen to death.

2006

🎧 THE REAPING
👤 SIXTH DOCTOR
✎ JOSEPH LIDSTER

A stranded Cyberleader from the far future forces the Doctor to take him to prehistoric Earth, where he plans to convert the earliest humans. Instead, the Doctor takes him to Earth's twin world of Mondas (p. 156). The Cybermen there conclude he is defective and deactivate him.

2005

💬 THE FLOOD
👤 EIGHTH DOCTOR
✎ SCOTT GRAY / MARTIN GERAGHTY

2005

Cybermen from the very far future create a form of liquid that produces extreme emotional reactions in humans—when they release it in London in the early 21st century, people beg to become emotionless Cybermen instead.

💬 THE FLOOD

The Doctor manages to destroy these, the most advanced Cybermen he's ever seen, by releasing the fragment of the Time Vortex they use to power their ship.

PLANETS OF
THE MONSTERS

ALFAVA METRAXIS

Alfava Metraxis is the seventh planet of the Dundra system in the Garn Belt. It has, according to the Doctor, an "oxygen-rich atmosphere, all toxins in the soft band, an eleven-hour day, and chances of rain later." It is a short warp journey from coordinates 777-5/3-4-9 x 10 0-12/acorn. Colonized by humans in the 49th century, 200 years later it was a terraformed human colony planet, with a population of six billion.

FIRST APPEARANCE

 *"The Time of Angels"*
(2010)

INHABITANTS

Aplans, human colonists, Weeping Angels

STATUS

Safe for now

HISTORY

The indigenous life form of the planet were the Aplans, a "lovely species" according to the Doctor, who once dined with their Chief Architect. They had two heads, both considered legally separate beings—there was a prohibition against self-marriage. Dead Aplans were entombed in an Aplan Mortarium, also known as a Maze of the Dead. These structures consisted of six levels, symbolizing the ascent of the soul. The Aplans died out in the 47th century; no one knew why for four centuries, until the Doctor, Amy, and River Song solved the mystery.

BEHIND THE SCENES

The two-part TV story "The Time of Angels" / "Flesh and Stone" consisted of the first episodes recorded with Matt Smith and Karen Gillan as the eleventh Doctor and Amy, but the fourth and fifth to be screened. These episodes set up or reintroduced many of the running story lines and recurring characters from the eleventh Doctor's era.

LEFT: The eleventh Doctor and Amy arrive on a rocky world infested with Weeping Angels.

TIMELINE

📺 "THE TIME OF ANGELS"
👤 ELEVENTH DOCTOR
✎ STEVEN MOFFAT

River Song escapes from the starliner *Byzantium* by carving a message for the Doctor into the ship's Home Box (the equivalent of a black box flight recorder); 12,000 years later, the Doctor finds the Home Box on display in the Delirium Archive, an asteroid that is the final resting place of the Headless Monks.

2010

📺 "FLESH AND STONE"

The Doctor is able to get aboard the *Byzantium* and neutralize the Weeping Angels by tricking them into falling into the crack in time.

2010

2010

📺 "THE TIME OF ANGELS"

The Doctor arrives in River's time zone at the moment she jumps out of the *Byzantium*'s airlock. She is working with the Church, which by her 51st century has become a military organization that hunts Weeping Angels. (The *Byzantium* is carrying one in its vault.)

📺 "FLESH AND STONE"
👤 ELEVENTH DOCTOR
✎ STEVEN MOFFAT

Alone for so long, the Weeping Angels had begun to waste away. The Angel from the *Byzantium* had crashed the ship there to flood the area with radiation that the Angels could feast upon. Once there, the Angels realized that there was a crack in time that promised to be an even greater feast.

2010

📺 "THE TIME OF ANGELS"

The Angel had been taken from the ruins of Razbahan at the end of the previous century and had been in a private collection.

📺 "THE TIME OF ANGELS"

The ship crashes into an ancient structure on Alfava Metraxis, the Maze of the Dead. The Doctor, Amy, and River arrive shortly afterward, and River calls in Father Octavian, a bishop leading a squad of 20 soldiers. The Maze is full of statues—but not Aplans. This is an army of Weeping Angels.

ARCTURUS

There are several Arcturan races, but the most prominent resemble shriveled human heads and can't survive in Earthlike conditions without life support. These Arcturans are members of the Galactic Federation and have long been enemies of the Ice Warriors[1] because the Martians settled on Nova Martia near Arcturus after fleeing Mars.[2] Arcturus is a swollen star, and one fleet of hundreds of ships left the dying solar system "many thousands of years" ago.

HISTORY

These Arcturans were an entirely peaceful race of frail, four-armed birdlike creatures who could no longer fly due to gravity fluctuations.[3] Beings from Arcturus resembling the Greek Gods abducted the *Marie Celeste*.[4]

One of Earth's earliest peaceful contacts with an alien race came in the late 21st century, when communications with Arcturus were detected. Humans gained much from the Arcturans, including scientific information.[5] Some of the earliest human missions outside the Solar System were to Arcturus, although the attempt to build an interstellar Stunnel (transmat corridor) to Arcturus II ended in disaster.[6] Arcturus VI is habitable by humans.[7] Humans settled Sifranos in the Arcturus Sector, but were wiped out by the Daleks.[8] There were civil wars in the Earth colonies on Arcturus.[9] A Von Neumann probe also landed there and began to build a city, unaware that the planet was already inhabited.[10]

BEHIND THE SCENES

We have seen at least three different alien races come from Arcturus over the course of *Doctor Who*, and it has been the site of a large number of events, although all of these have been alluded to rather than depicted.

FIRST APPEARANCE
The Curse of Peladon *(1972)*

STATUS
Federation member planet, prospering

ABOVE RIGHT: The second Doctor encountered the Arcturians of Arcturus.

RIGHT: The face of the Arcturus delegate to Peladon.

OPPOSITE: The tenth Doctor and Rose encountered an Arcturan.

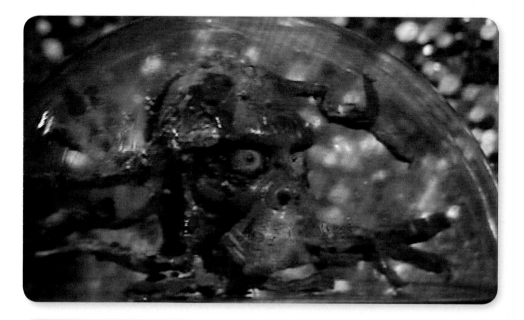

FOOTNOTES
[1] The Curse of Peladon • [2&9] GodEngine • [3] Only a Matter of Time • [4] The Mystery of the Marie Celeste • [5&8] Lucifer Rising • [6] Transit • [7] Love and War • [10] The Big Hunt

AXOS

The Axons are part of a single living organism, driven from its original worlds on the edge of the galaxy by solar flares. Axos is part world, part spacecraft. Being inside it is like being inside a body—fleshy walls, nervelike tendrils, and specialized organic structures. Axos is able to form itself into what appear to be individuals—beautiful people with gold, masklike faces—when it wishes to negotiate; duplicates of individuals when it wishes to infiltrate; spaghetti monsters with long, electrically charged tendrils when it wants to attack.

HISTORY

Axos is made from axonite, a miracle material that can change its structure. The first time the Axons came to Earth, they offered supplies of axonite as a panacea—it could be used to create food and enlarge food animals, solving world hunger. In reality, Axos wanted humanity to distribute axonite around the world so it could begin its feeding cycle. It would drain the life and energy from the entire world, growing until it covered the surface. Axos had learned some rudimentary time-travel techniques and knew of the Time Lords. It sought either the Doctor or Master's TARDIS so that it could travel through the whole of time and space to feed.

FIRST APPEARANCE
The Claws of Axos *(1971)*

STATUS
Timelooped

BELOW: The third Doctor and Jo confront the Axons within the heart of Axos.

TIMELINE

THE CLAWS OF AXOS

THIRD DOCTOR

BOB BAKER & DAVID MARTIN

UNIT detects an object approaching Earth, which makes a small time jump to avoid being shot down. The Axons have arrived on Earth, promising to solve the human race's problems using axonite to create unlimited resources.

1971

2011

THE FEAST OF AXOS

SIXTH DOCTOR

MIKE MADDOX

Billionaire Campbell Irons plans to travel to Axos and transmit its energy to Earth. The Axons duplicate the Doctor and try to break out of the time loop. The Doctor is able to keep Axos trapped, and it feeds for billions of years on a nuclear explosion intended to destroy it.

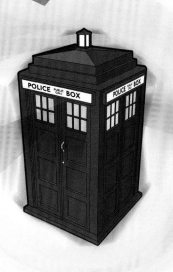

2010

1971

THE CLAWS OF AXOS

The Axons have trapped the Master, who forms an alliance with them as they secretly attempt to drain the Earth of its energy. When Axos betrays the Master, he works with the Doctor to trap it in a time loop.

THE GOLDEN ONES

The Doctor manages to draw electrical energy away from the power grid, draining Axos.

2010

THE GOLDEN ONES

ELEVENTH DOCTOR

JONATHAN MORRIS

Tens of thousands of children in Japan are drinking the energy drink Goruda, which contains axonite—they transform into Axons and begin rampaging.

PLANET OF THE CHEETAH PEOPLE

The Cheetah People are from a nameless, ancient world with a red sky, dusty ground, parched vegetation, and distant volcanoes. The whole planet was alive, but frequent earthquakes were a symptom that it was nearing the end of that life. Once there had been a thriving civilization, but that had fallen into ruins when they had tried to take control of the life force of the planet. They had become corrupt, and the planet transformed them into the Cheetah People—bestial, flesh-eating predators whose outer forms now resembled their inner nature.

BEHIND THE SCENES

Survival was the last story of the 26-year original run of the *Doctor Who* TV series.

HISTORY

The Cheetah People used Kitlings, telepathic creatures who could teleport to other worlds, to scout for prey. There was one other being on the living planet—the Doctor's old nemesis, the Master. Thanks to him, the Cheetah People found Earth. In 1989, they rode on horseback through the streets of Perivale, dragging human beings back to their world. The Cheetah People were linked to their world. As they fought, it wounded their dying planet. The Master knew that he had to escape this world, but his own savage nature was binding him to it.

BELOW: The Cheetah People were hunters from a dying planet.

FIRST APPEARANCE
📺 Survival *(1989)*

INHABITANTS
Cheetah People, Kitlings, abducted humans

STATUS
Destroyed

◎ TIMELINE

📺 **SURVIVAL**

The Doctor is able to suppress the urge to fight. The Cheetah Planet is in its death throes. The Doctor stops himself from killing the Master, and this triggers his return to Perivale. The Master is trapped as the Cheetah Planet tears itself apart.

📺 **SURVIVAL**

🧑 **SEVENTH DOCTOR**

✎ **RONA MUNRO**

Perivale, a London suburb, is the former home of the Doctor's friend Ace. They arrive on a quiet Sunday, and Ace manages to catch up with a number of her friends. A fair few people have "gone away," and it isn't clear where.

1989

1989 •

1989 •

📺 **SURVIVAL**

The Doctor begins turning into a Cheetah Person; he too will be trapped on the dying planet.

📺 **SURVIVAL**

Ace soon finds out: she is captured by a Cheetah Person and dragged to his home planet, where she meets other Perivale residents and discovers the plan is that they will be hunted for sport.

1989 •

📺 **SURVIVAL**

The Master returns to Earth but finds that he is becoming a Cheetah Person—and with such a link, he will inevitably find himself returning to their planet.

1989 •

📺 **SURVIVAL**

The Master is trapped, and he needs someone to guide him "home."

CHELONIA

Chelonia is home to a race of intelligent giant tortoises (Chelonians), roughly the size of a man when on their hind feet (they are usually, but not exclusively, quadrupeds). Each foot has opposable digits. They are strong, rugged creatures; well-armored; and have a life expectancy of over 100 years. They are also typically stubborn to the point of stupidity.[1] Chelonians are hermaphrodites (all able to lay eggs) and herbivores, usually eating flowers or seeds. They also love plants in all forms—they place a high value on flower arranging, and either conquer verdant worlds or transform the planets they conquer until they are covered in beautiful plants.[2]

BEHIND THE SCENES

Gareth Roberts created the Chelonians for a New Adventures novel and has since written a number of stories—including comic strips and short stories—in which they've returned. They've also been mentioned a number of times in other stories, including the TV episode "The Pandorica Opens" (Steven Moffat, 2010).

HISTORY

Chelonia is the seat of the God-Mother; he (Chelonians use the male pronoun) is the head of the Empire. Many factions and groups of Chelonians are warriors by nature, and they're rather belligerent, believing all non-Chelonians to be "parasites." (Many Chelonians have cyborg implants to improve both their senses and their fighting prowess.)

When they meet, it is customary to join in a rendition of the Chelonian Anthem, which has 185 verses.[3] Chelonian structures can serve as both vehicles and buildings.[4] They have fought wars with the Ice Warriors and attended the Armageddon Convention of 1609, when the major space powers agreed to limit their use of doomsday weaponry.[5]

FIRST APPEARANCE
The Highest Science *(1992)*

STATUS
Still stubborn, at least ten billion years from now

RIGHT: The tenth Doctor faces down a Chelonian warrior, armed only with his sonic screwdriver.

FOOTNOTES
[1] *The Highest Science* • [2&4] *The Well-Mannered War* •
[3] *Zamper* • [5] *The Empire of Glass*

TIMELINE

📖 *THE HIGHEST SCIENCE*

👤 SEVENTH DOCTOR

✏ GARETH ROBERTS

A slow time converter on the planet Hogsumm leads to a Fortean Flicker, a phenomenon that creates strange apparitions and coincidences. This includes the arrival of a group of angry Chelonians, together with a trainload of humans.

1992

2010

📺 "THE PANDORICA OPENS"

👤 ELEVENTH DOCTOR

✏ STEVEN MOFFAT

The Chelonians are among the races who form an Alliance to prevent the Doctor from destroying the universe.

1995

📖 *ZAMPER*

👤 SEVENTH DOCTOR

✏ GARETH ROBERTS

The Chelonian Empire sees the pacifist faction of Little Sister overthrow the warlike Big Mother. Forty years later, Big Mother leads a group of soldiers to the planet Zamper, a human weapons research facility, to acquire a Series 336c Delta-Spiral Sun Blaster battleship. The Chelonians learn that the Zamps, evil slug creatures, are planning to launch a war of galactic conquest, and sacrifice themselves to seal off Zamper from the rest of the universe.

1997

📖 *THE WELL-MANNERED WAR*

👤 FOURTH DOCTOR

✏ GARETH ROBERTS

In the Fifty-Eighth Segment of Time, the Black Guardian brings a Chelonian squad from the distant past in a time storm. The Chelonians claim the planet Barclow, close to the human world Metralubit, and the two planets fight a short war.

CHLORIS AND TYTHONUS

Chloris is a jungle planet; it is wild, misty, and overgrown. Its people resemble humans, but their technological development has been hampered by a lack of metal. While they are aware that space travel is possible, and that there is life on other worlds, they cannot build spaceships of their own—they can barely make clearings in the jungle. In a neighboring star system is the planet Tythonus. Tythonians are vast green blobs—hundreds of feet long, they feed by sucking chlorophyll through their skins. They have no vocal cords and communicate with other races using translator devices.

DR WHO

THE CREATURE FROM THE PIT

MYRA FRANCES AS ADRASTA

HISTORY

The people of Chloris have developed the art of astrology and tamed hostile moving plants, such as the Wolf Weeds. There is one mine on the planet, the Pit, owned by the cruel Lady Adrasta. It is nearly worked out, but Adrasta clings onto power because she can condemn her enemies to a terrible fate—throwing them into the Pit, where a lethal "Creature" lurks.

Tythonians are able to spin metal structures of various sizes and levels of complexity, including shells they fit photon drives to and use as spacecraft. Tythonians can live for 40,000 years. Their planet is rich in metal, but plant life is rare. Concluding that the people of Chloris, facing the opposite problem, would welcome a trading partnership, they sent an ambassador (Erato) to negotiate a deal. Unfortunately, his first encounter was with Adrasta, who stood to lose all her power if metals became more common. She trapped him in the Pit.

ABOVE RIGHT: Lady Adrasta ruled with a fist of iron, fittingly enough.

LEFT: The twelfth Doctor's favorite coffee came from Chloris.

FIRST APPEARANCE
📺 The Creature from the Pit (1979)

INHABITANTS
(Chloris) people of Chloris, Wolf Weeds; (Tythonus) Tythonians

STATUS
Rebuilding, free from dictatorship

TIMELINE

📺 **THE CREATURE FROM THE PIT**
👤 **FOURTH DOCTOR**
✏️ **DAVID FISHER**

Lady Adrasta demonstrates her great wealth by wearing metallic facepaint and nail polish, as well as a large metal girdle.

2014

📖 **LIGHTS OUT**
👤 **TWELFTH DOCTOR**
✏️ **HOLLY BLACK**

By the late 23rd century, Chloris is known for the production of supercaffeinated coffee beans, which the Doctor considers the third best in the universe.

1979

📺 **THE CREATURE FROM THE PIT**

The Doctor has Erato spin a shell of aluminum around the neutron star and spins it harmlessly out into space using the TARDIS's tractor beam.

1979

1979

📺 **THE CREATURE FROM THE PIT**

Erato is imprisoned for 15 years. The metal shell he uses to travel to Chloris lies abandoned in the jungle, baffling the scholars of the planet.

1979

📺 **THE CREATURE FROM THE PIT**

With Adrasta's death, you might think danger had passed, but the Tythonians consider the loss of their ambassador an act of war and launch a neutron star at the heart of Chloris's sun, which would destroy the entire solar system.

1979

📺 **THE CREATURE FROM THE PIT**

The Tythonian translation device resembles a metal shield. When a humanoid touches it, its Tythonian operator takes control of that person's vocal cords.

1979

📺 **THE CREATURE FROM THE PIT**

When Adrasta learns that the TARDIS can travel through time and space, she realizes she can use it to acquire metal—and maintain her monopoly. She orders Erato killed, but her people learn the truth and turn against her; she is killed by a pack of Wolf Weeds.

CHUMERIA

The Chimerons hatched from eggs and were the size of human babies, but with loose, translucent green skin; male Chimerons retained this in adulthood. The Chimeron Queen resembled a beautiful human woman, with a greenish tint to her skin and gray marks behind her ear (high-frequency antennae, giving her superhuman hearing). Queens were fed jelly, like bees on Earth, and in a day or so reached the size of a human adolescent. As she grew, a queen learned to emit high-frequency sounds ("the singing time") controlled to create beautiful music, a warning cry, or even a sonic attack.

HISTORY

Chumeria had a large moon visible in its sky. It was reputedly very beautiful, but its environment was ruined by an invasion by the Bannermen, a ferocious gang of marauders with a network of informers and mercenaries across time and space. It's unclear what motivated their leader, Gavrok, to launch a genocidal attack, beyond his obvious savagery. The Bannermen were humanoid, with red-rimmed eyes and webbed hands. They had powerful hand weapons and ships that they used to fire-bomb planets and that could travel through time as well as space. Chimerons themselves were technologically advanced, with a fleet of spacecraft (until the Bannermen fire-bombed them), laser guns, and portable incubation units. Chumeria was also close to Tollport G715, a gateway to time travel used by the Navarinos—squat, purple people from the tripolar moon of Navarro, with a notoriously high metabolic rate.

ABOVE & BELOW:
The seventh Doctor and Mel protected the Chimeron Queen.

FIRST APPEARANCE
Delta and the Bannermen
(1987)

STATUS
Rebuilding after invasion

TIMELINE

🖵 DELTA AND THE BANNERMEN
👤 SEVENTH DOCTOR
✎ MALCOLM KOHLL

The Bannermen wipe out every Chimeron apart from the Queen and two males, who sacrifice themselves to get the Queen to a Bannerman ship, which she steals and takes to Tollport G715. She arrives just as the Doctor and Mel show up in the TARDIS.

1987

🖵 DELTA AND THE BANNERMEN

Mel and the Queen join a Navarino Nostalgia Tours party planning to go to Disneyland in 1959.

1987

🖵 DELTA AND THE BANNERMEN

The Bannermen arrive shortly afterward, killing the Tollmaster. They send word to their network that they are offering a reward of one million units for the Chimeron Queen.

1987

🖵 DELTA AND THE BANNERMEN

The new Queen enters the singing time and uses a sonic attack on Gavrok that sends him reeling into an explosive trap he has set. The remaining Bannermen are arrested, and the Queen returns to her planet with the new queen and a Welshman named Billy, with whom she's fallen in love.

1987

1987

🖵 DELTA AND THE BANNERMEN

The Chimeron Queen has one egg with her. It hatches, to Mel's horror, and the Queen begins feeding it jelly so that it will grow into a new queen. The Doctor pledges to see that Gavrok will be tried for the crimes of invasion and genocide. The Queen knows that if she can get word to "the Brood Planet," then they will send an expeditionary force.

1987

🖵 DELTA AND THE BANNERMEN

The Nostalgia Tours bus malfunctions, ending up at a holiday camp in Wales rather than Disneyland.

DRACONIA

Draconia was a technologically advanced society of humanoid lizards, but one that had maintained a feudal system, with the people ruled by an Emperor and his Princes and court. Draconians had codes of honorable behavior and strict rules, such as banning women from speaking in the throne room.

HISTORY

In the 26th century, Earth fought a brief war with the Draconians, who closely matched the early Earth Empire in terms of territory and technological development. The fighting ended with an uneasy peace and the establishment of a neutral zone between their territories. For 20 years the Empires maintained diplomatic relations but were frosty and suspicious of each other. Like many planets in our galaxy, thanks to alien influence during its primitive days, some Draconians believed in a horned devil[1] and astrology.[2] The Doctor had visited Draconia 500 years before the time of the Space War, when he helped the 15th Emperor save his people from a space plague. Further in the future, Draconia was a member of the Galactic Federation,[3] and there had been a degree of progress when it came to women's rights;[4] 100,000 years from now, Draconia is a republic.[5]

FIRST APPEARANCE
📺 Frontier in Space *(1973)*

STATUS
Thriving empire

BEHIND THE SCENES

The Draconians have only made one appearance on TV, in Malcolm Hulke's *Frontier in Space* (1973), but good character design and hints at a sophisticated culture made an impression on an early generation of *Doctor Who* fans, and they have frequently popped up for cameo appearances or mentions in comics and books.

ABOVE: The third Doctor.

LEFT: The Draconians are a cultured, feudal race.

FOOTNOTES
[1] 📺 "The Satan Pit" • [2] 📺 *Secrets of the Stars* • [3] 🔍 *Cold-Blooded War!* • [4] 📖 *The Dark Path* • [5] 📖 *The Crystal Bucephalus*

TIMELINE

📺 FRONTIER IN SPACE

👤 THIRD DOCTOR

✎ MALCOLM HULKE

In 2540, Earth accuses Draconia of attacking its shipping, but the Doctor and Jo discover the real culprits to be the Ogrons, under the command of the Master.

1973

📺 FRONTIER IN SPACE

The Doctor is able to prove his case and accompanies a squad to the Ogrons' home planet to capture the Master. There, he discovers the true masterminds of the plan—the Daleks, who hope to set the two Empires fighting, then conquer both when they have exhausted their military resources.

1973

🎧 PAPER CUTS

👤 SIXTH DOCTOR

✎ MARC PLATT

2009

When Draconian Emperors are on the verge of death, they are sent to an orbiting space station and kept semidormant. The Doctor and Charley arrive to see the coronation of the 16th Emperor; instead, the previous 15 revive and fight among themselves.

2009

◯ COLD-BLOODED WAR!

👤 TENTH DOCTOR

🖌 GARY RUSSELL / ADRIAN SALMON

The Doctor and Donna help broker a peace between the Draconians and Ice Warriors, who are both members of the Galactic Federation.

1980

◯ STAR TIGERS

👤 ABSLOM DAAK

🖌 STEVE MOORE / STEVE DILLON & DAVID LLOYD

Abslom Daak, a criminal sentenced to being a Dalek Killer, flees a Dalek patrol and heads into Draconian space. He is met by high-ranking nobleman Salander.

1980

◯ STAR TIGERS

Soon after, Salander falls out of favor with the Emperor and is forced to escape in a prototype starship, the *Kill-Wagon*. Daak and Salander recruit Harma—an Ice Warrior—and the human tactician Mercurius, and together they become the mercenary group the Star Tigers.

DULKIS

The planet Dulkis was peaceful. The Dulcians resembled humans, but with two hearts. They were technologically advanced, but almost all its people lacked curiosity and lived completely safe lives. They did not believe in life on other worlds, but when confronted with aliens, they took it in their stride. In the temperate climate, only light clothing was needed, and it could be custom-made by special dispensers.

LOCATION
In one of "the Ten Galaxies," near Epsilon Four

INHABITANTS
Dulcians

STATUS
Safe for now

HISTORY

Dulkis's Capitol was a futuristic metropolis in the Northern hemisphere, with large buildings and networks of travel capsules. The ruling Council, led by Senex, endlessly deferred action. The planet itself was in "the Ten Galaxies," part of the vast tracts of space controlled by the Dominators, a large race notable for their sallow faces and large shoulders, which curved halfway up the back of their heads. The Dominators were warlike; flew powerful saucers that absorbed radiation for fuel; and used squat robots (Quarks) as guards, scouts, and for manual labor.

LEFT: The powerful Dominators were the masters of ten galaxies; the Quarks were merely their servants.

BELOW: The Doctor first encountered the Quarks in the Scottish highlands.

QUARKS!.. I'VE NEVER ENCOUNTERED THEM BEFORE BUT THEIR REPUTATION FOR DESTRUCTION IS UNPARALLELED THROUGHOUT THE GALAXIES.

 # TIMELINE

FIRES DOWN BELOW

👥 JOHN PEEL / JOHN STOKES

Major Whitaker and her UNIT squad defeat Dominator Haag and his Quarks in Iceland, when they attempt to destroy Earth in almost exactly the way the Dominators Rago and Toba had tried to destroy Dulkis.

1982

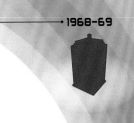

📺 **THE DOMINATORS**

👤 SECOND DOCTOR

✎ "NORMAN ASHBY" (PSEUDONYM FOR MERVYN HAISMAN & HENRY LINCOLN)

The Doctor visits Dulkis 200 years ago, finding a peaceful people on a beautiful world. Long ago, Director Olim of the Second Council had banned all weapons from the planet.

1968

1968–69

INVASION OF THE QUARKS, THE KILLER WASPS, JUNGLE OF DOOM, MARTHA THE MECHANICAL HOUSEMAID

👤 SECOND DOCTOR

The Doctor and Jamie defeat a Quark plan to invade the Earth, prompting the Quark leaders to order their pursuit through time and space. After attacking the Doctor using giant wasps on Gano, the pursuers are destroyed by bulldozers in a jungle on Earth. When the Doctor builds and markets robot maids (the Marthas), the Quarks take radio control of them and use them to soften up Earth for invasion. The Doctor turns the tables, and the army of Marthas send the Quarks packing.

1968

📺 **THE DOMINATORS**

Director Manus of the Seventh Council experiments with atomic fission 172 years ago, detonating an atom bomb on a small island in the Southern hemisphere. This becomes the "Island of Death," a monument to the follies of war, visited only by students.

1968

📺 **THE DOMINATORS**

The Doctor, Jamie, and Zoe land on the Island of Death at the same time as some sightseers and a group of students. The radiation has suddenly vanished. The incurious Dulcians accept this without need for further investigation.

1968

📺 **THE DOMINATORS**

The Doctor discovers the radiation has been absorbed by the Dominators and Quarks. They have landed on the Island and are preparing to drill a hole and irradiate the whole planet so that they can harvest the energy. The Doctor destroys the Dominator ship and turns the Island into a volcano.

PLANET OF THE GONDS

The Gonds lived on a world with two suns and low gravity, relative to Earth. The most important area was known as the Wasteland—a quarrylike zone, with mica for soil and a sulfurous smell in the air. The Gonds believed that the Wasteland was uninhabitable, and that had been the case, but the poisons in the air and soil had cleared.

HISTORY

In times of legend, the Gonds had been conquered by the Krotons. When they had resisted, the Krotons had rained poison on them, killing many hundreds of Gonds and turning the soil black.

After that time the Gonds had lived in a settlement close to the Wasteland, in low triangular buildings with triangular windows. The Krotons were never seen but maintained a "special area" in the settlement. They claimed they had raised the Gonds up from being primitives. This had been achieved by teaching machines in the Learning Hall. The goal of every Gond was to be selected as a "high mind"—if they passed a series of intelligence tests, a Gond was admitted into the Krotons' special area.

FIRST APPEARANCE
The Krotons *(1968–69)*

STATUS
Rebuilding after invasion

FACT FILE

THE KROTONS
The TARDIS landed in the Wasteland, and the second Doctor, Jamie, and Zoe saw a Gond disintegrated by some kind of gas jet. They wandered into the Gond settlement, baffling locals who thought nothing could survive there. The Doctor reported that the air in the Wasteland had a "rotten egg" smell but was perfectly breathable. He quickly worked out that the "special area" was a crashed spacecraft, the *Dynatrope*.

THE KROTONS
The Krotons were boxy, crystalline creatures who preferred the dark and had trouble seeing in bright light. They were harvesting the "high minds" for mental energy, which they used for fuel. The Doctor was able to use chemicals he found in the Wasteland to make sulfuric acid, dissolving the Krotons and freeing the Gonds from their slavery.

THE KROTONS
Zoe felt the Gond buildings had an Incan influence, but there's no evidence that the people of Earth ever had any contact with the Gonds.

ALIEN BODIES
The Krotons were from the planet Krosi-Aspai-Core. The central command of the Kroton Absolute was known as the First Lattice. They mimicked their prey's form; those on the Gond planet resembled a human servo robot they'd encountered. The Krotons fought a war with the Metatraxi.

RETURN OF THE KROTONS
The sixth Doctor defeated the Krotons on Onyakis by inducing hypoxia in their human captives, disrupting the flow of mental energy fueling the Kroton equipment.

BEHIND THE SCENES

The Krotons (Robert Holmes, 1968–69) was elevated from a rather forgettable story when a UK television repeat in the early 1980s made it the only story starring the second Doctor that many fans had seen in the era before home video. Krotons also made a memorable appearance in the book *Alien Bodies* (Lawrence Miles, 1997) and were the antagonists in the audio *Return of the Krotons* (Nicholas Briggs, 2008).

ABOVE: The second Doctor.

OPPOSITE: The Krotons are among the Doctor's most ruthless and fearsome foes.

JACONDA

There is a Jocondan legend that when the Queen offended the Sun God, he sent a swarm of half-human, half-slug creatures to ravage the planet. The Jocondans only survived when the Sun God relented and sent a great drought. The planet recovered and it returned to its natural state of thick forest, rich in animal life. The fourth Doctor learned of this legend when he visited his old friend Azmael, a Time Lord who had retired to become Master of Jaconda.

ABOVE: Mestor sits on the throne of Jaconda with a Jocondan in attendance.

HISTORY

When the newly regenerated sixth Doctor returned to Jaconda, he learned that the legends were true. Gastropod eggs had lain dormant—and now they had hatched. The head Gastropod, Mestor, had powerful telepathic abilities and had used them to take control of Azmael. They consumed all the plant life and sucked the nutrients from the soil. The Jocondans, a race of birdlike humanoids with silver skin, were condemned to worldwide famine. Mestor had an ambitious plan to move two other planets near to Jaconda. He led people to believe that he was doing this to make the planets fertile and to use them to feed the Jocondans. Mestor's plan was in fact far more ambitious…

FIRST APPEARANCE
The Twin Dilemma (1984)

LOCATION
The innermost planet of three in its star system

INHABITANTS
The Jocondans, the Gastropods, Azmael

STATUS
Rebuilding, free from dictatorship

TIMELINE

📺 *THE TWIN DILEMMA*
👤 SIXTH DOCTOR
✒️ ANTHONY STEVEN

Azmael had been one of the Doctor's tutors, the best he ever had. The fourth Doctor and Azmael later met on Jaconda, and Azmael became so drunk that the Doctor threw him into a fountain to clear his head.

1984

1984

📺 *THE TWIN DILEMMA*

Jaconda is advanced enough to have a spaceport, the Omega Intersection.

1984

📺 *THE TWIN DILEMMA*

Mestor sends Azmael to Earth, commanding him to kidnap the Sylvest twins, young mathematical geniuses, the only ones able to complete the calculations that will allow the outer planets to move into Jaconda's orbit. Earth launches interceptors, but Mestor destroys them.

1984

📺 *THE TWIN DILEMMA*

The Doctor and his allies travel to Jaconda and see firsthand evidence of the Gastropods' destruction. The Doctor realizes Mestor will create solar disturbances that will destroy Jaconda. This is the Gastropods' plan: their eggs will survive and be ejected into deep space. They will spread throughout the universe, hatching wherever they land.

1984

📺 *THE TWIN DILEMMA*

Azmael and the twins reach a safehouse on the barren asteroid of Titan III. By coincidence, the Doctor and Peri arrive there and discover the wreckage of a destroyed interceptor—and its injured pilot, Hugo Lang.

KARFEL

The surface of Karfel is gray, dusty, and quite possibly airless. The planet has a small population living in pyramid-shaped buildings. Society is centered around the Citadel, a vast pyramid topped with a squat tower, which seats the Council and 500 citizens. Below the surface, things are more lively, with caverns of lurid purple-streaked rocks inhabited by eels (the Morlox). In a neighboring solar system is Bandril, home of the Bandrils, natural allies of the Karfelons. One of the rooms of the Citadel is given over to beautiful plants from Bandril, such as the dracowlis, the "flower of many faces."

HISTORY

The third Doctor and Jo visited Karfel and saved the planet. A couple of generations later, the sixth Doctor and Peri arrived to discover that the planet was now under the dictatorial rule of an old man, the Borad—only ever seen on a television screen. Despite constant surveillance, armed android Guardoliers, and the threat of being thrown into the timelash and scattered throughout history, dissent was brewing. The Borad's obsession with time-travel experiments, and the withholding of grain supplies from the famine-stricken Bandrils, was causing many to quietly question their leader. Those loyal to the Borad were becoming increasingly more ruthless.

BEHIND THE SCENES

While *Doctor Who* books, audios, and comic strips have been keen to expand on many references to missing adventures, we have never seen the third Doctor's visit to Karfel depicted.

TOP RIGHT: The sixth Doctor.

ABOVE RIGHT: The third Doctor and Jo on an untelevised adventure.

LEFT: H. G. Wells's experience on Karfel proved inspirational.

FIRST APPEARANCE
Timelash *(1985)*

INHABITANTS
Karfelons, Borad (exiled), Morlox, purple acid-spitting flowers

STATUS
Rebuilding after years of tyranny

TIMELINE

1985

📺 *TIMELASH*

👤 SIXTH DOCTOR

✎ GLEN MCCOY

The Doctor and Jo uncover experiments being conducted by the mad scientist Megelen on the Morlox, savage reptilian eels that live in the caverns. The Doctor is considered to have saved the planet, and a large mural of him is painted in the Citadel.

1985

📺 *TIMELASH*

The Doctor traps Megelen in the timelash and sends him to 12th-century Scotland, to Loch Ness, where he will reach his true destiny, becoming a half-seen monster.

1985

📺 *TIMELASH*

The Doctor and Peri become trapped in the kontron tunnel in time formed by the timelash when a female rebel, Vena, fell into it. She appears as a ghostly vision, and the Doctor is able to follow her to Scotland in 1885. Her arrival is seen by a young H. G. Wells.

1985

📺 *TIMELASH*

All four return to Karfel. The Doctor is shocked by the changes to the planet and soon discovers that the Borad is not the old man seen in the television images but is a half-man, half-Morlox creature altered by his own experiments. This is the scientist Megelen, and he is planning to create a race of superbeings to lead conquests.

KASTRIA

Kastria is in our galaxy, at coordinates 7438000W811212729-double 1-E-8E by 4111309-11-5, with an Earthlike atmosphere and radiation count that is "a bit high." According to the Kastrian scientist Eldrad, it was a "cold, inhospitable planet," with "solar winds" dehydrating the planet. While survivors huddled in thermal caves beneath the surface, Eldrad built spatial or solar barriers to keep out the hurricane-force winds, and a "crystalline silicon form" for the Kastrian race itself, making it all but indestructible. He also granted them inexhaustible energy drawn from the planet's core and machines that replenished the earth and atmosphere.

FIRST APPEARANCE
The Hand of Fear *(1976)*

INHABITANTS
Kastrians

STATUS
Dead

HISTORY

Eldrad had dreams of using a fleet of starships to conquer the galaxy. When the Kastrians refused to depose King Rokon in Eldrad's favor, the scientist deactivated the barriers, killing almost all his people. The Race Banks were used to store 100 million crystal particles—using the Regeneration Chamber, a new race would one day be born. As the last systems began to fail, King Rokon ordered that Eldrad be executed. They faced the problem that he had given himself an almost indestructible body. If one particle remained, it could regenerate if exposed to enough radiation. Eldrad was launched "beyond all solar systems" in an Obliteration Module. The Module had to be detonated at 19 spans—there was a one in three million chance Eldrad survived.

RIGHT: The fourth Doctor and Sarah Jane parted ways after visiting Kastria.

TIMELINE

THE HAND OF FEAR

FOURTH DOCTOR

BOB BAKER & DAVID MARTIN

Sarah finds Eldrad's hand amidst the rubble of an English quarry. Eldrad is able to take mental possession of her and guide her to a nuclear reactor. There, he absorbs the radiation, regenerating a beautiful female body for himself.

1976

THE HAND OF FEAR

Eldrad forces the Doctor to take him to Kastria. However, the world has been dead for 150 million years. Rokon has left a message, telling Eldrad that they agreed to commit collective suicide, destroying the race banks rather than risking Eldrad returning and establishing a tyranny.

1976

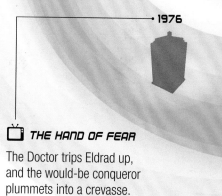

THE HAND OF FEAR

The Doctor trips Eldrad up, and the would-be conqueror plummets into a crevasse.

2013

ELDRAD MUST DIE!

Other fragments of Eldrad have survived—Mulkris the Executioner hunts them down and finally kills the original.

2013

ELDRAD MUST DIE!

FIFTH DOCTOR

MARC PLATT

Eldrad survives his encounter with the Doctor and crawls up out of the crevasse. Installing himself in the throne room, utterly mad, he spends his days bawling orders at the crumbled remains of the other Kastrians.

2001

THE QUANTUM ARCHANGEL

SIXTH DOCTOR

CRAIG HINTON

Hundreds of millions of years ago, the Kastrians fought alongside countless other ancient races in the Millennium War but saw their fleet wiped out and a devastating attack on their planet from the Mad Mind of Bophemeral.

LAKERTYA

What we see of Lakertya is an area of broken slate and small lakes under a pale pink sky. It is home to the Lakertyans, yellow reptile people with long crested heads, scaly faces, and golden manes of hair. Renegade Time Lord the Rani made the planet her base and used the Lakertyans as slave labor. Her verdict on them was harsh: "A race so indolent they can't be bothered to bury their dead ... a simple, primitive society, and the benevolent climate has induced lethargy. They've failed to realize their full potential."

FIRST APPEARANCE
Time and the Rani *(1987)*

INHABITANTS
Lakertyans, insects

STATUS
Rebuilding, free from dictatorship

HISTORY

The Rani worked many of the Lakertyans to death, building a headquarters for her. She harbored no hatred for them; she was simply a creature of scientific detachment, concerned with ends rather than means. She was also cautious. While few Lakertyans were inclined to rebel, she laid a minefield around her headquarters, fitted the locals with anklets that could reduce someone to a skeleton at the touch of a button, and set a globe of killer insects in the ceiling of their Centre of Leisure. Worst of all, she had a small army of vicious batpeople—the Tetraps, a race with four eyes, one on each side of their heads. The Tetraps hailed from the planet Tetrapyriarbus.

LEFT: The newly regenerated seventh Doctor and Mel outside the Rani's lair.

TIMELINE

📺 TIME AND THE RANI

The Doctor prevents the missile from launching—it explodes on the Launchpad, killing the brain. The Rani is captured by the angry Tetraps, and the Doctor returns the scientists to their own times.

1987

📺 TIME AND THE RANI
👤 SIXTH AND SEVENTH DOCTORS
✎ PIP & JANE BAKER

The Rani shoots down the Doctor's TARDIS with a Navigational Guidance System Distorter, which triggers the Doctor's regeneration into his seventh persona. The Rani takes advantage of his confusion to trick him into helping her complete a mysterious scientific project.

1987

1987

📺 TIME AND THE RANI

The answer is that exploding the strange-matter asteroid will create a shell of chronons around Lakertya, transforming the entire planet into a giant brain. This mental power would become a Time Manipulator, capable of turning the whole of time into an experiment in which the Rani could alter the results.

1987

📺 TIME AND THE RANI

Meanwhile, Mel wanders in the wilderness around the Rani's HQ. She finds Beyus, the only Lakertyan resisting the Rani and her Tetraps—a fact that makes him as disgusted with his own people as he is with the alien intruders.

1987

1987

📺 TIME AND THE RANI

The Rani plans to fire a missile at an asteroid made of strange matter. She also needs the Doctor's knowledge of time travel.

1987

📺 TIME AND THE RANI

The Doctor recovers his wits and tries to piece together what the Rani is attempting to do. She has assembled a group of geniuses from Earth history, including Hypatia, Pasteur, Einstein, Darwin, Za Panato, Ari Centos, and Niels Bohr.

📺 TIME AND THE RANI

The Rani has created a giant brain that acts as a gestalt repository for the mental power of the geniuses.

LOGOPOLIS

Logopolis was, according to the Doctor, a "quiet little planet," a cold, dusty world, home to "a retiring people." They were known for their mastery of block transfer computation, a technique for converting measurements of objects into precise mathematical models, which could then be overlaid as space-time events. When the Doctor visited in 1981, they had just acquired an exact copy of a radio telescope and computer from Earth in that period, as their researches required it. They were led by the Monitor, from a facility called the Central Register. The planet's population was essentially a living computer.

FIRST APPEARANCE
Logopolis *(1981)*

STATUS
Destroyed

HISTORY

The Logopolitans did not normally use computers as part of this process. The Monitor explained that "Block transfer computation is a complex discipline, way beyond the capabilities of simple machines. It requires all the subtleties of the living mind." As the process changed the physical world, it would change a computer, causing it to malfunction. While computers were used for preparation and recording, the programs the Logopolitans devised were never run on them. Instead, the Logopolitans did their work on abacuses, intoned the computations, and lived a monklike existence in the doorways of small cubicles. They never smiled or talked to each other. In the words of the Monitor, "We are a people driven not by individual need but by mathematical necessity. The language of the numbers is as much as we need."

RIGHT: Adric, Nyssa, and Tegan were brought together on Logopolis and saw the end of the fourth Doctor's era.

TIMELINE

📺 **LOGOPOLIS**

1981

The Doctor, his companions, and the Master hurry to Earth and the original radio telescope. If they can beam the signal to the CVE, they will save the universe. The Master attempts to blackmail the universe with the threat of total destruction, but the Doctor sacrifices his life to prevent this.

📺 **LOGOPOLIS**

👤 **FOURTH DOCTOR**

✎ **CHRISTOPHER H. BIDMEAD**

1981

The Doctor plans to take the TARDIS to Logopolis so that its chameleon circuit can be repaired. The Master follows him there, intent on learning the secrets of a project the Logopolitans are working on.

1981

📺 **LOGOPOLIS**

The universe is dissolving around them, and Logopolis itself falls victim to this, as does Nyssa's home planet of Traken (p. 220).

1981

📺 **LOGOPOLIS**

As he kills a number of mathematicians and otherwise disrupts the smooth running of the calculations, the Monitor is forced to reveal the secret of Logopolis.

1981

📺 **LOGOPOLIS**

Any closed system is subject to entropy—that includes the universe itself. The only thing keeping it from that fate is the work of Logopolis. The people there have punched holes in the universe (charged vacuum emboidments, or CVEs) to open it up. Their secret project is to devise a more permanent solution. The radio telescope they have copied has been sending signals to keep the CVEs open, but the Master's work means that all but one is now closed.

THE NIMON PLANETS

FIRST APPEARANCE
 The Horns of Nimon *(1979)*

INHABITANTS
The Nimon and their victims

The Nimon are a race of hyperadvanced beings who strongly resemble humanoid bulls—the minotaurs of Greek myth. Fittingly, their complexes are labyrinthine in nature, and unwary visitors find themselves trapped and terrified. The Nimon feed on the binding energy of organic compounds, so they maintain larders of frozen humans, which they drain until the bodies are reduced to husks. They feed on whole worlds, destroying everything and everyone. They then move to the next world.

HISTORY

The Nimon have a modus operandi—one Nimon arrives on a great or once-great world and promises powerful technology in return for "tributes"—rare material needed for their machines, such as hymetusite. They offered Soldeed of Skonnos, for example, "the power to conquer a galaxy" for what seemed like little cost. They secretly build a black hole near the planet and a powerful transmat system. This connects to the last planet the Nimon ravaged and allows more Nimon to arrive in transmat pods shaped like eggs. Each set of Nimon builds equipment to summon two more pods; their numbers grow exponentially until they are swarming across the planet like a plague of locusts.

BELOW LEFT: The Nimon, one of the most powerful adversaries the Doctor has encountered.

BELOW: The eleventh Doctor said his goodbyes to Amy and Rory after the experience with the Minotaur.

TIMELINE

📺 **"THE GOD COMPLEX"**

👤 ELEVENTH DOCTOR

✏️ TOBY WHITHOUSE

2011

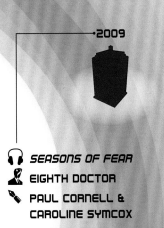

The Doctor, Amy, and Rory arrive in what looks like a large English hotel but is actually a shifting maze, stalked by a minotaurlike creature that demands praise. This is a hologram within a prison ship, and the creature is a cousin of the Nimon.

📺 **THE HORNS OF NIMON**

👤 FOURTH DOCTOR

✏️ ANTHONY READ

1979

There is a civil war on Skonnos (a "nasty race of people" known to the Doctor), and only the army survives. The one living scientist, Soldeed, builds the Power Complex for the Nimon in the heart of the Skonnan capital, who promises him technology that will forge a Second Skonnon Empire.

2009

🎧 **SEASONS OF FEAR**

👤 EIGHTH DOCTOR

✏️ PAUL CORNELL & CAROLINE SYMCOX

The Doctor and Charley travel to 1930s Singapore, Roman Britain, the time of Edward the Confessor, and the Hellfire Club as they fight a Nimon agent, the immortal Grayle.

1979

📺 **THE HORNS OF NIMON**

The Doctor, Romana, and K9 become drawn toward the black hole the Nimon is building near Skonnos, as is a ship containing the final tribute from Aneth. The Doctor rescues the ship, and it completes its journey to Skonnos. The Doctor and Romana meet Soldeed.

1979

📺 **THE HORNS OF NIMON**

The people of Skonnos worship the Nimon as "the Great God of Skonnos." Fearing the Nimon's wrath, the people of nearby Aneth—formerly enslaved by the First Skonnon Empire—are cowed into supplying Skonnos with human sacrifices and hymetusite (a highly radioactive crystalline fuel).

1979

📺 **THE HORNS OF NIMON**

Romana travels to Crinoth, a world already ravaged by the Nimon, and sees for herself what is in store for Skonnos. She and the Doctor manage to destroy the Power Complex, preventing the Nimon from spreading further.

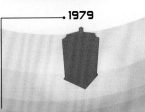

OGRON PLANET

The Ogrons are seven-foot apemen who've served as henchmen for the Daleks, the Master, and the Remote. They are strong and stupid. They are able to use blasters and follow simple instructions, but are easily fooled and cowed by authority. They are also literally weak-headed—a blow to the top of the skull could knock out an Ogron. Some have suggested that the Ogrons are feigning stupidity—if so, they're remarkably convincing. A couple of Ogrons have been augmented to genius-level intellects, and their combination of brains and brawn has made them formidable opponents.

BEHIND THE SCENES

While the dialogue, script, and novelization all refer to "the monster" as reptilian, the special effects budget didn't run to that, and what we see looks more like a large, bloblike orange creature.

HISTORY

The Ogrons come from a rocky planet at galactic coordinates 2349-6784, "a barren and uninteresting planet on the remote fringes of the galaxy," in a sector that 26th-century humans thought was completely uninhabited, and that you could not get to from Earth without passing through territory claimed by the Draconians. The Daleks and Master knew the Ogrons lived in scattered communities; the Doctor did not know the location of their planet, but knew that they worked as mercenaries for a number of different employers. The Ogrons were not the dominant life form; there was a large Ogron-eating reptile. They lacked the imagination to call it anything except "the monster," but they did erect an idol to it. They call their planet "Braah," but no one else does.

BELOW: The powerful Ogrons were used as muscle across the galaxy.

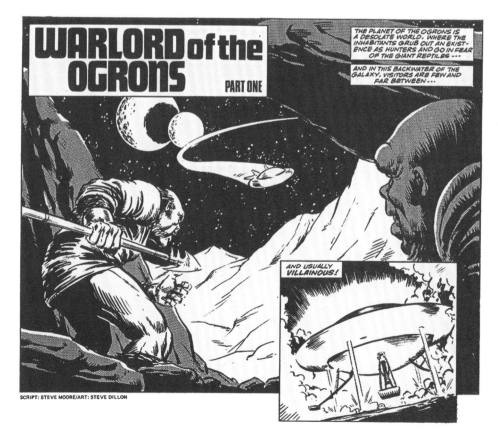

WARLORD of the OGRONS PART ONE

THE PLANET OF THE OGRONS IS A DESOLATE WORLD, WHERE THE INHABITANTS GRUB OUT AN EXISTENCE AS HUNTERS AND GO IN FEAR OF THE GIANT REPTILES ...

AND IN THIS BACKWATER OF THE GALAXY, VISITORS ARE FEW AND FAR BETWEEN ...

AND USUALLY VILLAINOUS!

SCRIPT: STEVE MOORE/ART: STEVE DILLON

FIRST APPEARANCE
Ogrons: Day of the Daleks (1972)
Ogron planet: Frontier in Space (1973)

INHABITANTS
Ogrons, "the monster"

STATUS
Unchanged

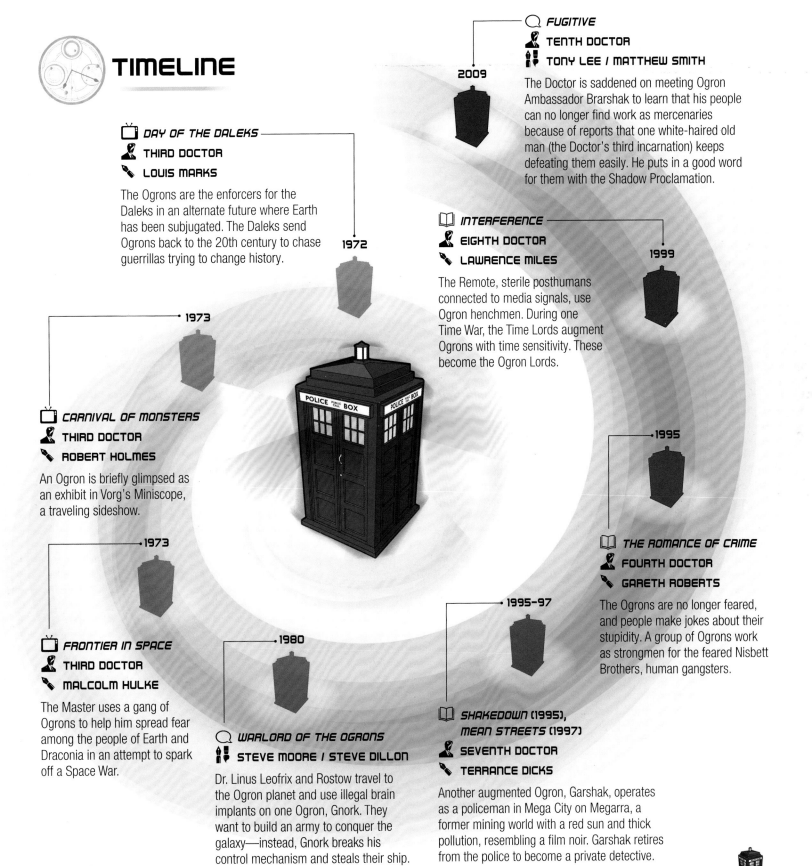

TIMELINE

FUGITIVE
TENTH DOCTOR
TONY LEE / MATTHEW SMITH

2009

The Doctor is saddened on meeting Ogron Ambassador Brarshak to learn that his people can no longer find work as mercenaries because of reports that one white-haired old man (the Doctor's third incarnation) keeps defeating them easily. He puts in a good word for them with the Shadow Proclamation.

DAY OF THE DALEKS
THIRD DOCTOR
LOUIS MARKS

1972

The Ogrons are the enforcers for the Daleks in an alternate future where Earth has been subjugated. The Daleks send Ogrons back to the 20th century to chase guerrillas trying to change history.

INTERFERENCE
EIGHTH DOCTOR
LAWRENCE MILES

1999

The Remote, sterile posthumans connected to media signals, use Ogron henchmen. During one Time War, the Time Lords augment Ogrons with time sensitivity. These become the Ogron Lords.

1973

CARNIVAL OF MONSTERS
THIRD DOCTOR
ROBERT HOLMES

An Ogron is briefly glimpsed as an exhibit in Vorg's Miniscope, a traveling sideshow.

1995

THE ROMANCE OF CRIME
FOURTH DOCTOR
GARETH ROBERTS

The Ogrons are no longer feared, and people make jokes about their stupidity. A group of Ogrons work as strongmen for the feared Nisbett Brothers, human gangsters.

1973

FRONTIER IN SPACE
THIRD DOCTOR
MALCOLM HULKE

The Master uses a gang of Ogrons to help him spread fear among the people of Earth and Draconia in an attempt to spark off a Space War.

1980

WARLORD OF THE OGRONS
STEVE MOORE / STEVE DILLON

Dr. Linus Leofrix and Rostow travel to the Ogron planet and use illegal brain implants on one Ogron, Gnork. They want to build an army to conquer the galaxy—instead, Gnork breaks his control mechanism and steals their ship.

1995–97

SHAKEDOWN (1995), MEAN STREETS (1997)
SEVENTH DOCTOR
TERRANCE DICKS

Another augmented Ogron, Garshak, operates as a policeman in Mega City on Megarra, a former mining world with a red sun and thick pollution, resembling a film noir. Garshak retires from the police to become a private detective.

PELADON

Peladon is a small, barbaric world in a future era, when the Earth is just one planet in the mighty and peaceful Galactic Federation. The third Doctor visited it twice. Peladon is ruled from the Citadel, a castle seemingly carved from the rock halfway up a mountain held sacred by the native Pels. The mountain is a honeycomb of mines. What we see of Peladon is concentrated around the Citadel—perhaps not typical of the planet—where it is consistently dark and wracked by electrical storms and strong winds.

FIRST APPEARANCE
The Curse of Peladon *(1972)*

CURRENT STATUS
Federation member ruled by Pelleas and the Doctor's former companion, Erimem

HISTORY

Peladon is "many light years from Earth," but at the time of the Doctor's first visit, the King (also named Peladon) was half-human, as his father had married an Earthwoman. It is a feudal monarchy in which the King or Queen has absolute power—within the strictures of the holy laws of Peladon—and takes advice from both a Chancellor and a High Priest. There is also a Grand Council and a court of nobles. While the Pels are aware that other societies strive for gender equality, only men of rank and women of noble blood are allowed in the throne room. The Pels are superstitious and they worship Aggedor, a mythical Royal Beast resembling a fierce tusked bear or boar. There is a dispute on the planet between those who are keen to become a member of the Galactic Federation and those who prefer to preserve the old ways and remain isolated.[1]

LEFT: The remote storm-wracked world of Peladon was of huge strategic importance.

FOOTNOTE
[1] The Curse of Peladon

TIMELINE

THE PRISONER OF PELADON

THIRD DOCTOR

CAVAN SCOTT & MARK WRIGHT

2009

Soon after joining the Federation, King Peladon finds room for Martian refugees fleeing a coup, including Lixgar, the young woman who is rightful heir.

THE CURSE OF PELADON

THIRD DOCTOR

BRIAN HAYLES

The Doctor and Jo help King Peladon to achieve Federation membership for his planet. The high priest Hepesh and Arcturus had tried to thwart this by playing on the fears of the people. The Doctor discovers that Aggedor is real, not a legend, and this is taken as greatly auspicious.

1972

2008

THE BRIDE OF PELADON

FIFTH DOCTOR

BARNABY EDWARDS

Fifty years later still, the Doctor, Peri, and Erimem (daughter of an ancient Egyptian pharaoh) discover that Peladon has been visited by the Osirians, the inspiration for the Egyptian gods. The tomb of Sekhmet is disturbed by miners. After defeating that threat, Erimem elects to remain behind as the Queen of Peladon, bride of King Pelleas.

1974

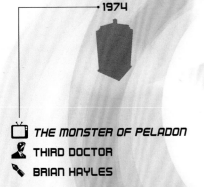

THE MONSTER OF PELADON

THIRD DOCTOR

BRIAN HAYLES

Fifty years after his previous visit, the Doctor and Sarah Jane find Peladon in the grip of a panic as the Ghost of Aggedor is appearing and killing people. The Federation is at war with Galaxy Five and keen to exploit the mineral wealth of Peladon for the war effort.

1994

1974

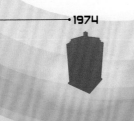

THE MONSTER OF PELADON

A group of renegade Ice Warriors are in league with Galaxy Five. When the Doctor exposes them, Galaxy Five quickly sues for peace.

LEGACY

SEVENTH DOCTOR

GARY RUSSELL

The Doctor, Ace, and Benny visit Peladon 50 years later. The ancient Diadem, a weapon of great power, has been brought to the planet. King Tarrol is shocked by the resulting devastation and wants to leave the Federation.

PELADON—WORLDS OF THE GALACTIC FEDERATION

The Galactic Federation that Peladon joined was an alliance of planets that had seen "war and violence" in their pasts—in the history of their own planets and between their planets—and had come together to cooperate instead.

📖 LEGACY

The Federation was formed after the collapse of the first Earth Empire (which fell around the year 3000). The Federation Chair was based on Jupiter's moon Io.

📺 THE CURSE OF PELADON

The planets were all signatories to the Galactic Charter, a set of rules that all member planets had to abide by in their dealings with each other.

📺 THE CURSE OF PELADON

Under the Galactic Articles of Peace, paragraph 29, subsection 2, planets have full sovereignty and Federation officials cannot violate or subvert local laws or customs. In the case of Peladon, for example, this meant they could not stop the Doctor from being sentenced to trial by combat, to the death, with the King's champion—however barbaric they found the practice.

📺 THE MONSTER OF PELADON

While the Federation was dedicated to peace, they "were the victims of a vicious and unprovoked attack by the forces of Galaxy Five." Little is known of this enemy, except that they refused to negotiate with the Federation.

📺 THE MONSTER OF PELADON

Federation technology is "based on" trisilicate, a glowing crystal used in "electronic circuitry, heat shields, inert microcell fibers, radionic crystals."

KNOWN MEMBERS OF THE GALACTIC FEDERATION

THE CURSE OF PELADON,
THE MONSTER OF PELADON

Alpha Centauri: A race of hermaphrodite hexapods, Alpha Centaurians have one giant eye in a spherical green head. The ambassador we see has a high-pitched voice and is rather jittery and over-excitable. They would appear to live longer than humans, as the same ambassador was present for the third Doctor's return visit to Peladon, 50 years after the first.

THE CURSE OF PELADON

Arcturus (p. 170): The delegate from Arcturus is the Arcturan species that resembles a shrunken head and needs a life-support system. Arcturus itself has few minerals.

THE CURSE OF PELADON

Earth: "A remote and unattractive planet" at this point, according to Alpha Centauri. This is perhaps an odd thing to say, as Alpha Centauri is one of the closest solar systems to our own, and Earth and Mars are even closer neighbors.

THE CURSE OF PELADON

Mars: While the Ice Warriors refer to themselves as "Martians" and call their own world "Mars," we could infer that they're actually from the planet that they settled after being displaced by the human race (pp. 62–63). "Mars and the world of Arcturus are old enemies," according to the Ice Lord Izlyr.

LEGACY

The Pakhars were members after that, and the Cybermen were long thought extinct by this time.

THE DARK PATH

Draconia (p. 182), Terileptus (p. 216), Veltroch, and Thoros Beta (p. 218) were all members of the Federation around the 35th century.

THE MONSTER OF PELADON

Vega Nexos: A race of practical mining engineers, the people of Vega have large eyes and manes.

THE MONSTER OF PELADON

At this time, there are reactionary factions of Ice Warriors who yearn for a return of Martian independence and military glory.

THE ROBOTOV EMPIRE

Halfway across the cosmos and millennia in the future, an entire sector of one galaxy is the dominion of the Robotov Empire. Aesthetically very similar to pre-Revolutionary Russia, the hub of the Empire is the Autumn Palace, which was constructed on a specially built platform in space. It is a luxurious complex, a home fit for the Tsar and Tsarina. There, elaborate meals are laid out on beautiful plates by servants. However, the meals are in fact only models made from Capo di Monte porcelain, and the only thing in the elegant wine goblets is dust.

HISTORY

The Robotovs may look human, and they have thoughts and emotions, but they are intricate mechanisms—androids. Centuries before, the robot servants overthrew their human masters. People were transferred to work in the numerous satellites, both natural and artificial, that orbit the palace, supplying resources to the Palace and the wider Empire. Many humans were sent to the caverns of the Bio-Moon, which generated energy for the palace. Robots and humans settled into this new pattern, and it became heresy to suggest that the robots had originally been designed and built by humans. The robots themselves thought the idea was absurd.

RIGHT: The cover of *Tsar Wars*.

BELOW: Tom Baker as Rasputin in *Nicholas and Alexandra*.

BEHIND THE SCENES

The first story in the *Serpent Crest* series of radio plays by Paul Magrs saw Tom Baker in the double role of the fourth Doctor and Father Gregory. Gregory was, in turn, closely based on Baker's portrayal of Rasputin in the 1974 movie *Nicholas and Alexandra*. Nicholas was played by Michael Jayston, who also played the Tsar in *Tsar Wars*.

FIRST APPEARANCE
🎧 Tsar Wars *(2011)*

STATUS
Uncertain

TIMELINE

The Doctor manages to steal the Skishtari egg, which has been implanted in Alex and would have hatched in ten years, releasing a Skishtari Emperor—a dragonlike creature that would devour everyone in a whole sector of space.

2011

🎧 *TSAR WARS*

👤 **FOURTH DOCTOR**

✎ **PAUL MAGRS**

The Doctor and his friend Fenella Wibbsey are kidnapped by servo robots and whisked across the universe to the heart of the Robotov Empire. The Doctor is mistaken for Father Gregory, and taken to Alex, the toddler son of the Tsarina—and a cyborg whose organic body is failing.

2011

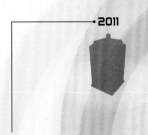

2011

🎧 *TSAR WARS*

Father Gregory has been a favorite at the court. Three years before, though, he was exiled and became a rabble-rouser on the Bio-Moon, spreading discontent among the human workers. This was not what he wanted to be: he had conceived Alex with the Tsarina to create a future leader who would unite the two factions.

2011

🎧 *TSAR WARS*

Gregory is in the thrall of the Skishtari, a race of evil serpents who want to take control of the Robotov Empire. They are advanced and vicious. Gregory sacrifices his life to give Alex his heart, thereby saving his life.

2011

🎧 *TSAR WARS*

The humans are now intent on storming the Autumn Palace, and the Tsar—who is furious with Gregory—plans to counter-attack using disruptors and war rockets.

RUTA III

The Rutans originated on Ruta III, an icy world. They feed on electricity, can survive in extreme cold, and can climb sheer surfaces. They are a hive-mind, ruled by the Rutan Queen. Earthmen have tended to see more of the Sontarans than their enemy, the Rutans, although Rutans may be hiding among us—since the early 20th century, they have possessed the "chameleon factor," a metamorphosis technique that allows them to shift their natural form (a sickly green, glowing jellyfish) to resemble individuals they have studied.

FIRST APPEARANCE

📺 *Rutans:* Horror of Fang Rock (1977)

📖 *Ruta III:* Shakedown *(1995)*

STATUS

At war

BELOW: The Rutan Host on their home planet.

HISTORY

For most of recorded history, the Sontarans have been at war with the Rutans, and the Sontaran–Rutan War has seen both races win great victories and suffer great losses. At the beginning of the 20th century, the Doctor thought the Rutans were on the verge of defeat,[1] but around 100 years later, the tables had turned and it was the Sontarans about to lose.[2] The Doctor eventually negotiated a peace, despite great skepticism from the Time Lords, who hosted the conference.[3] The two races eventually merged, becoming "a race of goblin shapeshifters."[4]

BEHIND THE SCENES

Although often mentioned in stories featuring the Sontarans, the Rutans have only been seen on screen once (as well as in the fan video-turned-novel *Shakedown*).

FOOTNOTES
[1] 📺 *Horror of Fang Rock* • [2] 📺 "The Sontaran Stratagem" / "The Poison Sky" • [3] 📖 *The Infinity Doctors* • [4] 📖 *Hope*

TIMELINE

HORROR OF FANG ROCK
FOURTH DOCTOR
TERRANCE DICKS

A Rutan scout ship crashes near Fang Rock, the site of an isolated lighthouse in the English Channel. It takes the form of the lighthouse keeper, Reuben, and concludes Earth would be a good place to launch a counterattack on the Sontarans. It sends a signal to the Rutan Battlefleet.

1977

2008

THE TAKING OF CHELSEA 426
TENTH DOCTOR
DAVID LLEWELLYN

The Doctor thwarts the plans of both the Sontarans and the Rutans at a Chelsea Flower Show held in the 26th century on a platform in Saturn's atmosphere.

1995

1977

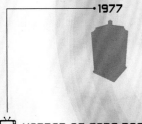

HORROR OF FANG ROCK

The Doctor knows that Earth would be destroyed in the crossfire if the Rutans got ahold of the lighthouse's lantern and were able to convert it into a primitive laser beam to destroy the Mothership.

1995

LORDS OF THE STORM
FIFTH DOCTOR
DAVID A MCINTEE

As he exposes a Rutan spy on a human colony world the Doctor realizes he is endangering humanity.

SHAKEDOWN
SEVENTH DOCTOR
TERRANCE DICKS

The Doctor travels to the Rutan home world in order to offer them information from the Sontaran computers in return for a pledge to leave the human colonies alone. The Rutan Queen agrees.

THE SHADOW PROCLAMATION

The Shadow Proclamation is the name of an intergalactic—possibly universal—legal charter, as well as the organization that enforces the laws in that charter. Or, as the Doctor put it, they're "outer space police." They claim to be able to operate "right across the universe." They are based in a complex constructed from three asteroids held together by artificial bridges. They are led by a humanoid who appears to be albino and is known as the "Shadow Architect."[1]

HISTORY

Invoking the Shadow Proclamation doesn't always work, but it is a clear sign that the person doing so is aware of galactic law and places the onus on the other party to behave in a way consistent with the expected standards. There's no evidence that Shadow Proclamation forces have the ability to time travel. They were active in both ancient Egypt[2] and the Classical period,[3] so they have been around for many thousands of years. The Shadow Proclamation was given strict rulings on the subject of manipulations in time and space before the Time Lords began fighting the Last Great Time War.[4]

FIRST APPEARANCE

(mentioned) "Rose" (2005)
Asteroid: "The Stolen Earth" (2009)

STATUS

Actively policing the universe

ABOVE: The tenth Doctor.

LEFT: A Sycorax, from a race scornful of the Shadow Proclamation.

BELOW: The tenth Doctor was once tried and imprisoned by the Shadow Proclamation.

OPPOSITE: The ninth Doctor and Rose.

FOOTNOTES
[1] "The Stolen Earth" • [2] *Agent Provocateur* •
[3] "The Fires of Pompei" • [4] *Fugitive*

FACT FILE

📺 "ROSE,"
📺 "THE CHRISTMAS INVASION"

Convention 15 is invoked when one party to hostilities demands a temporary cease-fire so there can be negotiations. When Rose tried this on the Sycorax, they weren't impressed.

📺 "THE ELEVENTH HOUR"

Article 57 bans the destruction of Level Five worlds (Earth is a Level Five world).

📺 "PARTNERS IN CRIME"

It is also illegal to seed a Level Five world (i.e., use it as a spawning ground).

🔍 AGENT PROVOCATEUR

The Shadow Proclamation dispatched a giant feline alien, Bubastion, to oversee the development of Earth from ancient Egypt, but he failed to save the life of the Pharaoh.

📺 "THE STOLEN EARTH," AND PRESUMABLY...
📺 "SMITH AND JONES,"
🔍 FUGITIVE

The Shadow Proclamation uses the Judoon as law enforcement officers. Ogrons have also been used.

📺 "FEAR HER,"
📺 "THE FIRES OF POMPEII"

The Shadow Proclamation establishes that anyone operating on a planet other than their own has to identify their place of origin and species designation.

🔍 SILVER SCREAM, FUGITIVE

When the tenth Doctor stopped the Terronites from draining the life energy from wannabe actors in Hollywood in the 1920s, he saved the life of Emily Winter. Her death, though, was a fixed point in time, and the Shadow Proclamation put the Doctor on trial for changing this. He was sentenced to life imprisonment and sent to the prison planet Volag Noc, along with Kraden of the Draconian Empire, Stomm the Sontaran, and Brarshak—an Ogron. (He had been framed by the Krillitanes.)

📺 "THE STOLEN EARTH"

The tenth Doctor and Donna went to the Shadow Proclamation asteroid to warn them that Earth had disappeared (p. 146).

SONTAR

The home world of the clone warriors the Sontarans is in the Melasaran Galaxy. Sontarans are squat and strong because their planet has a gravity six times stronger than that of Earth.[1] They reengineered their solar system so that their sun orbits Sontar.[2] Glimpses of the planet from orbit suggest a world with oceans, where all the available land mass has been built over,[3] possibly with arms factories, hatcheries, parade grounds, and barracks. So little is known, though, that some think the planet is actually called Sontara.[4] The one certain landmark is the Hall of the Fallen and the Brave.[5]

ABOVE: Fresh troops pour in from the clone banks of the Sontaran Empire.

BELOW: The fourth Doctor encountered the Sontarans on a number of occasions; this was in 16th-century China.

HISTORY

The Sontarans have been fighting the Rutans (p. 208) for about as long as Time Lord civilization has existed.[6] This was so far in the past that neither side remembers why they are fighting. They are led by General Sontar, the latest in a line of perfect clones of the first great leader of their kind—including all his memories of all his lifetimes.[7] A number of accounts exist of the origins of the Sontarans themselves, although all agree they were genetically engineered by the original natives of Sontar to fight a war, then overthrew their creators. Sontar was destroyed in the 26th century by a Rutan photonic missile strike.[8] It's possible—perhaps even likely—that different planets have served as the capital of the Sontaran Empire over the course of its long and bloody history.

(p. 208)

BEHIND THE SCENES

Earlier stories such as the comic *Pureblood* (opposite) and the book *The Crystal Bucephalus* (Craig Hinton, 1994) tended to call the Sontaran home planet "Sontara." The first official story to use the name "Sontar" was the novel *The Empire of Glass* (Andy Lane, 1995).

FIRST APPEARANCE

🔍 *(seen)* Pureblood
📖 *(named)* The Empire of Glass

STATUS

Reported destroyed

FOOTNOTES
[1&5] 🎬 *The Last Sontaran* • [2] 📖 *Empire of Glass* • [3] 🔍 *The Betrothal of Sontar* • [4] 📖 *The Crystal Bucephalus* • [6] 🔍 *Black Sun Rising* • [7] 📖 *The Infinity Doctors* • [8] 🔍 *Pureblood*

TIMELINE

THE FIRST SONTARANS
(RELEASED 2012)

🎧 SIXTH DOCTOR

✎ ANDREW SMITH

The Sontarans are created by the humanlike Kaveech, peaceful natives of Sontar, to fight a war against an invasion force of Rutans.

1985

1992

PUREBLOOD

Without the Sontarans, the Rutans will spread unchecked throughout the galaxy, so the Doctor ensures their survival.

1985

THE FIRST SONTARANS

Scientist Meredith Roath hatches the first batch of Sontarans—three million troops—on Elmenus, Sontar's moon. When the Sontarans turn on them, Roath and a few other survivors manage to use a time machine to escape them.

1992

PUREBLOOD

🎧 SEVENTH DOCTOR

✎ DAN ABNETT / COLIN ANDREW

The Rutans destroy Sontara with photonic missiles. The Sontarans have been betrayed by the "Purebloods," the original natives of Sontara, who resemble tall, gaunt Sontarans, and who have survived on one colony world.

TAU CETI

The Tau Ceti solar system is close to Earth—just under 12 light years—with a star slightly smaller and dimmer than our Sun. Three of its planets are known to support life: the home world of the Xaranti (destroyed)[1]; Diplos, inhabited by humanoids 4,000 years ago (and perhaps still is); and Ogros, home of the silicon-based Ogri, who resemble monolithic stone blocks. The Doctor described Ogros as a "repulsive place covered in great swamps full of amino acids, primitive proteins which they feed on by absorption." On Earth, the Ogri get the nutrients they need by feeding on blood.

HISTORY

Little is known of Diplos. It is a Class G world and subject to the legal code of the Galactic Charter. This places Diplosian criminals within the jurisdiction of the Megara, advanced "justice machines" who operate a complex system of extradition and criminal trials. Diplosians resemble human beings but have silver skin and a radically different metabolism, which leaves them unable to digest citric acid. They appear to be long-lived—the one Diplosian we've seen, Cessair of Diplos, lived for 4,000 years. Their civilization was advanced enough that the Great Seal of Diplos "had the powers of transmutation, transformation, and the establishing of hyperspatial and temporal coordinates."[2]

FIRST APPEARANCE
The Stones of Blood *(1978)*

STATUS
Xaranti destroyed; Diplos and Ogros not heard of for 4,000 years

RIGHT: Cessair of Diplos posed as the Goddess Cailleach.

FOOTNOTES
[1] *Deep Blue* • [2] *The Stones of Blood*

TIMELINE

1999

📺 THE STONES OF BLOOD
👤 FOURTH DOCTOR
✒️ DAVID FISHER

Cessair of Diplos has spent thousands of years posing as various people (and a Celtic goddess). She steals the Great Seal of Diplos and is being returned to her home planet for trial when she manages to divert the ship to Earth and lock it in hyperspace.

1978

📖 DEEP BLUE
👤 FIFTH DOCTOR
✒️ MARK MORRIS

The Doctor helps UNIT defeat the Xaranti, a race that has been nomadic since the destruction of their planet during a war with the Zygons. The Xaranti resemble giant scorpions and steal the technology of other races, rather than use their own. They breed by stinging living beings, which then transform into Xaranti.

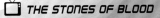

1978

1978

📺 THE STONES OF BLOOD

The Doctor, Romana, and K9 are searching for the third segment of the Key to Time in England in the present day. They discover a series of deaths have been caused by Ogri posing as a stone circle but roaming the area at night. They are the henchmen of Cessair.

📺 THE STONES OF BLOOD

The Doctor rouses the Megara justice machines, which sentence Cessair to perpetual imprisonment as a standing stone. The Great Seal is the third segment of the Key to Time, which the Doctor manages to retrieve as the sentence is being passed.

TERILEPTUS

The Terileptils' home planet was close to the Darkheart system, between spiral arms of the Mutter's Spiral and beyond Lasky's Nebula.[1] The Terileptils were an extremely advanced starfaring race who resembled reptile men, with some of the characteristics of tropical fish—brightly colored, with gills, webbed hands and feet, and pointed teeth. They breathed soliton gas and on worlds such as Earth would use portable atmospheric processors that wafted out the gas. With a single injection they could also genetically engineer rats to increase their lifespan. Much of their equipment was made from polygrite.[2]

HISTORY

After their ship was damaged by an asteroid, a small group of Terileptils crash-landed in 1666 in England, where they met the fifth Doctor. The Doctor was already familiar with their species: he mentioned that he was unable "to reconcile the Terileptils' love of art and beauty with their love of war," and when he saw the scarring on a Terileptil's face, he explained, "There's only one place in the universe a Terileptil can acquire such scarring: the tinclavic mines on Raaga." He did not know, though, that Raaga was a prison planet, and that the Terileptils he had met were fugitives. They were not interested in his offer to take them home; they planned to wipe out humanity with a plague before taking control of the world.

ABOVE RIGHT: The fifth Doctor.

RIGHT: The Terileptils were a colorful reptile species who crafted beautiful weapons.

FIRST APPEARANCE
Terileptils: The Visitation (1982)

STATUS
Destroyed in the 35th century

FOOTNOTES
[1] *The Dark Path* • [2] *The Visitation*

FACT FILE

📺 THE VISITATION

The Terileptils operated jewel-encrusted androids to perform manual labor. They also used vintaric crystals to power lighting and sophisticated holograms. Much of their equipment was made from polygrite.

📺 THE VISITATION

When the Doctor encountered the Terileptils, their leader had injected thousands of rats with a modified virus and was going to release them in London. At the base, a fire accidentally started—a blaze that soon became the Great Fire of London, which killed the Terileptils and their plague rats.

📺 THE AWAKENING

The Terileptils were mining tinclavic on Raaga almost exclusively in order to trade with the planet Hakol in the star system Rifta, hundreds of years before the 17th century.

📺 THE TRIAL OF A TIME LORD

A delegate from Posicar negotiating with the Mentors appeared to be a Terileptil.

📖 THE DARK PATH

Terileptus was destroyed around the 35th century, when an Adjudicator named Terrell activated the Darkheart, a device that could selectively rewrite history. The entire interplanetary civilization was wiped out, with only a few survivors. The Time Lord who would become the Master was working with Terrell and selected this option over the more drastic one of making every being in the galaxy human. Nevertheless, he understood the act to be evil, and that he was taking his first steps on a dark path.

📺 "THE PANDORICA OPENS"

The Terileptils joined the Alliance that imprisoned the eleventh Doctor in the Pandorica.

📺 "TIME HEIST"

A Terileptil was among the most notorious criminals in history.

THOROS ALPHA AND THOROS BETA

Thoros Alpha is a ringed planet with thick orange clouds. It looms in the sky of its twin planet, Thoros Beta. The Alphans look like dark-skinned humans and are transported to Thoros Beta to work as laborers and experimental test subjects. Thoros Beta is a lurid mix of pinks and green clouds. The surface, at least around the coast, is rocky, and the sky is fluorescent green. The names of the seas give some sense of what life is like here: Turmoil, Despair, and the Longing Sea of Sorrows. It is the home of the sixth Doctor's enemy, Sil.

HISTORY

Sil is one of the Mentors, an amphibious race that needs a constant spray of water to remain comfortable; they consider the leechlike "marsh minnow" a delicacy. The Mentors are small, with humanoid heads, torsos, and arms, but a segmented tail instead of legs. They vary in color—they can be brown, green, and yellow—and their bodies are covered in ridges and fins. They are arch-capitalists, obsessed with acquiring wealth. They traded with Earth and its colonies in the 23rd and 24th centuries, seeking, according to one of them, "cosmic mega-profit." Mentors pray to the Great Morgo and believe in an afterlife

in the Plague Hall of Mogdana. Mentors run the Search-Conv-Corp, which salvages derelict spacecraft and is active near Tokl, one of the Rim Worlds. Mentor companies compete with each other—Sil has faced rivals from the Amorb corporation—and they use mercenaries to protect their business interests.

BEHIND THE SCENES

Phillip Martin wrote three TV stories featuring Sil, memorably played by Nabil Shaban: *Vengeance on Varos*, *The Trial of A Time Lord* parts 5 to 8 (also known as *Mindwarp*), and an unmade story from 1986, *Mission to Magnus*, which was novelized in 1990 and adapted as an audio play in 2009.

BELOW: The Doctor's friend Peri met her fate on the planets of the Mentors.

FIRST APPEARANCE

📺 *Mentors:* Vengeance on Varos *(1985)*

📺 *Thoros Alpha & Beta:* The Trial of a Time Lord *(1986)*

INHABITANTS

Mentors, Raak, Thoros Alphans & Betans, marsh minnows

STATUS

Business as usual

TIMELINE

📺 VENGEANCE ON VAROS
👤 SIXTH DOCTOR
✎ PHILLIP MARTIN

Mentor-owned companies include the Galatron Mining Company.

1985

1990

📖🎧 MISSION TO MAGNUS
👤 SIXTH DOCTOR
✎ PHILLIP MARTIN

The Ice Warriors plan to alter the climate of Magnus, ushering in a new ice age. Sil spots a business opportunity and arrives to sell warm clothing and heaters.

1985

📺 VENGEANCE ON VAROS

When the Doctor first meets Sil, he is trading with the former prison planet Varos. Sil has told the people of Varos that zeiton-7 is very common, but it is actually an astonishingly rare mineral, used to fuel time machines (including the TARDIS).

1986

📺 THE TRIAL OF A TIME LORD PARTS 5-8
👤 SIXTH DOCTOR
✎ PHILLIP MARTIN

The Doctor tracks a consignment of energy weapons used by the Warlords of Thordon back to Thoros Beta, where he learns that Sil's boss, Kiv, is intending to prolong his life using an experimental brain transplant.

TRAKEN

The Traken Union was a utopian civilization in the solar system of Metulla Orionsis. The planet was temperate and abundant with trees and birds, and the populated areas were beautifully designed to incorporate gardens and groves and to hide advanced technology behind natural materials like wood, iron, and stone. The people of Traken wore fine clothes, a little reminiscent of fashions from the 16th century on Earth. The elite were scientists and scholars; the working men were Fosters—guards who doubled as gardeners.

BEHIND THE SCENES

Traken was destroyed in *Logopolis* (Christopher H. Bidmead, 1981). Nyssa of Traken would be the Doctor's companion until *Terminus* (Stephen Gallagher, 1983). Johnny Byrne wrote a follow-up, *The Guardians of Prophecy*, in 1983, but it was not made until 2012, when it was adapted for audio by Jonathan Morris.

HISTORY

The Union was, according to the Doctor, "famous for its universal harmony. A whole empire held together by … well, by people just being terribly nice to each other." Evil beings who set foot on the planet became calcified statuelike beings, known as Melkurs, which eventually eroded and passed harmlessly into the soil. Society was run by a group of Consuls, under the aegis of the powerful and benevolent Keeper of Traken—a person selected to spend the rest of his or her life connected to the Source manipulator, a bioelectronic machine with "limitless organizing capacity." His will was used to restructure reality.

ABOVE: Nyssa, a companion of the fourth and fifth Doctors, came from Traken.

FIRST APPEARANCE
The Keeper of Traken *(1981)*

STATUS
Destroyed

TIMELINE

Serenity is the site of the Tomb of Malador, an evil being who awakens and raises an army of Melkurs. A dimensional fracture opens, and the Doctor is able to trap Malador within it.

2012

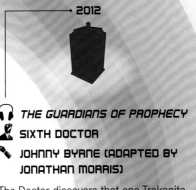

📺 **THE KEEPER OF TRAKEN**

👤 **FOURTH DOCTOR**

✒ **JOHNNY BYRNE**

The Doctor and Adric discover that the TARDIS of the ancient and decaying Master has become trapped as a Melkur. The Master is plotting to take control of the Source manipulator to gain a new body and then conquer worlds without number.

1981

2012

🎧 **THE GUARDIANS OF PROPHECY**

👤 **SIXTH DOCTOR**

✒ **JOHNNY BYRNE (ADAPTED BY JONATHAN MORRIS)**

The Doctor discovers that one Trakenite colony, Serenity, survived. It is far from a perfect society, but the Elect do what they can to rule the Benign Union wisely using Prophecy, a device a little like the Source manipulator.

1981

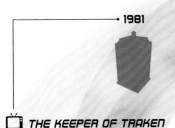

📺 **THE KEEPER OF TRAKEN**

The Doctor thinks he has defeated the Master with the help of Tremas and his daughter Nyssa, but his enemy possesses the body of Tremas and flees the planet.

2001

1981

🎧 **PRIMEVAL**

The illness has been contrived by the dark god Kwundaar, who was banished from Traken's Eden when the Union was forming and yearns to return. To defeat an omnipotent being, the Doctor has to become the very first Keeper of Traken—a title he quickly renounces.

2001

📺 **LOGOPOLIS**

👤 **FOURTH DOCTOR / WATCHER**

✒ **CHRISTOPHER H. BIDMEAD**

Nyssa is reunited with the Doctor by the mysterious Watcher, a ghostly version of the Doctor, on Logopolis. In trying to take control of that planet, the Master inadvertently releases forces that destroy much of the universe, including Traken.

🎧 **PRIMEVAL**

👤 **FIFTH DOCTOR**

✒ **LANCE PARKIN**

Nyssa is dying from a mysterious condition, and the Doctor takes her back to the ancient history of her planet to find a physician skilled in Trakenite medicine.

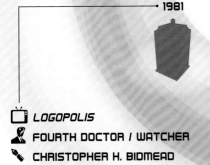

VOGA, PLANET OF GOLD

During the Cyber War it was discovered that the Cybermen had a vulnerability to gold dust. The noncorrodible metal plated their breathing apparatus and suffocated them. Ingenious human scientists built glitterguns, and the Cyber War ended in abject defeat for the Cybermen. Most of the gold used came from Voga. Even after the demands of the war, there was more gold on Voga than in the rest of the known galaxy.

FIRST APPEARANCE
Revenge of the Cybermen (1975)

STATUS
Rebuilding after invasion

HISTORY

The last act of the Cyber War was a devastating attack on Voga—then the last Cybermen just disappeared. The Guardians, leaders of the Vogans, were terrified by the prospect that the Cybermen would launch a revenge attack. Centuries after the end of the Cyber War, a small rogue planet entered Earth's Solar System. It was captured by Jupiter's gravity, becoming that planet's 13th moon. Astronomers named it Neophobus. Nerva Beacon was set up to warn shipping. Even after 50 years, a lot of the Great Circle freighters didn't have it on their charts. There was no prospect of any life on the planet—not after traveling the void between star systems for so long. A human exographer, Kellman, surveyed the planet, set up a transmat link to the world, and renamed it ... Voga.

LEFT: The Vogans cowered from the Cybermen in the aftermath of the Cyber War.

TIMELINE

REVENGE OF THE CYBERMEN
🧍 FOURTH DOCTOR
✎ GERRY DAVIS

The Doctor, Sarah, and Harry arrive on Nerva Beacon, a space station enduring the outbreak of a plague that's killed 47 crewmen. The Beacon is close to a planet that remains highly mysterious to the human race. The Doctor, though, recognizes the new name that Kellman has given it: Voga.

1975

1975

REVENGE OF THE CYBERMEN

The Doctor is able to connect the dots. He's seen the plague before—it was spread by the Cybermen. He knows of Voga's role in the Cyber War. It's clear to him that the Vogans have been hiding from their old foes and that the Cybermen have tracked them down.

REVENGE OF THE CYBERMEN

The Cybermen arrive, and they plan to destroy Voga by planting Cyber Bombs on Nerva and crashing it into the planet. The Doctor manages to get the Skystriker missile to hit the retreating Cybership, steadying the course of Nerva Beacon.

1975

1975

REVENGE OF THE CYBERMEN

One Vogan, Vorus, dreams of using his planet's gold to become wealthy and powerful. He has been working with Kellman to lure the last known Cybership to Voga, where he plans to destroy it with a Skystriker missile.

1975

1975

REVENGE OF THE CYBERMEN

Sarah becomes infected with the plague when she's bitten by a Cybermat, a cybernetic rodent used by the Cybermen as spies and saboteurs. The Doctor saves her life by transmatting her down to Voga.

REVENGE OF THE CYBERMEN

At the other end, Sarah's body is reassembled without the alien plague present. She and Harry discover the Vogans are alive and cowering in an underground bunker.

XEROS AND THE MOROK EMPIRE

Xeros was a world of crumbling rock and ground covered in thick dust, but with a pleasant climate. Xerons looked like humans but had large, neatly arched eyebrows. According to one Xeron, his planet "was a place of peace and knowledge, and the wisdom of our elders made us free from want." Unfortunately, it was only three light years from Morok, the center of an aggressive empire. The Moroks were warlike and easily subjugated Xeros. All adult Xerons were killed during the invasion, but the children were kept alive; when they were old enough, they were shipped off into slavery.

HISTORY

The Moroks looked a lot like humans, too. Their soldiers wore white uniforms with shoulder flaps and styled their hair swept back until it looked a little like a pinecone. They carried rayguns and weren't above pumping rooms full of poisonous Zaphra gas to smoke out their enemies. Once they had conquered Xeros, the Moroks built the Space Museum there—a vast complex celebrating their history of conquest. Its corridors went on for miles, and much of it seemed to be underground. From the surface, there was a squat black building with a single door, and the area just outside it was ringed with rocket ships from various eras.

Centuries later, though, the Morok Empire was not what it had been. The Governor of Xeros lamented, "Our civilization rests on its laurels. Galactic conquests are a thing of the past. Life, it is now said, is purely a thing to enjoy."

FIRST APPEARANCE
📺 The Space Museum *(1965)*

STATUS
Free from the collapsed Morok Empire

FACT FILE

📺 THE SPACE MUSEUM
The ennui of the Morok Empire affected attendance of the Space Museum. Governor Lobos told the Doctor, "Three hundred mimmians ago, sightseers filled this planet, marveling at what they saw. Today, the occasional spaceship from Morok calls."

📺 THE SPACE MUSEUM
A mimmian is a thousand days, so the Museum was built over 820 years ago.

📺 THE SPACE MUSEUM
Governor Lobos volunteered to run the Space Museum, as he was young and bored living on Morok.

📺 THE SPACE MUSEUM
The Space Museum exhibit included rockets, many examples of futuristic-looking machines, a couple of what appear to be mannequins wearing spacesuits, or similar outfits … and a Dalek casing from the planet Skaro.

📺 THE SPACE MUSEUM
The equipment also included devices Lobos could use to interrogate the Doctor by showing the contents of his mind, and another that could freeze his body "several hundred degrees below zero." The Doctor was able to resist both of these techniques.

📺 THE CHASE
When a revolution among the young Xerons proved successful, they smashed the contents of the museum—except for a Time/Space Visualizer that the Doctor asked to take away with him. It proved very useful in his next adventure, when he was chased through time and space by the Daleks.

ABOVE & OPPOSITE: The first Doctor, who would resist attempts to turn him into an exhibit in the Space Museum.

ZANAK

FIRST APPEARANCE
The Pirate Planet *(1978)*

INHABITANTS
People of Zanak (including the Mentiads), the Captain, his crew, the robot parrot Polyphase Avatron

STATUS
Rebuilding after dictatorship

The people of Zanak were so accustomed to ages of prosperity that they would leave gemstones just lying in the street: diamonds, rubies, and even Andromedan bloodstones. Almost everyone knew better than to ask why the night sky kept changing, or to challenge the sinister black-clad guards, although there were dissenters, particularly the Mentiads— men and women who fell ill and woke with psychic powers.

HISTORY

The secret was that, a century ago, the ship *Vantarialis* had crashed on Zanak. The Queen of Zanak, Xanxia, had fought galactic wars that had left her planet devastated. She fitted the ship's Captain with cyborg components, thus saving his life and also gaining control over him. One of the greatest hyper-engineers of all time, he was able to hollow out Zanak and fit it with engines capable of traveling through the Time Vortex.

Under his command, Zanak became a Pirate Planet. It would materialize around a world, then use mining machines to suck it clean of minerals and other valuable resources. This was not simply to acquire wealth. These raided planets were reduced to football-sized husks, with vast mass for their size, and by balancing their immense gravitational forces, the Captain was producing a staggering amount of power, fueling time dams to prevent the death of the ancient Xanxia.

BEHIND THE SCENES

Douglas Adams wrote *The Pirate Planet* at the same time as the original radio series of his *Hitchhiker's Guide to the Galaxy*. Ingredients for the notorious *Hitchhiker* cocktail, the Pan Galactic Gargle Blaster, include hypermint from Qualactin, one of the planets Zanak has destroyed, and water from the seas of Santraginus V (possibly the same place as "Bandraginus V," see opposite).

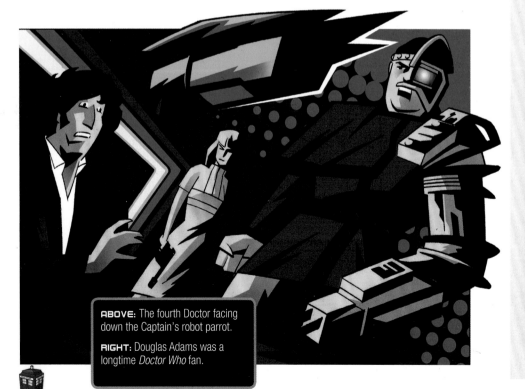

ABOVE: The fourth Doctor facing down the Captain's robot parrot.

RIGHT: Douglas Adams was a longtime *Doctor Who* fan.

TIMELINE

1978

THE PIRATE PLANET

The Captain refuses to listen and sets course for Earth, a source of quartz. The Mentiads throw a spanner in the works—literally, using their telekinetic powers. The Captain and Xanxia perish, and the Bridge is demolished.

THE PIRATE PLANET
FOURTH DOCTOR
DOUGLAS ADAMS

The planets Zanak destroys include Bandraginus V (home to a billion people, lost a century before), Granados, Qualactin, Aterica, Bibicorpus, Lowiteliom, Temesis, and Tridentio III.

1978

1978

1978

THE PIRATE PLANET

The Doctor tells the Captain that not even the staggering amounts of power he is able to generate using crushed planets will be able to stave off time forever: Xanxia will inevitably die, and soon.

THE PIRATE PLANET

The Pirate Captain frequently bellows out oaths that name other planets—the X-ray storms of Vega, the Moons of Madness, Flaming Moons of Heretes, the Flaming Moons of Hell, and the Bursting Suns of Banzar.

1978

1978

THE PIRATE PLANET

The Doctor meets up with the Mentiads and learns the secrets of the Pirate Planet. He is captured and brought to the Bridge, the stronghold of the Captain, built from the remains of the *Vantarialis*.

THE PIRATE PLANET

The Doctor, Romana, and K9 are searching the universe for the six segments of the Key to Time. To the Doctor's chagrin, they locate the second segment on the dismal world of Calufrax. However, they find turbulence as they materialize, and as they explore, they find a pleasant, populated world. They have arrived just as Zanak has materialized around Calufrax, the only source in the universe for the mineral madranite 1-5.

ZOLFA-THURA AND TIGELLA

Twin planets in the Prion System, across the Milky Way from Earth, Zolfa-Thura is a featureless, lifeless desert and Tigella is a jungle planet with a subterranean civilization. The Zolfa-Thurans wiped themselves out in a war 10,000 years ago, leaving only the mysterious Screens of Zolfa-Thura as evidence that they ever existed. This set of five giant pentagonal metal plates, hundreds of feet tall, was remarked upon in records of the planet, but no one knew what they were for. The entire rest of the planet had been reduced to a level wilderness of sand.

FIRST APPEARANCE
📺 Meglos *(1980)*

INHABITANTS
Meglos, Tigellans, Bell Plants

STATUS
Zolfa-Thura destroyed, Tigella rebuilding

HISTORY

Tigella is covered in vegetation that is at least partially mobile and aware—a good example being the Bell Plants, which prey on humans. The Tigellans live underground to avoid this, in a complex powered by the Dodecahedron, which fell from the sky 10,000 years before. This event split the Tigellans into two factions—the Deons, who thought it was a gift from the god Ti, and whose religion includes human sacrifice and an absolute prohibition on studying the Dodecahedron; and the Savants, scientists who harnessed power from the Dodecahedron to run their civilization. The Doctor had visited 50 years before and made a friend in the future leader of the planet Zastor.

RIGHT: The cactus creature Meglos was able to impersonate the fourth Doctor and infiltrate Tigella.

TIMELINE

📺 MEGLOS

🎭 FOURTH DOCTOR

✏️ JOHN FLANAGAN & ANDREW MCCULLOCH

A group of Gaztaks, space scavengers, take on a job that involves them bringing a random human from Earth to the Screens of Zolfa-Thura. A building emerges from the sand, and they go in to discover Meglos, last of the Zolfa-Thurans.

1980

1980

📺 MEGLOS

Without their power source, the Tigellans will have to move back to the surface.

1980

1980

📺 MEGLOS

The Zolfa-Thurans are a race of super-advanced cacti who have mastered the ability to switch bodies (corporeal transference), create objects from thin air (mass conversion), and engineer time loops (chronic hysteresis).

📺 MEGLOS

Despite the Doctor's best efforts, Meglos is able to steal the Dodecahedron and return it to Zolfa-Thura. The Doctor manages to realign the screens, and so when Meglos fires a shot intended to destroy Tigella, it backfires, reducing Meglos, the Screens, the Dodecahedron, and all of Zolfa-Thura to dust.

1980

1980

📺 MEGLOS

Their greatest achievement is the Dodecahedron, which generates enough energy to power an entire galactic civilization. When placed among the legendary Screens of Zolfa-Thura, the Dodecahedron becomes a component of one of the most powerful weapons ever built, able to disintegrate whole planets.

1980

📺 MEGLOS

The Dodecahedron is somehow propelled to the neighboring planet of Tigella. Meglos wants it back to resume his dreams of conquest. He takes possession of the human body the Gaztaks procure for him, and they travel to Tigella.

📺 MEGLOS

The Doctor, Romana, and K9 arrive on Tigella and navigate the politics of the planet to reveal the truth about the Dodecahedron.

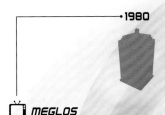

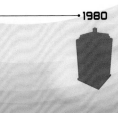

ZYGOR

The Zygons are a race of long-lived humanoids with large domed heads, rows of suckers, and bright orange skin. They are shapeshifters, although this seems to be at least in part a technological ability rather than a natural one. They have to immobilize the person they are impersonating, at least for some time. The Zygon technology is organic in nature, with cybernetic augmentations. They drink the milk of the plesiosaurlike Skarasens,[1] and they have venom sacs in their mouths.[2] Zygons start life as female; they are small and have almost white skin. They become male as they grow older.[3]

HISTORY

The Zygon home planet was called Zygor.[4] It was warmer than Earth, covered in lakes, and there were no ice caps. The planet was destroyed … but different events have been credited with this destruction. It may have been in a war with the Xaranti,[5] or in the early days of the Last Great Time War.[6] Different groups of Zygons survived the end of their world, and many have made it to Earth, a world that they feel could be reengineered to be more like their home world. Zygor's sun was part of a star cluster in the Biphaelides System.[7]

ABOVE: The eleventh Doctor and Clara's TARDIS was airlifted by Zygons posing as UNIT personnel.

LEFT: Young Zygons are white, and not as strong.

FIRST APPEARANCE
📺 Terror of the Zygons *(1975)*

INHABITANTS
Zygons, Skarasens

STATUS
Destroyed

FOOTNOTES
[1] 📺 *Terror of the Zygons* •
[2&6] 📺 "The Day of the Doctor" •
[3] 📖 *The Sting of the Zygons* •
[3, 4, 5, 7] 📖 *The Bodysnatchers* .

TIMELINE

TERROR OF THE ZYGONS
FOURTH DOCTOR
ROBERT BANKS STEWART

The Doctor, Sarah, and Harry are called back to Earth by the Brigadier, who is investigating attacks on North Sea oil rigs by a sea monster. The creature is tracked back to Loch Ness and revealed to be controlled by a small group of Zygons led by Broton who has lurked in the loch for centuries. They now seek to flood the Earth and take control.

1975

2013

"THE DAY OF THE DOCTOR"
The Doctors force the Zygons to negotiate with UNIT.

1975

TERROR OF THE ZYGONS
The Doctor is able to free the Skarasen, and UNIT launches an air strike to blow up the Zygon ship.

2013

"THE DAY OF THE DOCTOR"
WAR, TENTH & ELEVENTH DOCTORS
STEVEN MOFFAT

A group of Zygons infiltrate Elizabethan England and hide in paintings, storing themselves until the early 21st century. They have the misfortune of doing this while the Moment is showing the War Doctor his Tenth and Eleventh selves.

1997

THE BODYSNATCHERS
EIGHTH DOCTOR
MARK MORRIS

In 1894 London, the Doctor and Sam team up with the Doctor's old friend Professor Litefoot and discover a group of Zygons, led by Balaak, who plan to conquer Earth.

BATTLEGROUND PLANETS

There are worlds in a state of perpetual war. There are some races on a permanent war footing, such as the Sontarans (see p. 212); or with a martial culture, like the Ice Warriors (p. 58); with aggressive neighbors, like Draconia (p. 182); or with long-standing civil wars or internecine conflicts, like Vortis (p. 264). Some worlds have a combination of these, like Skaro (p. 140) … and Earth. There are some worlds, though, that have become the sites of perpetual wars, and these planets are known for little else.

HISTORY

In these cases, either the inhabitants have become locked in a permanent struggle against an equally matched foe, or caught in the cross fire of an external struggle. The same patterns are repeated: Weapons become more and more deadly, and leaders find it harder and harder to recruit troops to the cause. On some worlds, conflicts that started for pragmatic reasons, or because of some burning ideological dispute,

become simple struggles for survival as new generations emerge to continue the fight.

It usually becomes all but impossible to live on the surface, and in many cases, the population starts altering their soldiers—genetically engineering them, adding cyborg implants. When the war is over, the surviving warriors are often incapable of ending the fight. There are also races that kidnap people from other planets to serve in their armies.

ABOVE: Many worlds have been devastated by war.

LEFT: Sarah Jane Smith saw her fair share of planets devastated by war.

TIMELINE

WARRIORS OF KUDLAK
SARAH JANE
PHIL GLADWIN

2007

Kudlak of the Uvodni uses the Laser Tag game Combat 3000 to recruit children from England to fight in the Ghost Wars against the Malakh. Sarah Jane and her friends succeed in uncovering the scheme and shut it down.

THE ARMAGEDDON FACTOR
FOURTH DOCTOR
BOB BAKER & DAVE MARTIN

On the edge of the Helical Galaxy, the twin planets of Atrios and Zeos go to war. Wave after wave of spaceships are sent by both sides, dropping nuclear bombs. The people of Atrios live in deep shelters, so their view of their opponent is obscured by a dark asteroid, "the planet of evil."

1979

2007

1979

"THE DOCTOR'S DAUGHTER"

There are massive casualties, and the war continues for 6,680 generations … the Doctor, Donna, and Martha arrive and discover that the war has only been fought for a week. The Doctor manages to activate the terraformer, transforming the world into a beautiful garden.

THE ARMAGEDDON FACTOR

Unknown to the Atrians, the Zeons have gone, and their only opponent is Mentalis, the Zeon war computer. The Doctor, Romana, and K9 are able to neutralize Mentalis.

2007

2007

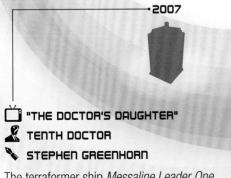

"THE DOCTOR'S DAUGHTER"
TENTH DOCTOR
STEPHEN GREENHORN

The terraformer ship *Messaline Leader One* arrives on a cold, radioactive planet with a crew of humans, Hath, and robots who plan to construct an underground city and populate it using a Progenator, a device that can create fully grown clones.

"THE DOCTOR'S DAUGHTER"

The leader of the mission dies of fever, and the humans and Hath split, each creating armies of clones. The original settlers are quickly wiped out, leaving just clones endlessly being born, fighting, and dying.

DEAD PLANETS

FIRST APPEARANCE
Dead planets: The Daleks
(1963)

INHABITANTS
...?

It takes a great deal to kill a whole planet's biosphere—Earth, for example, saw mass extinctions like the explosion that wiped out the dinosaurs, as well as ice ages and solar flares—but all it took were a few surviving plants and animals and, in time, life flourished once again. Even the "dead planet" Skaro (p. 140) saw vestigial, mutated survivors. There are some worlds, though, that are now utterly devoid of life. So while worlds like Mars (p. 58) and Uxarieus are merely dying, those like Kastria (p. 192), and Zolfa-Thura (p. 228) are truly dead worlds.

HISTORY

There is almost always a malevolent reason, and often the monster, weapon, plague, or whatever it was that killed the planet survives, waiting to be unleashed on another world. Sometimes there are a handful of survivors; at other times there is just a single one. As fate would have it, if an individual's actions were responsible for the death of their world, then it would be that individual who was the last survivor of their race.

ABOVE RIGHT: K9 helped defeat the Etydions.

RIGHT: The tenth Doctor and Christina de Souza went to the dead world of San Helios.

TIMELINE

🖵 **"THE CUSTODIANS"**

👤 K9

✏️ SHAYNE ARMSTRONG & S P KRAUSE

2010

The Etydions are green-skinned, horned telepaths who hire themselves out to inspire fear in the enemies of their clients. The races affected by this team up to attack the Etydion home planet, wiping out all life on it.

🖵 **PYRAMIDS OF MARS**

👤 FOURTH DOCTOR

✏️ "STEPHEN HARRIS" (PSEUDONYM FOR LEWIS GREIFER & ROBERT HOLMES)

The planet of the Osirians is left utterly desolate by the rampage of Sutekh. To show Sarah Jane why they had to fight Sutekh in 1911, the Doctor takes her to Earth in 1980, which is now a howling wilderness.

1975

🖵 **"PLANET OF THE DEAD"**

The Doctor, Christina de Souza, and a busload of Earthmen find themselves in a lifeless desert, along with a marooned Tritovore ship that has come to San Helios to trade. The stingrays travel to other planets via wormholes—the Doctor uses one to return to Earth and seals off the others, trapping the stingrays.

2009

1980

2009

• 1980

🗨 **BLACK LEGACY**

👥 ALAN MOORE / DAVID LLOYD

The Deathsmiths of Goth were renowned creators of weapons, until they died out. An expedition of Cybermen arrive looking to scavenge items from the war museum.

🖵 **"PLANET OF THE DEAD"**

👤 TENTH DOCTOR

✏️ RUSSELL T DAVIES & GARETH ROBERTS

San Helios is an advanced, trisolar world in the Scorpion Nebula, with beautiful tree-lined cities and a population of 100 billion. It is obliterated in a year by creatures like flying stingrays.

• 1980

🗨 **BLACK LEGACY**

The Cybermen are hunted down and killed by the Apocalypse Device, a sentient weapon that spreads every disease and virus, as well as the ability to provoke fear—even in the emotionless Cybermen.

• 2001

• 1980

🗨 **BLACK LEGACY**

The Cybermen blow up their ship rather than let the Apocalypse Device escape Goth.

🎧 **THE EXTINCTION EVENT**

✏️ LANCE PARKIN

At an auction event, Bernice Summerfield learns that the Gulfrargs have removed some items from the planet Halstad and deliberately wiped out that planet's biosphere, smashing the surface to dust, knowing that any surviving artifacts from the dead world will become very valuable to art collectors.

DEMONS RUN

"Demons run when a good man goes to war." The first line of a children's poem inspired the name of an asteroid military base set up in the 52nd century as a hideout for forces working against the eleventh Doctor. This was a remote asteroid, with an industrial-looking structure built into the side. The base was well defended, not least by a powerful forcefield. There were large hangar bays and defense systems.

HISTORY

The group based on Demons Run, led by Madame Kovarian, included factions from within the Church, and Silents. From here, they enacted a decades-long plan, working throughout time and space, to kill the Doctor.

Madame Kovarian came from the Doctor's future, during the Siege of Trenzalore (p. 244). She knew that Melody Pond was unique because she'd been conceived in the Time Vortex, and so planned to shape the child into a weapon, one to kill the Doctor before he got to Trenzalore.

RIGHT: The Silence fought the Doctor's army at Demons Run.

ABOVE RIGHT & FAR RIGHT: The eleventh Doctor did not rest until he was reunited with Amy at Demons Run.

FIRST APPEARANCE

📺 (by inference) "The Curse of the Black Spot" (2011)
📺 (named) "A Good Man Goes to War" (2011)

BEHIND THE SCENES

The name of the asteroid probably ought to be "Demons Run," given the origin of the name, and it's spelled that way on a sign we see. A caption, though, names it "Demon's Run."

TIMELINE

"A GOOD MAN GOES TO WAR"

Rory and Amy return to Earth in the 21st century. Vastra and Jenny take Strax back with them to Victorian London.

2011

"A GOOD MAN GOES TO WAR"
ELEVENTH DOCTOR
STEVEN MOFFAT

The Doctor's companion, Amy Pond, is kidnapped by Kovarian's operatives and brought to Demons Run. Amy has recently married Rory and is pregnant.

2011

2011

"A GOOD MAN GOES TO WAR"

Most of the Doctor's forces, however, are killed by the Headless Monks, and Madame Kovarian escapes with baby Melody. The Doctor pursues them, charging River Song with returning the survivors home.

2011

"A GOOD MAN GOES TO WAR"

Amy is replaced with a Ganger, an artificial duplicate. The real Amy is immobilized and kept linked to the Ganger, so she experiences everything the duplicate does, and—except for rare glitches—is unaware anything is wrong … or that she is pregnant. The Doctor detects anomalies around Amy but cannot decipher the readings.

2011

"A GOOD MAN GOES TO WAR"

The Doctor attacks Demons Run with an army of Silurians and Judoon, under the command of the Sontaran Strax. Spitfires sent by Winston Churchill destroy the communications system, isolating the asteroid. His friends Vastra, Jenny, and Dorium help the Doctor get to the base's computer.

2011

2011

"A GOOD MAN GOES TO WAR"

When the Doctor realizes, he immediately terminates the link, causing the Ganger to dissolve. Amy wakes to discover that she is a captive and about to give birth. She names the baby "Melody Pond."

"A GOOD MAN GOES TO WAR"

The Doctor and Rory trek across time and space to locate Amy, and to assemble an army to rescue her. It takes them a month, and they finally learn of the location of Demons Run by threatening the Twelfth Cyber Legion with destruction.

LIBRARY AND MUSEUM PLANETS

Many species have the urge to collect, preserve, and curate artifacts from their own cultures and those of other beings. The Daleks, for example, maintained a vast museum celebrating their scientific and military achievements on Skaro (p. 140), but a Dalek casing also somehow found its way into an exhibition at the Space Museum of the Morok Empire (p. 224).

HISTORY

The Doctor tends to stumble across such places, but he also finds them extremely useful—such institutions preserve and catalog items, and this can be an invaluable resource for a curious time traveler. Other beings can have more sinister intent, and are keen to find knowledge, weapons, or other devices that will further their malevolent ambitions.

There are countless small museums in the universe—in quick succession, the second Doctor visited one commemorating a nuclear test on Dulkis (p. 184) and Daniel Eldred's privately run museum of space travel on Earth.[1] There are, though, some extraordinary museums, galleries, and libraries in the universe—places like the Louvre, the Academia Stellaris on Sirius V, the Solarian Pinacotheque on Stricium, and the Braxiatel Collection (p. 90)[2]—while the Royal Collection aboard *Starship UK* collects the treasures of the United Kingdom.[3]

ABOVE: Biblios was the location of a long stand off.

BELOW LEFT: The Library was the size of a planet and had a copy of every book published.

FIRST APPEARANCE
The Dalek Book *(1964)*

STATUS
Various, but mostly intact

FOOTNOTES
[1] *The Seeds of Death* • [2] *City of Death* • [3] "The Pandorica Opens"

TIMELINE

☐ "THE TIME OF ANGELS"

☐ **"THE TIME OF ANGELS"**

🎗 **ELEVENTH DOCTOR**

✎ **STEVEN MOFFAT**

2010

The Delirium Archive, last resting place of the Headless Monks, is a museum on an asteroid. The Doctor visits it frequently to "keep score"—to track the big events of history and his role in them. In roughly 62,000 AD, the Doctor and Amy visit and find a message left for him 12,000 years before by River Song.

🔍 **WAR OF THE WORDS**

🎗 **FOURTH DOCTOR**

👥 **STEVE MOORE / DAVE GIBBONS**

1981

The Vromyx and Garynth have battled over the library planet Biblios, both trying to get to data on weapons—even though the robot librarians have told them repeatedly the library doesn't have that information. No one has been able to visit the library for 50 years.

2008

🔍 **WAR OF THE WORDS**

1981

☐ **"SILENCE IN THE LIBRARY" / "FOREST OF THE DEAD"**

🎗 **TENTH DOCTOR**

✎ **STEVEN MOFFAT**

The Doctor arrives in the TARDIS and convinces the two sides he is a powerful warlord who has taken control of the data. The warring sides flee.

The Doctor and Donna visit the Library, a planet-sized facility containing a paper copy of every book ever written, around a core that is the largest computer hard drive ever built. The place is haunted by the Vashta Nerada, creatures that lived in the dark forests cut down to make the books.

2000

📖 **HEART OF TARDIS**

🎗 **FOURTH DOCTOR**

✎ **DAVE STONE**

The Doctor and Romana retrieve K9 from the Big Huge and Educational Collection of Old Galactic Stuff, where he has accidentally been exhibited. It is an institution run by the Collectors, amorphous, undiscriminating accumulators of stuff.

PEACEFUL PLANETS

It's not all doom and gloom. Some utopian civilizations exist where the people spend their days as they wish. These societies share many characteristics. They often live in well-organized cities, with access to a unique supply of energy. They dress in opulent robes and dedicate themselves to scholarly pursuits. Their technology can perform miracles but is not ostentatious. They are ruled by a wise council that ensures justice yet tolerates some dissent. They hate violence and do not impose their beliefs on others. The ultimate exemplars of this way of life were the Time Lords of Gallifrey.

FIRST APPEARANCE

Seemingly utopian civilization: The Keys of Marinus *(1964)*

HISTORY

However, many of these Edens also have a snake. For every peaceful, ordered society under benevolent rule (Traken, p.220; Dulkis, p. 184) there's at least one Karfel (p. 190), where such statements are merely the propaganda of a tyrant. The luxury of the city of Morphoton (p. 154) was literally an illusion—visions of silk robes placed in the minds of hypnotized people in rags. The second Doctor visited an Earth colony that resembled a holiday camp but was really a front for Macra slave camps (p. 89). More often than not, the civilization harbors a dark secret behind its serene facade. Either that, or its wealth and power proves attractive to an aggressive alien race, and the peaceful world can offer little resistance. And in times of universal crisis, these utopian civilizations face the choice of annihilation or the abandonment of their most cherished principles.

BEHIND THE SCENES

Presumably, there are many peaceful civilizations in the *Doctor Who* universe that we don't see because they offer no prospect of adventure. The Doctor left Gallifrey, according to most accounts, because he was bored with the unadventurous life on his home planet.

RIGHT: The tenth Doctor and his companion Martha visiting a utopian planet.

TIMELINE

📺 THE SAVAGES
👤 FIRST DOCTOR
✎ IAN STUART BLACK

In the distant future, an advanced civilization lives in peace and prosperity in a city lit by an artificial sun. Just beyond the walls, though, is desolation—in the Valley of Caves, patrols from the City round up "savages" and take them to be drained of their life force, the fuel for this utopia.

2005

📖 THE GALLIFREY CHRONICLES
👤 EIGHTH DOCTOR
✎ LANCE PARKIN

After the interior of the TARDIS is damaged in an atomic explosion, the Doctor thinks the best place for it and him to recuperate is Klist in the Northern Constellations, a planetary string controlled by the benevolent Ruling Mind.

1966

1966

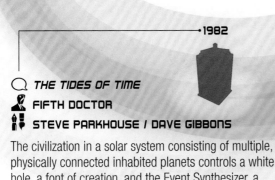

📺 THE SAVAGES

When the leader of the Elders, Jano, absorbs some of the Doctor's life force, he gains his conscience and leads an attack that smashes the transference machines.

1982

🔍 THE TIDES OF TIME

One of their kind, Melanicus from the Kalichura, tries to seize control of Althrace but is forced to flee to another dimension. He will return and take control of the Event Synthesizer, sparking war on a thousand worlds in a thousand times—the Millennium War—but the Doctor will defeat him.

1982

🔍 THE TIDES OF TIME
👤 FIFTH DOCTOR
👥 STEVE PARKHOUSE / DAVE GIBBONS

The civilization in a solar system consisting of multiple, physically connected inhabited planets controls a white hole, a font of creation, and the Event Synthesizer, a device controlled by the Prime Mover that maintains the harmony of time. The system is ruled by the Lords of Althrace, and the population, biomechanical technology, and the planets themselves are effectively one being.

PRISON PLANETS

Countries on Earth once transported their most dangerous prisoners to remote locations—the British Empire, for example, sent violent criminals to Australia, and they exiled Napoleon to the island of St. Helena. Once the human race spread to the stars, they adopted the same principle. The Earth Empire maintained a penal colony on the Moon (p. 52) from its earliest days. Prison planets were not meant to be comfortable, but some managed to develop a functioning society.

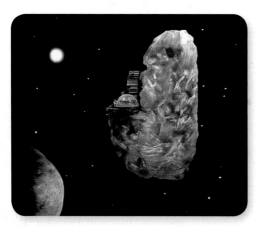

FIRST APPEARANCE
Prison planet Desperus: The Daleks' Master Plan *(1965)*

BEHIND THE SCENES

Terry Nation would go on to write *Blake's 7*, and his depiction of Cygnus Alpha in that 1978 series was almost identical to Desperus in *The Daleks' Master Plan*.

HISTORY

The human race was not the only group to set up prison planets. The Terileptils exiled prisoners to the tinclavic mines of Raaga (p. 216). The Time Lords had a number of punishments for the most heinous crimes—with reluctance, they were quite capable of destroying or timelooping whole worlds, and they had been known to execute renegade Time Lords. They also, though, maintained the prison asteroid of Shada. There are some immortal beings whose crimes demand they be imprisoned for eternity—the universe is littered with the "tombs" of such monsters.

ABOVE: Shada, the prison planet of the Time Lords.

RIGHT: The twelfth Doctor faced an impenetrable prison station.

ABOVE RIGHT: The twelfth Doctor tried to escape from a prison planet.

OPPOSITE: The Moon will serve as a penal colony for thousands of years.

📺 DESPERUS (*THE DALEKS' MASTER PLAN*)

In 4000 AD, Earth exiled violent crimes to the "Devil's Planet" Desperus—
a planet so far from the Solar System it was close to Kembel, a planet chosen
for the Daleks precisely because it was so remote. Desperus was rocky,
home to screaming bats. There were no guards; prisoners were left to
fend for themselves.

📺 SHADA (*SHADA*)

The Time Lords had a secret prison on the asteroid Shada—so secret, even
they had forgotten it. It was accessed via a code in the old book *The Ancient
and Worshipful Law of Gallifrey*. Prisoners were kept in suspended animation.
(One of them, Salyavin, was a Time Lord who could mentally dominate all
others. He escaped to Earth and became the kindly Cambridge don,
Professor Chronotis.)

📺 SARN (*PLANET OF FIRE*)

Sarn was a dying world, rich in numismaton gas, a substance with miraculous
healing powers. The people of Trion—the race the Doctor's companion
Turlough came from—colonized Sarn and set up an extraction plant in a
volcano, leaving the humanlike natives to think they had been visited by the
gods. In reality, the Trion Empire was fading, and the planet was a dumping
ground for political dissenters. The Master attempted to heal himself using
numismaton gas but only succeeded in devastating the planet in an eruption.
Turlough arranged for Trion to evacuate the planet and elected to return with
them to his home planet.

📺 VAROS (*VENGEANCE ON VAROS*)

Varos was a prison asylum for the criminally insane in the constellation of
Cetes. The population lived in metal domes on a planet with a harsh red sky.
The indigenous life included gee-jee flies and clinker moles. Centuries after
it was set up, the planet functioned as a mining colony, with the descendants
of the warders in charge and a population with an appetite for the violent
punishment of rebels. The planet traded zeiton-7 ore with the Galatron Mining
Company (p. 219).

📖 THE GLASS PRISON (*THE GLASS PRISON*)

The future human fascist group the Fifth Axis ran a jail with transparent walls
on Dierbhile. Bernice Summerfield gave birth to her son Peter while being
held there.

📖 JUSTICIA (*THE MONSTERS INSIDE*)

The Blathereen infiltrated the six-planet prison solar system of Justicia, but
the ninth Doctor and Rose were on hand to prevent them harnessing the
spacewarping properties of that region of space.

📺 VOLAG-NOC (*THE INFINITE QUEST*)

The coldest planet in the galaxy was home to a brutal prison camp.

📺 STORMCAGE (FIRST SEEN IN "THE PANDORICA OPENS")

River Song was imprisoned at the Stormcage Containment Facility, as
punishment for murdering the Doctor.

📖 THE PRISON (*THE BLOOD CELL*)

In the far future, the humans of HomeWorld built The Prison on a remote
asteroid. Its Governor was a disgraced former President.

TRENZALORE

Trenzalore should have been entirely unremarkable. A small blue planet with two moons and the trace of planetary rings, it was settled by humans to become a Level Two colony sometime before the 52nd century. There was a permanent layer of snow, and daylight only lasted for a few minutes a day, but it was a pleasant, peaceful place, and the settlers called their main city Christmas, laying it out all year round with lights and decorations. They made their living as snow farmers in rather idyllic surroundings, watched over by a large clock tower.

FIRST APPEARANCE

📺 (mentioned) "The Wedding of River Song" (2012)
📺 (seen) "The Name of the Doctor" (2013)

CURRENT STATUS

Devastated by the long siege, but not a dead world

HISTORY

Trenzalore became the site of one of the most enduring sieges, then consequential battles, in the history of the universe. The Doctor always knew he would die one day. Time Lords live a long time but can only regenerate 12 times, so the eleventh Doctor knew the end was near. He had used up a spare regeneration saving himself from a Dalek blast.[1] He also had a secret one between his eighth and ninth incarnations—the "War Doctor," who had done terrible things in the name of peace and sanity during the Last Great Time War, an incarnation shunned by his other selves, who renounced his claim on the name of the Doctor.

One of the perils time travelers face is stumbling across information about their own future. The eleventh Doctor discovered his grave on Trenzalore, so he understood that one day he would go there and make his last stand.

BELOW LEFT: The eleventh Doctor faced down many old foes on Trenzalore.

BELOW: The beautiful planet of Trenzalore, before the epic battle that scarred it.

FOOTNOTE
[1] 📺 "Journey's End"

BBC
DOCTOR WHO
THE ELEVENTH DOCTOR'S LAST STAND
TALES OF TRENZALORE
Justin Richards, Mark Morris, George Mann & Paul Finch
READ BY DAVID TROUGHTON

TIMELINE

📺 "THE TIME OF THE DOCTOR"

2013

The Papal Mainframe and the Doctor spend centuries defending against countless forces attempting to reach Trenzalore. The Doctor grows old repelling the Cybermen, Sontarans, Monoids, Krynoids, Mara, Weeping Angels, and many more. Finally, the Papal Mainframe falls to the Daleks, the forcefields protecting the planet fail, and the Doctor faces his death … but the Time Lords pour energy through the crack, regenerating him and destroying the Daleks.

📺 "THE WEDDING OF RIVER SONG"
👤 ELEVENTH DOCTOR
🖊 STEVEN MOFFAT

2011

Madam Kovarian has an elaborate plan to kill the Doctor on Earth in 2011, using River Song as her agent. Amy, Rory, and River Song herself had seen this happen and believe it to be inevitable—a "fixed point in time."

2013

📺 "THE TIME OF THE DOCTOR"
👤 ELEVENTH DOCTOR
🖊 STEVEN MOFFAT

A crack is discovered in the Christmas clock tower. This has inadvertently been created by Madame Kovarian and will allow the Time Lords to return to our universe, provoking a new Time War.

2011

📺 "THE WEDDING OF RIVER SONG"

However, the Doctor is able to survive. He is warned by the trader Dorium about events on "the fields of Trenzalore"—the first time he has heard that name.

2013

📺 "THE NAME OF THE DOCTOR"
👤 ELEVENTH DOCTOR
🖊 STEVEN MOFFAT

The Doctor is lured to Trenzalore by the Great Intelligence and discovers a ruined world covered in gravestones. His future self is entombed in a mausoleum constructed from his dying TARDIS. His "body" is a scar in space time, which the Great Intelligence hopes to destroy, wiping the Doctor from existence.

THE WAR PLANET

It was one of the most ambitious plans of conquest the universe has ever seen—and the first time the Doctor had to admit he could not resolve a situation and was forced to call in his people, the Time Lords. A race of aliens led by their War Lord formed an alliance with the renegade Time Lord the War Chief and created the War Games.

HISTORY

On a planet sectioned off by impenetrable mists, the aliens created a series of battlefields, then kidnapped thousands of soldiers from the "most vicious species of all," one that "for a half a million years" had been "systematically killing each other"—humans. The aim was to create the ultimate army and then unite the thousand inhabited worlds of the galaxy under the rule of the War Lord.

The second Doctor and his companions, Jamie and Zoe, thought things were bad enough because they had landed in No Man's Land during the Great War. As they explored, they came across a bank of mist, through which lurched a Roman chariot. They were not on Earth, but on a planet where ten distinct zones were separated by mysterious barriers, with the War Chief in the central Zone One. When the Doctor's intervention triggered revolutions across every zone, the War Lord arrived to take command.

FACT FILE

The War Lord and his people came from an unnamed "home planet." They might have escaped justice, but the Doctor was able to trick the War Lord into revealing that his planet was in Galactic Sector 9-7-3.

The Time Lords surrounded the planet with an impenetrable forcefield … and dematerialized the War Lord, erasing him entirely from history. They then set about the mammoth task of returning the surviving troops to their home times, with their memories erased.

The Time Lords also returned Jamie and Zoe to their home times, leaving them with only the memories of their first adventure with the Doctor.

FIRST APPEARANCE
The War Games *(1969)*

ABOVE LEFT: The War Lords survey their map of the War Games.

ABOVE: What looked like a breakdown in the structure of time was actually something far more sinister.

WAR ZONES

ZONE ONE—the central command zone, a futuristic series of control rooms, processing centers, and the machinery necessary to maintain the War Planet.

1917 ZONE—the latest of the time zones: beyond this point, the humans' "greater technological knowledge would be dangerous." This was the first zone the Doctor and his companions arrived in and was adjacent to the…

ROMAN ZONE (also known as Sector Five). This seemed to border…

- the American Civil War Zone
- the Crimean War Zone
- the Russo-Japanese War Zone
- the Thirty Years' War Zone
- the Boer Wars Zone
- the English Civil War Zone
- the Peninsular War Zone
- the Greek Zone and
- the Mexican Civil War Zone

We also see or hear about soldiers from the Jacobite Rebellion, Napoleon's advance on Russia, and the Boxer Rising.

BEHIND THE SCENES

This ten-part story (Terrance Dicks & Malcolm Hulke, 1969) was the last regular adventure of the second Doctor, who was captured by his people, the Time Lords, at the end; put on trial; and then sentenced to exile on Earth for interfering in the histories of other planets.

5

DISTANT PLANETS

THE ANDROMEDA GALAXY

FIRST APPEARANCE

📖 Doctor Who and the Invasion from Space *(1965)*

The nearest large spiral galaxy to our own Milky Way, Andromeda clearly has its own vast and diverse array of civilizations, creatures, and landmarks. Star Pioneers from Earth first reached Andromeda after solar flares caused Earth to be evacuated. They found the galaxy to be infested with the Wirrn, large insects that reproduced by infecting live hosts, who became Wirrn larvae. The two races fought each other for 1,000 years, until all the Wirrn breeding grounds were destroyed. Some Wirrn, though, were able to make the journey to Earth's Solar System.

HISTORY

Millions of years in the future, there is a human civilization in Andromeda—the conman Sabalom Glitz, who met both the sixth and seventh Doctors, comes from Salostopus, in Andromeda, a society where women can take multiple husbands. Andromedans are advanced, building powerful robots and harnessing black light energy. They are able, indeed, to steal secrets from the Matrix, the repository of all Time Lord knowledge. When the subsequent cover-up comes to light during the Doctor's second trial, it is enough to spark a revolution on Gallifrey and see the High Council deposed.[1]

ABOVE: The One, the godlike controller of the Andromedan fleet that was scattered by the first Doctor.

LEFT: Galactic conman Sabalom Glitz comes from Andromeda.

FOOTNOTE
[1] 📺 *The Trial of a Time Lord*

📖 THE INVASION FROM SPACE

In the distant future, Andromeda is ruled by The One (an artificial intelligence containing the memories of all Andromedans) for millions of years, but it comes to a point where it is running out of natural resources. The One orders the construction of an armada of a million artificial planets and sets out on a 400-million-year journey to the Milky Way. The first Doctor arrives on one of these planets and is able to sabotage the systems, so the fleet ends up drifting aimlessly in space.

📺 THE DALEKS' MASTER PLAN

Mavic Chen attended a conference of Galactic leaders in Andromeda. The Outer Galaxies sent a single representative, Trantis.

📖 DANGER DOWN BELOW

A lot of Andromedan planets are full of Migrators, large amoebalike creatures protected by external antibodies.

📖 EVOLUTION

The fourth Doctor encountered hybrid mer-children, results of an experiment, in Victorian England. He rehoused them on a water planet in the Andromeda Galaxy.

📺 THE PIRATE PLANET

The ground of the Pirate Planet of Zanak was littered with Andromedan bloodstones (p. 226).

📺 CASTROVALVA

Castrovalva is a planet in the Phylox series in Andromeda—at least according to an entry in the TARDIS Information File that the Master may have faked.

📺 TIMELASH

The Doctor contemplated visiting the Constellation of Andromeda.

📖 THE GALLIFREY CHRONICLES

The currency in Andromeda is the Andromedan Euro.

📖 THE LAST DODO

The Museum of the Lost Ones has a single specimen of each extinct species in the Milky Way and Andromeda.

📖 SHINING DARKNESS

There is a highly advanced Andromedan galactic civilization where biological and machine life coexist in relative harmony.

THE ACTEON GALAXY

The third Doctor was exiled to Earth in the 20th century by the Time Lords, unable to travel time and space except on the rare occasions they sent him on a mission to another world. When his exile was lifted, the first planet he wanted to visit was Metebelis III, "the famous blue planet of the Acteon group." Never very good at programming the TARDIS, the Doctor "slightly overshot," and he and his companion, Jo Grant, instead arrived on Inter Minor, another planet in the group. The third Doctor would have better luck on a later occasion, visiting Metebelis III twice.

FIRST APPEARANCE
Carnival of Monsters *(1973)*

CURRENT STATUS
Inter Minor adopting a more liberal regime; Metebelis III recovering from the rule of the Spiders

HISTORY

The Doctor also referred to the Acteon group as the "Acteon Galaxy," and it's clear that Inter Minor and Metebelis III are a long way from Earth. The Lurmans, a humanlike race, lived close enough that the showman Vorg and his lovely assistant, Shirna, could travel there, and were well known enough for the leader of Inter Minor, President Zarb, to agree that Lurmans could be the first aliens to visit their world when immigration restrictions were lifted. Vorg had done national service with the Old Fourteenth Heavy Lasers, and his battery sergeant was a Crustacoid mercenary, suggesting the galaxy was not an entirely peaceful one. Vorg and Shirna were not, though, as some of the isolationists on Inter Minor feared, the spearhead for the Lurman battlefleets.

RIGHT: The third Doctor got to Metebelis III eventually … but it wasn't what he was expecting.

TIMELINE

PLANET OF THE SPIDERS

1974

The Doctor defeats the Great One, the giant spider Queen who leads the Eight Legs, but as the crystal chamber is highly radioactive, it costs him his life. At the end of this adventure, he returns to Earth to regenerate.

CARNIVAL OF MONSTERS

THIRD DOCTOR

ROBERT HOLMES

1973

Inter Minor has been an isolated world for thousands of years, following a virulent space plague. It allows Vorg and Shirna to present their *Carnival of Monsters* show, using a Miniscope that contains living specimens kept in time bubbles.

1974

PLANET OF THE SPIDERS

THIRD DOCTOR

ROBERT SLOMAN

The "Eight Legs" of Metebelis III travel across time and space to recover the blue crystal. These are superevolved spiders (mutated by the blue crystals) who need the crystal the Doctor has taken to complete their plan to dominate the universe as they have dominated the human colonists of their world.

1973

CARNIVAL OF MONSTERS

The Doctor is able to calm the fears of the more xenophobic Inter Minorians … but not before a deadly Drashig monster has escaped the Miniscope.

1973

THE GREEN DEATH

THIRD DOCTOR

ROBERT SLOMAN

The Doctor makes a very brief visit to Metebelis III, but instead of the promised paradise, he is attacked by spear-throwing natives and a giant bird. He returns with a fabulous blue crystal that can be used to clear confused or hypnotized minds.

GALAXY 4

Little is known about Galaxy 4, or the Fourth Galaxy. In the year 4000, it was considered one of the Outer Galaxies. In public Mavic Chen celebrated the signing of a complicated mineral agreement with Galaxy 4; in private they were working against the interests of the Solar System, both in league with the Daleks. One of the Delegates who met with Chen and the Daleks on Kembel was from Galaxy 4 (although it's unclear which one).[1]

HISTORY

We know that the Semestran Interlude[2] and The Suffering[3] were natives of Galaxy 4. We have only ever seen one planet in Galaxy 4, which was visited by the first Doctor—a world with three suns that was warm, oxygen-rich … and utterly devoid of life other than some dessicated vegetation. This was a fact that piqued the Doctor's scientific curiosity. There were, in fact, two other parties present on the planet, neither of them native to this world.

RIGHT: The Drahvins crash-landed on a dying world in Galaxy 4.

FIRST APPEARANCE
Galaxy 4 (1965)

INHABITANTS
The Rill, the Drahvins, the Chumblies, Trantis, the Semestran Interlude, the Suffering

FACT FILE

GALAXY 4
Two ships had crashed on this unnamed world following a battle in space. The first the Doctor encountered were the Drahvins. They were a race of beautiful but cruel women from Drahva, a planet with limited resources in the grip of global cooling, who operated a strict caste system.

GALAXY 4
Most Drahvins were menial workers, created artificially and with limited creativity. They had numbers instead of names and ate food pills. The Elite were born naturally—a few males were kept alive for breeding purposes—and ate real food. The Drahvin ship was old and had already been in need of repair. It was commanded by the fearsome Maaga.

GALAXY 4
Not far away was the crashed ship of the Rills. At first, they did not reveal themselves, sending out small robot servants, which the Doctor's companion, Vicki, named "Chumblies" because of the peculiar noises they made. The Rills were monstrous—large, tusked walruslike creatures who could only breathe ammonia. They communicated telepathically. The Rills needed "sunray" energy for their ship but could not collect enough with the equipment they had.

GALAXY 4
Despite appearances, it was the Drahvins who were the monsters. If they had cooperated with the Rills, both could have left the planet, but instead both were trapped. Both races knew that the planet had only around 400 days before it would be destroyed. The Drahvins planned to fight the Rill and steal their technology.

GALAXY 4
The Doctor had bad news: the planet did not have 400 dawns; it had two. The day after tomorrow, the planet would disintegrate. The Doctor offered to power the Rill ship using energy from the TARDIS to get it off the planet and close enough to a star to recharge its sunray banks. Despite the Drahvins' best efforts, the Doctor got the Rill ship into space and left Maaga and her soldiers to their fate as the planet exploded.

THE DYING DAYS
UNIT fought the Drahvins.

"THE PANDORICA OPENS"
The Drahvins also took part in a massive alliance to imprison the Doctor in the Pandorica.

FOOTNOTES
[1] *The Daleks' Master Plan* • [2] *Voyage to the New World* •
[3] *The Suffering*

HYSPERO

FIRST APPEARANCE
📖 The Scarlet Empress *(1998)*

STATUS
Prosperous

Hyspero is on the edge of the universe, a place from which the Obverse can be reached (see p. 15). Hyspero is the name of both the planet and its capital city. The city looks like something of a storybook, with steeples, domes, minarets, and towers. It also contains a bazaar where buyers and sellers from countless worlds trade. Almost anything can be found there, although it has a particular reputation for fine silks. Goods are paid for in the local currency, the dirna (one being worth about 30 cents). The Doctor has visited Hyspero many times.

HISTORY

Visitors to Hyspero are colorful and cosmopolitan, but the city's locals are beige-skinned, with lugubrious expressions. They are wary of the Scarlet Guard, who are covered in blue tattoos and don't hesitate to arrest troublemakers. The people of Hyspero love stories of thieves and assassins—but only if they're never caught.

The planet also has many other principalities. Fortalice has a library containing exactly 1,001 books. Kesthaven is a forest full of bears that shave their golden fur off every day. There are also alligator men; mock turtles; at least one giant walrus; a race of intelligent giant spiders; Ifrits

(who eat the dead); Kabikaj (large orange men who can control insect life); and reptile, warthog, and heron people. The terrain includes deserts, ice fields, and oceans. Hyspero is ruled by the ancient Scarlet Empress, 900th of her line. She has powerful magical abilities and hates anyone who claims they can see the future.

RIGHT: The cover of *The Scarlet Empress*, in which the eighth Doctor visited Hyspero.
BELOW: Landscapes of Hyspero.

TIMELINE

2002

📖 *THE SCARLET EMPRESS*

👤 EIGHTH DOCTOR

✒ PAUL MAGRS

The Doctor and Sam visit Hyspero in the third decade of the Abbasid era. Sam finds a crocodile man, Gila, chained up in a bus. The bus belongs to an old flame of the Doctor's, Iris Wildthyme, who is working for the Scarlet Empress to reassemble Gila's old band of mercenaries, the Four. After a series of colorful adventures across Hyspero, the Four are reunited—Gila the Duchess (mechanical, except for her heart), Major Angela, the Bearded Lady, and the Mock Turtle.

1998

🎧 *EXCELIS DAWNS*

👤 FIFTH DOCTOR

✒ PAUL MAGRS

Iris Wildthyme claims that her handbag was bought in Hyspero's bazaar.

1999

📖 *THE BLUE ANGEL*

👤 EIGHTH DOCTOR

✒ PAUL MAGRS & JEREMY HOAD

Daedalus, the jade elephant king, once tried to boost his reputation by going to Hyspero.

1998

📖 *THE SCARLET EMPRESS*

The Scarlet Empress lives in a glass cylinder full of preserving honey. Her predecessors are all alive and kept in smaller jars. The Scarlet Empress wants Cassandra, the first empress, who lives in a jar that has disappeared. Cassandra disapproves of the rule of the current empress and bends time to undo it.

KROP TOR, THE IMPOSSIBLE PLANET

Krop Tor was called the "Impossible Planet" because it was in a stable orbit around the black hole K37 Gem 5. The name appears in the scriptures of the Valtino; in their language it means "bitter pill"—legends spoke of a demon spitting it out. The planet was remote. Even by the 42nd century, the era of the Second Great and Bountiful Earth Empire, it would take 500 years to reach Earth from Krop Tor. It was desolate, too—airless, covered in volcanic rock, and unstable due to gravitational forces from the black hole.

FIRST APPEARANCE
📺 *"The Impossible Planet"* (2006)

STATUS
Destroyed

LEFT: Ood servants were possessed by the Beast.

HISTORY

There were ruins of a lost civilization on Krop Tor—the Disciples of the Light—and there was a city ten miles beneath the surface, with monumental architecture, but little else had survived apart from shards of pottery.

The Walker Expedition, working for the Torchwood Archive, arrived from Earth to study the Impossible Planet. Whatever was keeping the planet from falling into the black hole was an immense power source, and so it was of great interest to the Empire. The mission lost its captain as soon as it arrived, but they were able to establish their Sanctuary Base and commence drilling and investigation of the planet. They soon faced other problems. Their Ood servants, their electronic equipment, and eventually some of the humans became possessed by a strange force.

TIMELINE

"THE IMPOSSIBLE PLANET"
TENTH DOCTOR
MATT JONES

The Doctor and Rose arrive at Sanctuary Base to be confronted with graffiti declaring "Welcome to Hell," as well as a language so old the Doctor can't translate it.

2006

"THE IMPOSSIBLE PLANET"

The base is hit by an earthquake, during which the TARDIS drops into the depths of the planet. The Ood are acting strangely. The Doctor helps calculate the power of an artificial gravity funnel that allows Krop Tor to survive. They tunnel down to the depths of the planet, and as they reach the center, the Ood, clearly possessed, declare themselves the "Legion of the Beast."

2006

"THE IMPOSSIBLE PLANET"

The Doctor locates the TARDIS in the caverns below the base and finds the Pit, which contains a demonic being who is now free.

"END OF DAYS"
CHRIS CHIBNALL

In early 21st century Cardiff, Torchwood fights the "Son of the Beast," Abaddon, when he is released from his own imprisonment underneath the space-time rift under that city.

2007

2006

"THE SATAN PIT"

Rose sends Toby's body into the black hole, and the gravity funnel is cut off. The Doctor, though, is able to use the TARDIS to tow the Earthmen's ship away from Krop Tor. The Impossible Planet plunges into the black hole, the Ood are killed, and the Beast's body is destroyed.

2006

"THE SATAN PIT"
TENTH DOCTOR
MATT JONES

The being is the Beast, chained here since the dawn of time, and very possibly the Devil of human mythology. The expedition attempts to fend off his army of Ood, who are trying to ensure his release. The Beast places his spirit in Toby, one of the humans, leaving his own body merely a mindless animal.

ABOVE: The diverse giant insects of Vortis, in the Isop Galaxy.

RIGHT: The Abzorbaloff, native of Clom.

THE ISOP GALAXY

A distant galaxy … but one whose inhabitants find it surprisingly easy to get to Earth, the Isop Galaxy is notable as the location of both Vortis—planet of the Zarbi and Menoptra (see p. 264)—and Raxacoricofallapatorius, home of the Slitheen (p. 262). The latter is senior partner of the Raxas Alliance, a union of four planets: Raxacoricofallapatorius, Raxacoricovarlonpatoris, Clix, and Clom.[1]

HISTORY

The Abzorbaloff came from Clom, which was the sister planet of Raxacoricofallapatorius, and Rose spotted a family resemblance to the Slitheen—he was fast for his vast bulk, had sickly green skin and three-fingered hands, and was able to disguise himself as human. His face was far more like a human being's. He was able to absorb people, gaining their memories and knowledge, their faces remaining visible in his immense folds of fat. It's unclear if everyone from Clom was of this nature, or whether the Abzorbaloff was unique. He hated the inhabitants of Clom's twin planet.[2] Clom was, somewhat to the Doctor's astonishment, stolen by the Daleks as part of one of their most ambitious schemes.[3]

FIRST APPEARANCE
The Web Planet *(1965)*

STATUS
Rebuilding after misrule

BEHIND THE SCENES

A reference to Venom Grubs in the TV story "Boom Town" led fans to speculate that the Slitheen were from the same galaxy as Vortis (p. 264), home of the Venom Grubs. This was confirmed in the installment of the extra feature *Sarah Jane's Alien Files* that ran alongside the TV story titled *The Empty Planet*.

FACT FILE

TWILIGHT OF THE GODS
The Rhumons are from the Isop Galaxy—they resemble beautiful, copper-skinned humans and originated on Rhumon Prime but settled the neighboring New Rhumos long ago. Following the first Doctor's defeat of the Animus, Vortis drifted into the Rhumons' solar system. The second Doctor was able to unite the warring factions of all the worlds involved.

THE DARKSMITH LEGACY: THE GAME OF DEATH
The Silver Devastation is in the Isop Galaxy. It is a vast, lifeless sector of space, but with so many stars it looks like a silver sea.

"THE END OF THE WORLD"
The Face of Boe came from the Silver Devastation …

"UTOPIA"
… and the infant who would grow up to be Professor Yana was found there—Yana was secretly the Master, so well disguised that not even he knew.

REVENGE OF THE SLITHEEN
"Clom" is a Slitheen expletive, as in the phrase, "For the love of Clom."

SHINING DARKNESS
The Doctor has a copy of the *Rough Guide to the Isop Galaxy*, which names the robotic inhabitants of Napir Prime as the best hosts in the universe.

THE GIFT
Raxacoricofallapatorians enjoy eating land prawns harvested on Clom.

"THE GIRL WHO WAITED"
There is a Disneyland on Clom.

FOOTNOTES
[1] *The Gift* • [2] "Love and Monsters" •
[3] "The Stolen Earth"

RAXACORICOFALLAPATORIUS

Raxacoricofallapatorius is home to the race commonly known as the Slitheen, although that is actually just the name of the former ruling clan of the planet. The Slitheen used to run the Grand Council, with the head of the family serving as Lord Predator, but have recently been overthrown by the Blathereen. Members of the Slitheen are plotting their return. The planet was also the home of the giant squirrel creatures, the baaraddelskelliumfatrexius beasts (before they were hunted to extinction), the bartleboigle tree, and rakweed.

FIRST APPEARANCE
📺 *"Aliens of London" (2005)*

STATUS
Ruled by the Blathereen, attempting to restore their reputation

HISTORY

Adult Raxacoricofallapatorians are tall, fat humanoids with faces resembling human babies. They are fast and strong, with three-clawed hands. Their skin can be various sickly shades, ranging from yellow-green to brownish-orange. They hatch from large eggs and grow more slowly than humans. They have the best sense of smell in the galaxy (the Isop Galaxy, presumably) and are able to identify and track human beings by their scent. They have some sort of empathic sense for others of their kind—for example, they are able to know when another of their kind has died, even over many miles distance. Their bodies are calcium-based. They are easily killed using household vinegar. Females naturally produce poison darts and breathe poison from their mouths. The species is advanced, and they are active scavengers, meaning they have access to a variety of exotic technologies. Their society retains the death penalty.

LEFT: The Slitheen nearly destroyed the Earth in pursuit of profits.

TIMELINE

📖 THE SLITHEEN EXCURSION
👤 TENTH DOCTOR
✎ SIMON GUERRIER

2009

A group of Slitheen pose as gods at the time of King Acteus. They are running time-travel tours back to Ancient Greece —and the alien tourists become the basis for many of the monsters of Greek myth.

📺 "ALIENS OF LONDON" / "WORLD WAR THREE"
👤 NINTH DOCTOR
✎ RUSSELL T DAVIES

2005

Using compression fields that allow them to squeeze into the skins of (fat) people they have killed and hollowed out, the Slitheen infiltrate the upper echelons of British society. They then fake a first-contact scenario, crashing a spaceship containing a genetically modified Space Pig into London. In the confusion, they take control of the UK's nuclear codes and attempt to destroy the Earth, converting it into radioactive fuel they could then sell. The Doctor and Rose manage to stop them.

2009

📺 THE GIFT
👤 SARAH JANE & K9
✎ RUPERT LAIGHT

The Blathereen arrive on Earth offering a plant native to their world—rakweed—which grows so quickly it could solve world hunger. The weed spreads uncontrollably, and Sarah Jane and K9 realize this had been the plan all along. They track the Blathereen to their lair in Antarctica.

2005

📺 "BOOM TOWN"
👤 NINTH DOCTOR
✎ RUSSELL T DAVIES

One Slitheen survives the explosion in London: Blon Fel-Fotch Passameer-Day Slitheen, who escapes to Cardiff and, as Margaret Blaine, becomes Lord Mayor. She plans to build an unstable nuclear reactor in the city. The Doctor and Rose are, once again, able to stop her. She is rejuvenated by the power of the TARDIS.

2008

📺 REVENGE OF THE SLITHEEN
👤 SARAH JANE
✎ GARETH ROBERTS

Other Slitheen try to shut off the Sun to avenge the deaths of their family members but Sarah Jane Smith and her friends are able to sabotage their plans.

VORTIS

Vortis, in the Isop Galaxy, was a beautiful world of flower forests populated by the Menoptra, butterfly people who raised giant ants, the Zarbi, as livestock. The Menoptra worshipped the light, but their flightless (and rather stupid) cousins, the Optera, lived underground and practiced a more barbaric religion. Life on Vortis was peaceful. The Doctor made a number of visits, mostly during his first incarnation.

HISTORY

The world was invaded by the Animus, a spiderlike being that could take control of the minds of others. The ecology of Vortis collapsed, and it became a world of gray mica soil and formic acid pools, with such a thin atmosphere that humans could not survive without special breathing equipment. The Animus built a vast fortress, the Carsinome, at the north pole of Vortis. It dragged two planetoids to Vortis, which became new moons, and the Menoptra fled to one of them—Pictos.[1]

FIRST APPEARANCE
The Web Planet *(1965)*

STATUS
Under the control of the Menoptra, for now

FOOTNOTE
[1] *The Web Planet*

RIGHT: The first Doctor is menaced by a Zarbi.

TIMELINE

THE WEB PLANET
FIRST DOCTOR
BILL STRUTTON

The Animus is planning to spread its influence across the universe. The Doctor and his companions are able to defeat the Animus by teaming up with the Menoptra and using the Isop-Tope, a weapon that can destroy the cells of its body.

1965

1965

ON THE WEB PLANET
FIRST DOCTOR
NEVILLE MAIN

Skirkon invaders take control of the Zarbi and use them to enslave the Menoptra to mine Galvinium X—an explosive the Doctor is able to use to blow up the Skirkon base.

1965

THE LAIR OF ZARBI SUPREMO
FIRST DOCTOR
WALTER HOWARTH

An intelligent Zarbi evolves, three times the normal size, and becomes the leader of its kind, the Zarbi Supremo. The Supremo orders great engines built to move Vortis into the orbit of the planet Jupiter. The Supremo wants Earth's water and vegetation.

TWILIGHT OF THE GODS
SECOND DOCTOR
CHRISTOPHER BULIS

1996

The Doctor returns hundreds of years after the Animus was defeated to find that Vortis has mostly recovered and drifted into the Rhumos solar system. Two Rhumon groups want to take control of the planet to mine the rare antigravity mineral isocryte. A seed of the Animus begins to grow, and the Doctor persuades the Rhumons to unite and join forces with the Menoptra to defeat it.

1965

THE LOST ONES
FIRST DOCTOR
WALTER HOWARTH

The Zarbi force the Menoptra off Vortis. A scout party returns and is attacked by giants from Atlantis. The Atlanteans are caught in the crossfire as the Menoptra seek to take back their world.

1965

THE LAIR OF ZARBI SUPREMO

The Doctor arrives and learns of the Supremo's plan, thanks to some human astronauts who have arrived on the planet and are trying to warn Earth. With the help of the Menoptra, the Doctor and the astronauts kill the Zarbi Supremo.

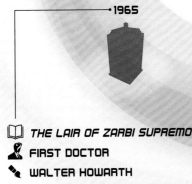

THE SENSE-SPHERE

FIRST APPEARANCE
The Sensorites *(1964)*

INHABITANTS
The Sensorites

The Sensorites are small humanoids, with large heads and bulging black eyes. They all look very similar, even to each other. They were shaped by their environment. The Sense-Sphere has two suns and is in perpetual daylight. The atmosphere is thicker than Earth's, meaning sound travels farther. The Sensorites cannot see in the dark and are upset by loud noises. One group of Sensorites live in a futuristic city surrounded by the Yellow Mountains. They collect "crystal water" from a spring there, of such quality that the Elders drink nothing else.

HISTORY

When Earth survey ships found the Sense-Sphere, all they saw was an ordinary planet with a slightly higher than average land mass. When the results were studied, though, it became clear the planet had vast deposits of molybdenum. The element was used as an alloy to increase the melting point of steel, so it was a vital part of spaceship construction. The astronaut who made that discovery, John, pictured himself growing rich when fleets of ships came from Earth to mine the Sense-Sphere. The Sensorites' greatest invention, however, was the mind transmitter, which gave them the ability to send and receive on "mind frequencies"—telepathy. Unfortunately for John, this ability to read minds meant that the people of the Sense-Sphere were horrified by what they saw in his.

BEHIND THE SCENES

The Sensorites appeared once on TV and once in a story from the first *Doctor Who Annual*, a year later. In the *Annual* story, the Doctor has never met the Sensorites, which we can infer makes it a very rare example of an entire story set before the TV series started.

ABOVE: The Sensorites kept human astronauts under control with their psychic powers.

TIMELINE

📺 "TIME HEIST"
👤 TWELFTH DOCTOR
✎ STEVE THOMPSON & STEVEN MOFFAT

2014

A Sensorite is among the most notorious universal criminals of his age.

📺 THE SENSORITES
👤 FIRST DOCTOR
✎ PETER R. NEWMAN

1964

The Doctor, Ian, Barbara, and Susan arrive in a spaceship in orbit around a mysterious world. The crew appears to be dead but they revive. They are a survey team being kept there by the Sensorites.

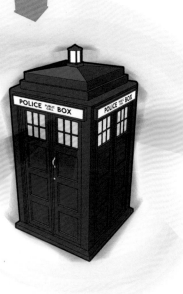

2009

📺 "PLANET OF THE OOD"
👤 TENTH DOCTOR
✎ KEITH TEMPLE

While on Ood Sphere, the planet of the Ood, the Doctor and Donna see a map that confirms it is in the same solar system as the Sense-Sphere. The Ood and Sensorites are both dome-headed telepathic humanoids, so they possibly share an ancestor.

1964

📺 THE SENSORITES

John, an astronaut who dreams of exploiting the mineral wealth of the planet, is living below the Sensorite city with other survivors of an earlier expedition and poisoning their leaders. The Doctor finds him and frees the other astronauts.

1965

📖 THE MONSTERS FROM EARTH
👤 FIRST DOCTOR
✎ WALTER HOWARTH

Earlier in their history, the Doctor accidentally brings Earth children Amy and Tony Barker (and their dog Butch) to the Sense-Sphere. They escape a giant spider, a creature the Sensorites are terrified of, and call the Zilgan. The Sensorites capture the Doctor but run away at the sound of Butch's barking.

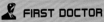

WORLDSPHERE

FIRST APPEARANCE
The Also People *(1995)*

STATUS
Masters of the Home Galaxy

Many millions of years ago, many spacefaring civilizations of what they called "Home Galaxy" united to become "the People." They genetically engineered themselves so that all species could interbreed, creating an extraordinarily diverse population that looked human, but with an almost infinite variety of skin tones and body shapes. They also developed powerful artificial intelligences, citizens in their own right. Finally, they enclosed the star Whynot within a large shell—creating a Dyson Sphere—and moved to its inner surface, which was 600 million times larger than Earth's.

BEHIND THE SCENES

Ben Aaronovitch freely declared that *The Also People* was inspired by imagining the Doctor visiting the Culture, the advanced utopian civilization seen in many of the science-fiction novels by Iain M. Banks, and the People of the Worldsphere share many characteristics. Later New Adventures novels added to our knowledge of this civilization.

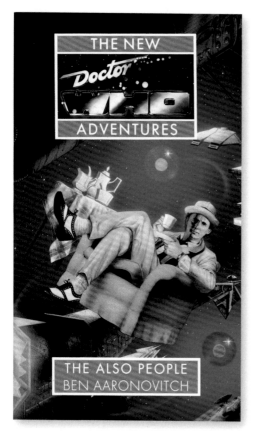

HISTORY

Two trillion people are watched over by the artificial intelligence, God. They have no government as such, just elaborate hobbies, and they form interest groups on everything from pottery to intergalactic warfare.[1] They are one of a few civilizations that have signed a non-aggression pact with the Time Lords (the Doctor was part of the negotiating team). The People of the Worldsphere are so advanced that they rival the Doctor's people technologically, and in terms of potential, although they have agreed not to conduct any time-travel experiments.

The devastating war against the Great Hive Mind of Insects saw the development of Very Aggressive Ships, run by powerful and dangerous artificial intelligences; 26 billion people died, and dozens of worlds were destroyed or devastated. The Insects joined the People, who now had no rivals in their own galaxy.[2]

LEFT: The seventh Doctor and his friends solved a murder in paradise.

RIGHT: The People fought in a great army of races alongside the sixth Doctor in the Millennium War.

FOOTNOTES
[1,2] *The Also People*

TIMELINE

2001

📖 *THE ALSO PEOPLE*

👤 SEVENTH DOCTOR

✏️ BEN AARONOVITCH

The Doctor, Benny, Chris, and Roz manage to visit the utopian society at a time when it suffers its first violent crime in over 300 years, the murder of the drone viCari.

1995

📖 *THE QUANTUM ARCHANGEL*

👤 SIXTH DOCTOR

✏️ CRAIG HINTON

Although they are not from our galaxy, the People fought alongside many other civilizations in the Millennium War in the distant past of the Mutter's Spiral galaxy.

1997

📖 *DOWN*

✏️ LAWRENCE MILES

The concept of "hollow worlds" appears in the mythology of many planets, thanks to the real-life example of the Worldsphere. They are also responsible for the MEPHISTO meme: Mankind Expects Pain, However It Seems To Outsiders, which stated that feeling pain is necessary even when all is "perfect."

1999

📖 *THE SHADOWS OF AVALON*

👤 EIGHTH DOCTOR

✏️ PAUL CORNELL

President Romana leads negotiations to resolve Gallifrey's disputes with the Worldsphere, knowing that the Time War is on the horizon.

1997

📖 *WALKING TO BABYLON*

✏️ KATE ORMAN

Two drones, !Ci!ci-tel and WiRgo!xu, try to goad the Time Lords into a war by time-traveling to ancient Babylon. The Doctor's former companion, Bernice Summerfield, is sent back by the People to prevent them from destroying Earth with a singularity bomb.

6

THE LAST PLANETS

REFUGEES FROM EARTH

"Fleeing from the imminence of a catastrophic collision with the Sun, a group of refugees from the doomed planet Earth..." Ten million years in the future, the Earth plunges into the Sun. The human race has time to plan their escape. As they did at the time of the solar flares, they construct giant arks and evacuate the planet.

HISTORY

This time, the arks are sent into deep space on voyages to specific planets selected to be new Earths. We know of two arks, and perhaps there were more. This was the 57th segment of time. Time Lord knowledge was a little patchy about events so far in the future, but Earth had survived the Primal Wars, flirted with developing time-travel technology, and emerged as a technically advanced, peaceful people.

Refusis II is identified as a future home for the human race because when they look through telescopes, it is clearly a beautiful, Earthlike world, complete with seemingly abandoned buildings. The planet Frontios, in the Veruna system on the edge of the universe, is selected because it looks perfect for settlement. In both cases, the arks face technical, political, and external problems that threaten the existence of the entire human race.

FIRST APPEARANCE
The Ark (1966)

BEHIND THE SCENES

While we seem to see the Earth destroyed in *The Ark*, set ten million years from now, the final and definitive end comes five billion years from now, and we see it in "The End of the World" (p. 48). Earth clearly survives whatever happened in *The Ark* (it seems like something knocked Earth out of its normal orbit).

LEFT: A Monoid abducts the Doctor's friend Dodo.

TIMELINE

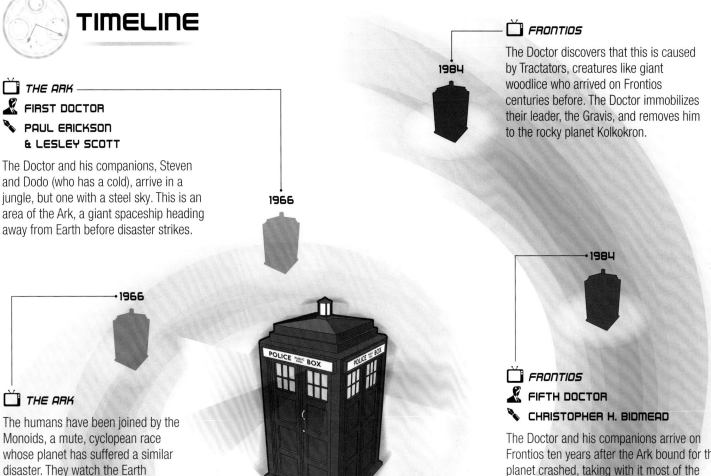

THE ARK

FIRST DOCTOR

PAUL ERICKSON & LESLEY SCOTT

The Doctor and his companions, Steven and Dodo (who has a cold), arrive in a jungle, but one with a steel sky. This is an area of the Ark, a giant spaceship heading away from Earth before disaster strikes.

1966

FRONTIOS

1984

The Doctor discovers that this is caused by Tractators, creatures like giant woodlice who arrived on Frontios centuries before. The Doctor immobilizes their leader, the Gravis, and removes him to the rocky planet Kolkokron.

1984

1966

THE ARK

The humans have been joined by the Monoids, a mute, cyclopean race whose planet has suffered a similar disaster. They watch the Earth destroyed, then leave, knowing the Ark is safely on its way …

FRONTIOS

FIFTH DOCTOR

CHRISTOPHER H. BIDMEAD

The Doctor and his companions arrive on Frontios ten years after the Ark bound for that planet crashed, taking with it most of the people and technology. The planet is experiencing strange anomalies with its gravity, which sees asteroids (and the TARDIS) drawn to Frontios and people sucked into the soil.

1966

1966

THE ARK

… and immediately land on the same spot, 700 years later. The Monoids have taken over the Ark, making humanity their slaves.

THE ARK

To add to the problems, Refusis II turns out to be inhabited by invisible giants. With the Doctor's help, the Refusians destroy the more militant Monoids and welcome the two races—if they can live in peace.

NEW EARTH

Following the final destruction of the Earth, five billion years from now (p. 48), humans and catkind settle an almost identical world. They have to travel some way to find it—50,000 light years to Galaxy M87. There are what appear to be two moons or planets prominent in the sky, even during the day. One large city, New New York, is the 15th New York, so it should probably have 16 "New"s in front of its name.

HISTORY

New New York has a New Fifth Avenue, a towering skyline of futuristic buildings, and a great deal of aircar traffic; it is policed by the NNYPD; and sits in what looks like pristine grassland (applegrass, grass with an apple scent), with forests and a crystal clear body of water—possibly the "New Atlantic." The New New York hospital is a large freestanding building within sight of the city run by the Sisters of Plenitude, an order of catkind nuns. They can cure almost every human disease, including exotic ones. One prominent citizen is the Duke of Manhattan.[1] Underground is the Motorway, a vast loop for aircars that divides into at least 50 vertical lanes, with the Fast Lane at the bottom. Traffic news is broadcast by the AI Sally Calypso.[2] New Earth is the home of the New Earth Empire and is close to the planet New Savannah, home of catkind.[3] Catkind fear sabrewolves, so they may be natives of New Savannah.[4]

FIRST APPEARANCE
 "New Earth" (2006)

ABOVE RIGHT: The tenth Doctor and his companion Martha.

RIGHT: The Sisters of Plenitude, an order of catkind nuns, can cure every disease known to man … and some that aren't yet.

FOOTNOTES
[1] "New Earth" • [2] "Gridlock" • [3] *Agent Provocateur* • [4] "The God Complex"

TIMELINE

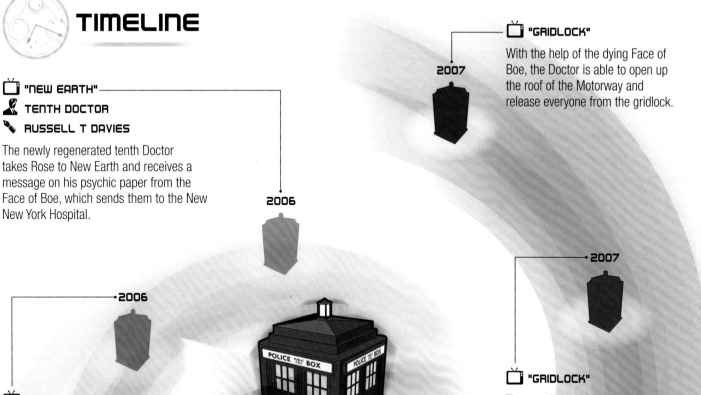

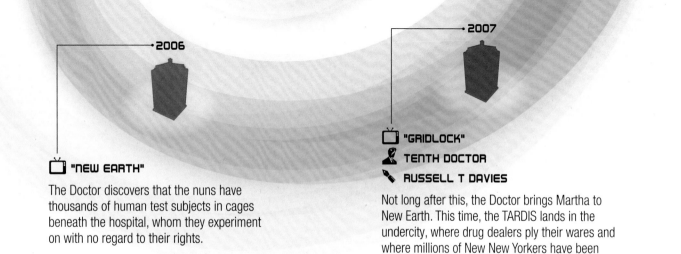

📺 **"NEW EARTH"**

👤 TENTH DOCTOR

✎ RUSSELL T DAVIES

The newly regenerated tenth Doctor takes Rose to New Earth and receives a message on his psychic paper from the Face of Boe, which sends them to the New New York Hospital.

2006

2006

📺 **"NEW EARTH"**

The Doctor grows suspicious that the nuns can treat diseases like Petrifold Regression, Marconi's Disease, and Pallidome Pancrosis, conditions that human science should be a thousand years away from curing. The nuns are very coy about their skills.

2006

📺 **"NEW EARTH"**

The Doctor discovers that the nuns have thousands of human test subjects in cages beneath the hospital, whom they experiment on with no regard to their rights.

📺 **"GRIDLOCK"**

2007

With the help of the dying Face of Boe, the Doctor is able to open up the roof of the Motorway and release everyone from the gridlock.

2007

📺 **"GRIDLOCK"**

The population of the overcity has died out from a mutant disease, and the planet has been placed in quarantine. The Macra are deep in the system, preying on commuters.

2007

📺 **"GRIDLOCK"**

👤 TENTH DOCTOR

✎ RUSSELL T DAVIES

Not long after this, the Doctor brings Martha to New Earth. This time, the TARDIS lands in the undercity, where drug dealers ply their wares and where millions of New New Yorkers have been trapped on the Motorway in a giant aircar jam.

THE LAST PLANETS

The universe will eventually wind down. Trillions of years from now, the last stars will be dying and the vestiges of the surviving species will huddle in the dark. The human race survives, and what it yearns for is found in the names of the places they're trying to get to: Hope, Utopia. One feature of the universe at this point is the Silver Devastation, which may (or may not) be named for a cybernetic would-be dictator of this period.

BELOW: The universe of the last civilizations contained much vying for power.

HISTORY

There are remnants of familiar races, divided into Houses and Factions. There are four surviving Time Lords, but the Children of Kasterborous are, surely, their heirs. A race of shape-shifting goblins can only be hybrids of the Sontarans and the Rutans. The Klade are a race of blond supermen, obsessed with the supremacy of their race and exterminating their enemies, who operate fleets of time-traveling flying saucers. One of the Time Lords was proclaimed the first Emperor of the whole universe. He ruled from the Needle, a light-year-long structure created when a TARDIS died trying to escape from a black hole.

FIRST APPEARANCE
📖 Father Time *(2000)*

TIMELINE

FATHER TIME
👤 EIGHTH DOCTOR
🖊 LANCE PARKIN

In the very distant future, rival Factions vie for the Imperial Throne. The Emperor is deposed in a civil war, but his baby daughter Miranda is taken to safety in 20th-century Earth. The winners of the war are the Klade, who vow to hunt the Last One down and finally claim victory in their eternal war.

2000

2002

HOPE
👤 EIGHTH DOCTOR
🖊 MARK CLAPHAM

Endpoint is a planet of stilt cities on frozen, polluted oceans. The Endpointers are descended from humans, and the largest city, Hope, is run by Silver, a powerful cyborg. Silver is building an army of synthetic soldiers and plans to attack the Imperial Throneworld.

2002

HOPE

The Doctor and his companions, Anji and Fitz, redirect the Hypertunnel Silver is using, marooning him on the barren rock A2756.

2007

📺 "UTOPIA"
👤 TENTH DOCTOR
🖊 RUSSELL T DAVIES

The Doctor, Martha, and Jack end up on Malcassairo 100 trillion years in the future, where the last remnants of the human race are barricaded in a compound to protect them from the savage Futurekind, bestial posthumans.

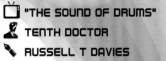

📺 "THE SOUND OF DRUMS"

The Master converts the humans bound for Utopia into Toclafane—shriveled heads in spiky, floating balls. He then sends them, in their billions, to invade the warm, resource-rich present day.

2007

2007

📺 "THE SOUND OF DRUMS"
👤 TENTH DOCTOR
🖊 RUSSELL T DAVIES

… and ends up in modern-day London. The TARDIS is damaged, only able to travel from the present day to the end of the time and back.

2007

📺 "UTOPIA"

Unknown even to himself, Yana is the Doctor's old arch nemesis, the Master, who fled from the Last Great Time War and is so perfectly disguised that he doesn't even recognize himself. His true nature is revealed, and he steals the Doctor's TARDIS but is shot by Chantho and is forced to regenerate …

2007

📺 "UTOPIA"

Malcassairo used to be the home of the Malmooth, a blue-skinned race with insectile facial features, but now only one of them, Chantho, survives. She is working with wise Professor Yana to construct a giant rocket that will take the human race to Utopia, the last stronghold of humanity.

THE END OF THE UNIVERSE

The Time Lords call it Event Two—the last moment of the universe. Since the Big Bang, the universe has been spreading outward, growing colder and more diffuse. Some contemporary scientists think it will eventually start falling back in on itself and collapse into a Big Crunch. This is not what happens—nor does the universe go on forever.

BELOW: The eighth Doctor fought the Council of Eight's attempt to control the entire universe.

HISTORY

There will be a discrete moment around 100,000,000,000,000,000,000,000,000,000,000,000 AD when the universe will end. At this point it is a cold and desolate place. Virtually everything is dead, and the survivors are just the vestiges of great hyper-powers.

To exist at the moment when the universe is complete—and so everything that can be known can be observed—will grant omniscience to a being. This is the so-called Omega Point, and fittingly, one of the beings that will survive is Omega, first of the Time Lords. He had been trapped in a black hole, but even the black holes were starting to disintegrate. The Needle (p. 276) survived, with a handful of people sitting around a fire, surrounded by the art and relics of an entire universe.

FIRST APPEARANCE

📖 *The Omega Point:* Timewyrm: Apocalypse *(1991)*

TIMELINE

THE CHAOS POOL

FIFTH DOCTOR

PETER ANGHELIDES

2009

Sixty-six minutes from the end of time, the Doctor prevents either of the Guardians from a final attempt to assemble the Key to Time.

TIMEWYRM: APOCALYPSE

SEVENTH DOCTOR

NIGEL ROBINSON

1991

The Panjistri, rulers of Kirith, try to create a being that has reached the Omega Point, but it has the wisdom to destroy them, and itself.

2004

SOMETIME NEVER

The Council understands that the Doctor is a threat to their plans and assembles forces across time and space to attack him and his companions. They think that by erasing humanity from history, they will unleash vast amounts of energy, enough to survive the end of the universe.

1998

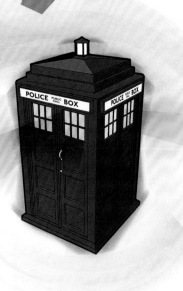

THE INFINITY DOCTORS

THE DOCTOR

LANCE PARKIN

The Needle hosts the last few survivors of the universe—Gordel, Willhuff, Pallant, and Helios, although the four men have forgotten their origins. They guard the entrance to Omega's universe of antimatter. The Doctor passes through it and is able to contain Omega's emergence.

2004

SOMETIME NEVER

EIGHTH DOCTOR

JUSTIN RICHARDS

The Council of Eight is an organization that constructs a Vortex Palace at the end of time and uses special crystals seeded throughout the universe from its early days to create a perfect map of the cosmos.

THE CITY OF THE SAVED

… and then every human being wakes up in the City of the Saved. The definition of "human being" is wide enough to encompass hominid ancestors of homo sapiens and its posthuman, transhuman, half-human descendants. It not only includes fictional characters, but where those characters have been subject to radical reinterpretations, it includes each iteration of those characters, too. Everyone has been reborn in perfect, invulnerable bodies.

FACT FILE

📖 OF THE CITY OF THE SAVED

The City was constructed by, and from the fabric of, Compassion (who had evolved from being a member of the posthuman Remote into a TARDIS while she'd been a companion of the Doctor's) and UniMac (the perfect conceptual human databank) during the last days of the War in Heaven (p. 122).

📖 OF THE CITY OF THE SAVED

The presence of Antipathy, Compassion's child, disrupted a number of the protocols that allowed the City to function. Antipathy was annihilated by Godfather Avatar.

📖 OF THE CITY OF THE SAVED

It posed a great threat to the future of the City if weapons existed that could kill people there.

📖 OF THE CITY OF THE SAVED

Investigator Laura Tobin tried to trace these so-called "potent" weapons and discovered the nature of the City. In a former life, Compassion had been Laura Tobin. Tobin refused to work with … herself, and returned to her work.

📖 BURNING WITH OPTIMISM'S FLAMES

Later, there would be a civil war in the City of the Saved, with at least four trillion deaths.

📖 THE BOOK OF THE WAR

The human race had survived the end of the universe. There had been universes before ours; there will be universes after ours.

HISTORY

The entire City—as best as anyone can make out—is about the size of the Milky Way galaxy. It is vast and defies easy categorization, but it is broadly a place where a polymorphous mass of humanity shares a single urban environment.

While theories abound, the origins and purpose of the City are entirely mysterious to the vast majority of the people resurrected there. The population is immeasurable, but certainly in the septillions (tens of trillions of trillions—more people than there are stars in the universe). The early years of the City are spent with people settling into their new circumstances. New work by the writer Philip K Dick proves popular, and a council of Sherlock Holmeses helps solve a number of mysteries.

FIRST APPEARANCE
📖 The Book of the War (2002)

INHABITANTS
Every single human being who has or will ever live. No one else.

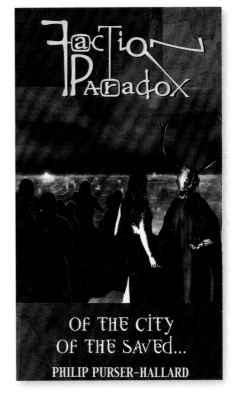

ABOVE: There are a septillion stories in the City. This is one of them.

INDEX

PICTURE CREDITS

iStock

Page 82 Foreground: © REX

Page 84: Screencap of *Time Heist* © BBC

Page 86: ©Hudson Garron (Pending)

Page 87: © Photoshot/Getty Images

Page 88: © World Distributors from *The Doctor Who Annual* (1975)

Page 90 Left: © Adrian Salmon

Right: © Paul Hanley

Page 92: © Mirrorpix, staff photo

Page 95 Top: © Daryl Joyce

Bottom: Image © Panini UK/*Doctor Who Magazine*, Steve Moore/John Stoke

Page 96 Top: © Magic Bullet

Bottom: © Adrian Salmon

Page 98 Left: Hudson Garron (Pending)

Right: © Mirrorpix, photo by Arthur Sidey

Page 100 Left: © Big Finish Productions

Right: © Dan Kitwood/Getty Images

Page 102: © Adrian Salmon

Page 104: © Daryl Joyce

Page 105: © Mirrorpix

Page 106 Left: © Joseph Branston/Future Publishing/REX

Right: © BBC Books

Page 107: © Mark Campbell/REX

Page 108: © Daryl Joyce

Page 109: © Daryl Joyce

Page 110: © PavelSmilyk via iStock

Page 113: © Paul Hanley

Page 114: © Paul Hanley

Page 116: Image © Panini UK/*Doctor Who Magazine*, Alan Moore/John Stokes

Page 117: © Paul Hanley

Page 118 Background: Image courtesy NASA

Top: © ITV/REX

Bottom: Screencap of *The Sound of*

Drums © BBC

Page 120 Top: © World Distributors from *The Doctor Who Annual* (1975)

Bottom: © Adrian Salmon

Page 122 Top: © Cambridge Jones/Getty Images

Bottom Left: ©Mad Norwegian Press

Bottom Right: © BBC Books

Page 124–25: © Paul Cooke

Page 126 Top: © City Magazines from TV Century 21

Bottom: Screencap of *Remembrance of the Daleks* © BBC

Page 127: © Mirrorpix, photo by Dan Smith

Page 128 Top: © Screencap from *The Magician's Apprentice* © BBC

Bottom: © World Distributors, from *The Dalek Outer Space Book*

Page 129: © World Distributors, from *The Dalek Annual* (1979)

Page 130: © Chris Balcome/REX

Page 131: © Daryl Joyce

Page 132 Top: © City Magazines from TV Century 21

Bottom: © Everett Collection/REX

Page 134 Top: © City Magazines from TV Century 21

Bottom: © Mirrorpix, staff photo

Page 136 Top: © Big Finish Productions

Bottom: © BBC Magazines, from the *Doctor Who Special* (1973)

Page 138 Top: © World Distributors, from *The Dalek Outer Space Book*

Bottom: Mirrorpix, photo by Freddie Cole

Page 140 Top: Screencap of *Remembrance of the Daleks* © BBC

Bottom: Screencap of *Asylum of the*

Daleks © BBC

Page 142: © St Martin's Press from the *Doctor Who and the Daleks Omnibus*

Page 144 Top: PDN/VILLARD/SIPA/REX

Bottom: © Paul Hanley

Page 146: © Philip Boyes

Page 147: Screencap of *Journey's End* © BBC

Page 148: Screencap of *Victory of the Daleks* © BBC

Page 150–51: © Paul Hanley

Page 152: © Philip Boyes

Page 154 Top: © Richard Jennings/Cadet Sweets

Bottom: © Daryl Joyce

Page 155: © Mirrorpix

Page 156: © Polystyle from TV Comic

Page 157: © Adrian Salmon

Page 158: © Mirrorpix, photo by Victor Crawshaw

Page 160: © Paul Hanley

Page 162: © Richard Gardner/REX

Page 164 Top: © Chris Jackson/Getty Images

Middle: Image © Panini UK/*Doctor Who Magazine*, Scott Gray/Martin Geraghty

Bottom: © Darren Griffiths/Huw Evans Agency/REX

Page 166: © Paul Hanley

Page 168: © REX

Page 170 Top: © World Distributors, from *Doctor Who Annual* (1969)

Bottom: Screencap from *The Curse of Peladon* © BBC

Page 171: © REX

Page 172: © Adrian Salmon

Page 174: © Richard Gardner/REX

Page 176: © Dan McDaid

Page 178 Top: Hudson Garron (Pending)

Bottom: © Ray Tang/REX

Page 180 Top: ©REX

Page 180 Bottom: © REX

Page 182 Top: © Fox Photos/Getty Images

Bottom: © Philip Boyes

Page 184 Left: © Dan McDaid

Right: © Polystyle from TV Comic

Page 186: © Paul Cooke

Page 187: © Mirrorpix, photo by Peter Stone

Page 188: © Paul Hanley

Page 190 Top: Eddie Wing/REX

Middle: © Science & Society Picture Library/Getty Images

Bottom: © British Library/Robana/REX

Page 192: © Mirrorpix, photo by Ron Burton

Page 194: © South West News Service/REX

Page 196: © Bill Zygmant/REX

Page 198 Left: © Daryl Joyce

Right: © REX

Page 200: Image © Panini UK/*Doctor Who Magazine*, Steve Moore/Steve Dillon

Page 202: © Daryl Joyce

Page 204–5 © hadzi3 via iStock

Page 206 Top: © BBC Worldwide

Bottom: © Moviestore Collection/REX

Page 208: © Daryl Joyce

Page 210 Top: © Huw John/REX

Bottom left: © REX

Bottom right: © IDW

Page 211: Huw John/REX

ACKNOWLEDGMENTS

FROM THE AUTHOR

Thanks to Brie Parkin.

And to Adrian Salmon, Dan McDaid, Daryl Joyce, Paul Hanley, Paul Cooke, Philip Boyes, Allan Bednar; Mark Jones; Lars Pearson; Tom Spilsbury; Brandy Schillace; Kate Orman and Jon Blum; Jim Cooray Smith, Eddie Robson, Mark Clapham; Isheeta Mustafi, Jane Lanaway, Angela Koo; Simon Flavin, Dimity Telfer; Philip Purser-Hallard, Stuart Douglas; Becky Gissel.

PICTURE ACKNOWLEDGEMENTS (CONTINUED)

Page 212 Top: Image © Panini UK/*Doctor Who Magazine*, Steve Moore/Dave Gibbons

Bottom: Image © Panini UK/*Doctor Who Magazine*, Steve Moore/David Lloyd

Page 214: © Adrian Salmon

Page 216 Top: Associated Newspapers/REX

Middle: © Eaglemoss Publications

Bottom: Romolo Tavani via iStock

Page 217: Jonathan Hordle/REX

Page 218: © Adrian Salmon

Page 220: © Bill Zygmant/REX

Page 222: © Daryl Joyce

Page 224: © Mirrorpix/Sunday Mirror

Page 225: © Clive Limpkin/Express/Getty Images

Page 226 Left : © Adrian Salmon

Right: © Mirrorpix, photo by Alisdair MacDonald

Page 228 Top: © Neville Mariner/Daily Mail/REX

Bottom: © gkuna via iStock

Page 230 Top: © Beretta/Sims/REX

Bottom: © Paul Cooke

Page 232 Top: © St Martin's Press from *The Doctor Who and the Daleks Omnibus*

Bottom (L–R): © Rob Monk/Future Publishing/REX

© Matthew71 vi iStock

© Huw John/REX

© Bobby Bank/WireImage/Getty Images

Page 234 Top: © Metal Mutt Productions

Bottom: © REX

Page 236 Top: MediaPunch/REX

Bottom Left: Alexandra Thompson/REX

Bottom Right: © Mirrorpix, photo by NCJ

Page 238 Top: Image© Panini UK/*Doctor Who Magazine*, Steve Moore/Dave Gibbon

Bottom: © Screencap of *Silence in the Library* © BBC

Page 240: © Dan McDaid

Page 242 Top: © BBC Books

Middle: Screencap of *Shada* © BBC

Bottom: © Ray Tang/REX

Page 244 Left: © BBC Books

Right: Screencap of *The Time of the Doctor* © BBC

Page 246: Screencap of *The War Games* © BBC

Page 247: © Adrian Salmon

Page 248: Image courtesy NASA

Page 250 Left: © United News/Popperfoto/Getty Images

Right: © World Distributors, from *Doctor Who and the Invasion from Space*

Page 251: © forplayday via iStock

Page 252: © Daryl Joyce

Page 255: © Mirrorpix, photo by Tony Eyeles

Page 256 Top: © BBC Books

Bottom (L–R): © A330Pilot/ iStock; © Avatar_023

/iStock; © andrej67/iStock; © archives/iStock

Page 258: © REX

Page 261: © Mirrorpix, photo by Alisdair MacDonald

Page 262: © REX

Page 263: © Chris Balcombe/REX

Page 264: © Mirrorpix/Sunday Mirror

Page 266: © Adrian Salmon

Page 268 Left: © Virgin Publishing

Right: Eddie Wing/REX

Page 270–71: Images courtesy NASA

Page 272: © Mirrorpix/Manchester Mirror

Page 274 Top: Huw John/REX

Bottom: © REX

Page 276: © Allan Bednar

Page 278 Top: © BBC Books

Bottom: © Image courtesy NASA

Page 280: © Traffic_analyzer via iStock and courtesy NASA

Page 281: © Mad Norwegian Press